The Daily Laws

The Daily Laws

366 Meditations on Power,

Seduction, Mastery, Strategy,

and Human Nature

ROBERT GREENE

P

PROFILE BOOKS

First published in Great Britain in 2021 by
Profile Books Ltd
29 Cloth Fair
London
EC1A 7JQ
www.profilebooks.com

First published in the United States of America in 2021 by
Viking, an imprint of Penguin Random House LLC

1 3 5 7 9 10 8 6 4 2

Printed and bound in Great Britain by
Clays Ltd, Elcograf S.p.A.

A CIP catalogue record for this book is available from the British Library.

ISBN 978 1 78816 853 3
Export edition ISBN 978 1 78816 854 0
eISBN 978 1 78283 874 6

FSC
www.fsc.org
MIX
Paper from
responsible sources
FSC® C018072

To the memory of Brutus, the greatest cat who ever lived.

Contents

PREFACE

From the beginning of our existence as a species, we humans have depended on our connection to reality for our very survival and success. What this meant for our ancestors was that they had to become highly sensitive to their environment, detecting any changes in the weather, anticipating the presence of predators, discerning where opportunities for food might lie. They had to be aware, alert, and continually thinking about what the environment was telling them.

In such an atmosphere, with the pressures so immediate and the consequences of any inattention being life or death, the human brain evolved as an instrument for helping humans to not only detect dangers, but also to slowly gain control of a treacherous environment. The moment our ancestors began to turn inward and give in to wishes and fantasies, reality rigorously punished them for their delusions and bad decisions.

Today, so many hundreds of thousands of years later, we have the same brain designed for the same purpose. But because we have increasingly gained control of our environment and the physical pressures have loosened dramatically, the dangers have become much more subtle—they come in the form of people (not leopards) and their tricky psychology, and the delicate political and social games we have to play. And because of these less obvious dangers, our greatest problem is that our minds tend to become less sensitive to the environment; we turn inward, absorbed in our dreams and fantasies. We become naive.

To add to this dangerous brew, our culture tends to fill our heads with all kinds of false notions, making us believe things about what the world and human nature should be like, rather than what they are actually like. We take all of this for the truth and act on these misconceptions and, just as in the past, the environment and reality eventually punish us for our delusionary behavior. We may not lose our lives, but our careers and relationships take wrong turns. We blame other people for our woes when all along the problem is inside us, stemming from our naiveté and the fantasies we've absorbed, which unconsciously guide our actions.

The following are some of the common false notions in our culture that can lead us astray: For instance, when it comes to our career, we believe that where we went to school, who we know, and who we are connected to is the key to our future success. We think that making mistakes or failing or any kind of conflict are to be avoided at all costs, and that we need to be in a hurry to make money, gain attention, and rise to the top. We imagine that work should be fun, that boredom is bad, and that we can take shortcuts to becoming really good at things. We have the idea that creativity is something we are born with, a natural gift. We feel that everyone is equal, and that hierarchies are a thing of the past.

With people, we operate under the belief that most of our friends and colleagues like us and want the best for us. We think that those with a pattern of bad behavior can be trusted if they say they've reformed, that people full of conviction and a sense of outrage must be telling the truth, and that those in power, including our bosses, are not insecure. We imagine that people who are extremely nice and accommodating are not potentially masking a dark and devious nature, that those who espouse progressive ideas have a corresponding virtuous character, and that people will be grateful for any favors we do for them.

With ourselves, we think that it's important to be honest and to tell others what's exactly on our minds. We feel that it's good to show off our best qualities—our intelligence, our industriousness, etc. We think that if bad things happen to us, we're just victims and not responsible in any way. We of course see that some people are narcissistic, aggressive, envious, grandiose, and manipulative, but we believe that these are just a few bad apples and that we ourselves have none of these qualities.

What often happens is that at a fairly young age, burdened with such delusions, we enter the work world, and reality suddenly slaps us in the face. We discover that some people have fragile egos and can be devious and not at all what they seem. We are blindsided by their indifference or sudden acts of betrayal. Being ourselves and just saying what we think can land us in all kinds of trouble. We come to realize that the work world is riddled with political games that nobody has prepared us for.

Some of our career decisions, based on the desire for money and attention, lead to emotional burnout, disenchantment, and dead ends. And by not looking at ourselves in an honest way, and glossing over our own flaws and weaknesses, we become trapped in patterns of behavior that we cannot control. As the years go by, and the misreadings, missteps, and unrealistic decisions pile up, we can become bitter, confused, and damaged.

The Daily Laws is designed to reverse these toxic patterns and to reconnect you to reality. It takes aim at the various delusions we have all absorbed and seeks to attune your mind instead to the most entrenched traits of human nature and how our brains actually operate. Its goal is to transform you into a radical realist, so that when the book is finished, you will continue, on your own, to see people and events through this clarifying lens, and become ever more sensitive to the dangers and opportunities in your social environment. It is based on twenty-five years of intense research on the subjects of power, persuasion, strategy, mastery, and human nature, and is the distillation of all the lessons in my books.

The entries in the first three months will help rid you of all the external voices telling you about which career path to follow, and instead will connect you to your own voice, to what makes you unique, to your purpose and calling in life. Once this connection is made, you will have a guide for all your subsequent career decisions. These entries will show you that what matters is not education or money, but your persistence and the intensity of your desire to learn; that failures, mistakes, and conflicts are often the best education of all; and how true creativity and mastery emerge from all this.

The next three months will train you to see the political nature of the work world and how dangerous it is to take appearances for reality. They will help you to recognize the toxic types before they immerse you in their emotional maelstroms and teach you how to consciously outwit the great manipulators out there.

The ensuing three months will attempt to show you how real persuasion and influence work—not by thinking first of yourself and saying what's on your mind, but from getting into the mindset of others and appealing to their self-interest. They will also help you to become a superior strategist in life, effectively advancing those causes you so deeply believe in and realizing your goals.

And the last three months will immerse you in the underlying motivations that drive human behavior, including your own. By making you reflect on who you are and realize that you are a flawed human being like everyone else, you will not only have greater empathy and acceptance of people, but you will have the key to altering your own negative patterns. These entries will show you that by confronting your deepest fears about mortality, you can open yourself up to the truly awesome nature of life, appreciating every moment that remains to you for absorbing its sublimity.

The entries have been culled from five of my books, and from part of the book I am currently working on, *The Law of the Sublime*; from interviews and talks over the years; and from blog posts and online essays I have written. At the end of each entry, I share the title and the chapter of the book the entries come from, so that you can deepen your study on any specific idea. Each month has a specific title and subtheme, and begins with a short essay. These essays illustrate the connection of the ideas in my books to my own experiences, the hardships that I have encountered, and the realistic lessons I have derived from them.

This book can be read in a pick-and-choose manner, skipping around as you desire, fitting the ideas to your own issues at this particular moment in your life. But it is best to read *The Daily Laws* from cover to cover, beginning with whichever date the book happens to land in your hands. In this way the book will immerse you in each subject, infiltrating your mind and helping you develop the essential habit of seeing things as they are. As part of this habit, it's best to take notes as often as you can, relating the entries to your own experiences past and present. And it's even better to occasionally put some of the ideas into practice and reflect on the real-world experiences that ensue.

Finally, consider *The Daily Laws* as a kind of bildungsroman. The *bildungsroman*—from the German meaning a "development" or "education novel"—was a literary genre that began in the eighteenth century and continues into the present. In these stories, the protagonists, often quite young, enter life full of naive notions. The author takes them on a journey through a land teeming with miscreants, rogues, and fools. Slowly, the protagonists learn to shed themselves of their various illusions as the real world educates them. And they come to see that reality is infinitely more interesting and richer than all the fantasies they had been fed on. They emerge enlightened, battle-tested, and wise beyond their years.

The Daily Laws will take you, the protagonist, on a similar journey through a land full of dangerous and toxic types of people, helping you shed your illusions and hardening you for the battles ahead so that you may find solace and pleasure in seeing people and the world in their true light.

We are not provided with wisdom, we must discover it for ourselves, after a journey through the wilderness which no one else can take for us. . . . The lives that you admire, the attitudes that seem noble to you are not the result of training at home, by a father, or by masters at school, they have sprung from beginnings of a very different order, by reaction from the influence of everything evil or commonplace that prevailed round about them. They represent a struggle and a victory.

—MARCEL PROUST

January

Your Life's Task

PLANTING THE SEEDS FOR MASTERY

≈

All of us are born unique. This uniqueness is marked genetically in our DNA. We are a one-time phenomenon in the universe—our exact genetic makeup has never occurred before nor will it ever be repeated. For all of us, this uniqueness first expresses itself in childhood through certain primal inclinations. They are *forces* within us that come from a deeper place than conscious words can express. They draw us to certain experiences and away from others. As these forces move us here or there, they influence the development of our minds in very particular ways. Let us state it in the following way: At your birth a seed is planted. That seed is your uniqueness. It wants to grow, transform itself, and flower to its full potential. It has a natural, assertive energy to it. Your Life's Task is to bring that seed to flower, to express your uniqueness through your work. You have a destiny to fulfill. The stronger you feel and maintain it—as a force, a voice, or in whatever form—the greater your chance for fulfilling this Life's Task and achieving mastery. The month of January is all about discovering and developing your Life's Task, your purpose, what you were put here to do.

I had known from a very young age—perhaps the age of eight—that I wanted to become a writer. I had a tremendous love of books and of words. I thought at first, when I was young, that I would be a novelist, but after graduating university, I had to make a living, and I realized being a novelist was too impractical. And so, living in New York, I drifted into journalism as a way to at least make a living. Then one day, after several years of working as a writer and editor, I was having lunch with a man who had just edited an article I had written for a magazine. After downing his third martini, he finally admitted to me why he had asked me to lunch. "You should seriously consider a different career," he told me. "You are not writer material. Your work is too undisciplined. Your style is too bizarre. Your ideas—they're just not relatable to the average reader. Go to law school, Robert. Go to business school. Spare yourself the pain."

At first, these words were like a punch in the stomach. But in the months to come, I realized something about myself. I'd entered a career that didn't suit me, and my work reflected this incompatibility. I had to get out of journalism. This realization initiated a period of wandering in my life. I traveled all across Europe. I worked every conceivable job. I did construction work in Greece, taught English in Barcelona, worked as a hotel receptionist in Paris and a tour guide in Dublin, served as a trainee for an English company making television documentaries. I tried writing novels and plays. I wandered back to Los Angeles, California, where I was born and raised. I worked in a detective agency, among other odd jobs. I entered the film business working as an assistant to a director, as a researcher, story developer, and screenwriter. In these long years of wandering, I had totaled some sixty different jobs. By the year 1995, my parents (God bless them) were beginning to get seriously worried about their son. I was thirty-six years old, and I seemed lost and unable to settle into anything. I too had moments of great doubt and even depression, but I did not really feel lost. Something inside kept pushing and guiding me.

I was searching and exploring, I was hungry for experiences, and I was continuously writing. That same year, while in Italy for yet another job, I met a man there named Joost Elffers—a packager and producer of books. One day while we were walking along the quais of Venice, Joost asked me if I had any ideas for a book.

Suddenly, seemingly out of nowhere, an idea just gushed out of me. I told Joost that I was constantly reading books on history and the stories that I read of Julius Caesar and the Borgias and Louis XIV, these were the exact same stories that I had personally witnessed with my own eyes in all my different jobs, only less bloody. People want power and they want to disguise this wanting of power. And so, they play games. They covertly manipulate and intrigue, all the while presenting a nice even saintly front. I would expose these games.

As I was improvising this pitch to him, which would eventually become my first book, *The 48 Laws of Power*, I felt something click inside me. I felt this tremendous sense of excitement welling up. It felt natural. It felt like destiny. When I saw that he was excited, I became even more excited. He said that he loved the idea and that he would pay me to live while I wrote half the book and then he would try to sell it to a publisher, himself being the packager, designer, and producer of it. When I returned home to Los Angeles and began working on *The 48 Laws*, I knew that this was my one chance in life, my one avenue of escaping all the years of wandering. So, I went all in. I put every single ounce of energy I had into it, because either I would make this book a success, or I would end up a failure in life. And I poured into this book all the lessons I had learned, all my training as a writer, all the discipline I'd gained from journalism, all the good and bad experiences I had accumulated in my sixty different jobs, all the horrible bosses that I had dealt with. And my pent-up excitement in writing the book could be felt by the reader and, much to my surprise, and beyond anything I'd imagined, the book had tremendous success.

Now looking back on all this some twenty-five years later, I realized that that thing that was pushing and guiding me (that I mentioned earlier) was a sense of purpose, a sense of destiny. It was like this voice inside of me whispering, "Don't give up. Keep trying. Keep trying." This voice, which had first appeared to me as a child, was guiding me toward my Life's Task. It took many years, many experiments, many mistakes, and obstacles, but it kept me advancing and oddly hopeful.

And now, many books later, I remain dedicated to that task. Like every person, I still need that sense of purpose to guide me, day in and day out. Each book I write has to feel like it's part of that destiny, like it was meant to happen. And this sense of purpose I've had for my whole life that became so much clearer twenty-five years ago is what I believe has guided me through all the hard moments in my life. And I think it could do that for anybody, once you sense it within you, once you search for it.

The real lesson here is that it took me a long time to get there, with many twists and turns. And so, it can come even later in life—in your thirties or forties, or beyond. But my existence forever changed the moment I embraced my Life's Task.

Discover Your Calling

Everyone holds his fortune in his own hands, like a sculptor the raw material he will fashion into a figure. But it's the same with that type of artistic activity as with all others: We are merely born with the capability to do it. The skill to mold the material into what we want must be learned and attentively cultivated.

—JOHANN WOLFGANG VON GOETHE

You possess a kind of inner force that seeks to guide you toward your Life's Task—what you are meant to accomplish in the time that you have to live. In childhood this force was clear to you. It directed you toward activities and subjects that fit your natural inclinations, that sparked a curiosity that was deep and primal. In the intervening years, the force tends to fade in and out as you listen more to parents and peers, to the daily anxieties that wear away at you. This can be the source of your unhappiness—your lack of connection to who you are and what makes you unique. The first move toward mastery is always inward—learning who you really are and reconnecting with that innate force. Knowing it with clarity, you will find your way to the proper career path and everything else will fall into place. It is never too late to start this process.

Daily Law: Mastery is a process and discovering your calling is the starting point.

Mastery, I: Discover Your Calling—The Life's Task

Reconnect with Your Childhood Obsession

When Marie Curie, the future discoverer of radium, was four years old she wandered into her father's study and stood transfixed before a glass case that contained all kinds of laboratory instruments for chemistry and physics experiments. She would return to that room again and again to stare at the instruments, imagining all sorts of experiments she could conduct with these tubes and measuring devices. Years later, when she entered a real laboratory for the first time and did some experiments herself, she reconnected immediately with her childhood obsession; she knew she had found her vocation.

Daily Law: You were obsessed with it as a child for a reason. Reconnect with it.

Mastery, I: Discover Your Calling—The Life's Task

The Voice

The way to recover the meaning of life and the worthwhileness of
life is to recover the power of experience, to have impulse voices from
within, and to be able to hear these impulse voices from within.

—ABRAHAM MASLOW

From the time I was young, I was entranced with words. I can remember
in the fourth grade the teacher did this activity where she put up the
word *carpenter*, and she asked us to come up with as many words as we
could with just those letters. "Ant," "pet," "car," et cetera. And I just thought,
"Wow! You mean you can take letters like this and recombine them into
words?" I was entranced. These childhood attractions are hard to put into
words. Abraham Maslow called it "impulse voices." He noticed that children know exactly what they like and dislike from a very early age. It is
extremely human and powerful. You had those impulse voices too. You
hated this kind of activity and you loved that other one. You didn't like
math but you were drawn to words. You were exhilarated by certain kinds
of books and fell promptly asleep with other kinds. The importance of
recognizing these early inclinations is that they are clear indications of an
attraction that is not infected by the desires of other people. They are not
something embedded in you by your parents, which come with a more
superficial connection, something more verbal and conscious. Coming
instead from somewhere deeper, these inclinations can only be your own,
reflections of your unique chemistry.

Daily Law: Do something today that you used to love doing as a kid.
Try to reconnect with your impulse voices.

Robert Greene in conversation at Live Talks Los Angeles, February 11, 2019

It Is Already within You

Sooner or later something seems to call us onto a particular path.
You may remember this something as a signal calling in childhood
when an urge out of nowhere, a fascination, a peculiar turn of
events struck like an annunciation: This is what I must do, this is
what I've got to have. This is who I am.

—JAMES HILLMAN

As you become more sophisticated, you often lose touch with these signals from your primal core. They can be buried beneath all of the other
subjects you have studied. Your power and future can depend on reconnecting with this core and returning to your origins. You must dig for
signs of such inclinations in your earliest years. Look for its traces in visceral reactions to something simple; a desire to repeat an activity that you
never tired of; a subject that stimulated an unusual degree of curiosity;
feelings of power attached to particular actions. It is already there within
you. You have nothing to create; you merely need to dig and refine what
has been buried inside of you all along. If you reconnect with this core at
any age, some element of that primitive attraction will spark back to life,
indicating a path that can ultimately become your Life's Task.

Daily Law: Ask someone who recalls your childhood what they remember about your interests. Get reacquainted with those early passions.

Mastery, I: Discover Your Calling—The Life's Task

Know What You're Drawn to and Immerse Yourself in It

The contemporary anthropologist-linguist Daniel Everett grew up on the California-Mexico border, in a cowboy town. From a very early age, he found himself drawn to the Mexican culture around him. Everything about it fascinated him—the sound of the words spoken by the migrant workers, the food, the manners that were so different from the Anglo world. He immersed himself as much as he could in their language and culture. This would transform into a lifelong interest in the Other—the diversity of cultures on the planet and what that means about our evolution.

Daily Law: What's something you've always felt a pull toward? Dive deep into it today.

Mastery, I: Discover Your Calling—The Life's Task

Change Is the Law

In dealing with your career and its inevitable changes, you must think in the following way: You are not tied to a particular position; your loyalty is not to a career or a company. You are committed to your Life's Task, to giving it full expression. It is up to you to find it and guide it correctly. It is not up to others to protect or help you. You are on your own. Change is inevitable, particularly in such a revolutionary moment as ours. Since you are on your own, it is up to you to foresee the changes going on right now in your profession. You must adapt your Life's Task to these circumstances. You do not hold on to past ways of doing things, because that will ensure you will fall behind and suffer for it. You are flexible and always looking to adapt. If change is forced upon you, you must resist the temptation to overreact or feel sorry for yourself. Before he became the great boxing trainer, Freddie Roach was forced to retire from boxing. He instinctively found his way back to the ring because he understood that what he loved was not boxing per se, but competitive sports and strategizing. Thinking in this way, he could adapt his inclinations to a new direction within boxing. Like Roach, you don't want to abandon the skills and experience you have gained, but to find a new way to apply them. Your eye is on the future, not the past. Often such creative readjustments lead to a superior path for us—we are shaken out of our complacency and forced to reassess where we are headed.

Daily Law: Adapt your inclinations. Avoid having rigid goals and dreams. Change is the law.

Mastery, I: Discover Your Calling—The Life's Task

Money and Success

For many people, the pursuit of money and status can supply them with plenty of motivation and focus. Such types would consider figuring out their calling in life a monumental waste of time and an antiquated notion. But in the long run this philosophy often yields the most impractical of results. We all know the effects of "hyperintention": If we want and need desperately to sleep, we are less likely to fall asleep. If we absolutely must give the best talk possible at some conference, we become hyperanxious about the result, and the performance suffers. If we desperately need to find an intimate partner or make friends, we are more likely to push them away. If instead we relax and focus on other things, we are more likely to fall asleep or give a great talk or charm people. The most pleasurable things in life occur as a result of something not directly intended and expected. When we try to manufacture happy moments, they tend to disappoint us. The same goes for the dogged pursuit of money and success. Many of the most successful, famous, and wealthy individuals do not begin with an obsession with money and status. One prime example would be Steve Jobs, who amassed quite a fortune in his relatively short life. He actually cared very little for material possessions. His singular focus was on creating the best and most original designs, and when he did so, good fortune followed him.

Daily Law: Concentrate on maintaining a high sense of purpose, and the success will flow to you naturally.

The Laws of Human Nature, 13: Advance with a Sense of Purpose—The Law of Aimlessness

Occupy Your Own Niche

As a child growing up in Madras, India, in the late 1950s, V. S. Ramach-andran knew he was different. In his loneliness he would often wander along the beach, and soon he became fascinated by the incredible variety of seashells that washed up on shore. He began to collect them and study the subject in detail. Soon he was drawn to the strangest varieties of sea-shells, such as the Xenophora, an organism that collects discarded shells and uses them for camouflage. In a way, he was like the Xenophora—an anomaly. In nature, these anomalies often serve a larger evolutionary purpose—they can lead to the occupation of new ecological niches, offer-ing a greater chance of survival. Over the years, he transferred this boy-hood interest into other subjects—human anatomical abnormalities, peculiar phenomena in chemistry, and so on. He went to medical school then became a professor in visual psychology at the University of Califor-nia at San Diego. He became intrigued by the phenomenon of phantom limbs—people who have had an arm or leg amputated and yet still feel a paralyzing pain in the missing limb. He proceeded to conduct experi-ments on phantom limb subjects. These experiments led to some exciting discoveries about the brain itself, as well as a novel way to relieve such patients of their pain. Studying anomalous neurological disorders would be the subject to which he could devote the rest of his life. It was as if he had come full circle to the days of collecting the rarest forms of seashells.

Daily Law: Embrace your strangeness. Identify what makes you differ-ent. Fuse those things together and become an anomaly.

Mastery, I: Discover Your Calling—The Life's Task

Find Inspiration from Your Heroes

As a young boy growing up in North Carolina, John Coltrane felt different and strange. He was much more serious than his schoolmates; he experienced emotional and spiritual longings he did not know how to verbalize. He drifted into music more as a hobby, taking up the saxophone and playing in his high school band. Then a few years later he saw the great jazz saxophonist Charlie "Bird" Parker perform live, and the sounds Parker produced touched Coltrane to the core. Something primal and personal came through Parker's saxophone, a voice from deep within. Coltrane suddenly saw the means for expressing his uniqueness and giving a voice to his own spiritual longings. He began to practice the instrument with such intensity that within a decade he transformed himself into perhaps the greatest jazz artist of his era. You must understand the following: In order to master a field, you must love the subject and feel a profound connection to it. Your interest must transcend the field and border on the religious. For Coltrane, it was not music but giving voice to powerful emotions.

Daily Law: Are there people whose work affects you in a powerful way? Analyze this and use them as models.

Mastery, I: Discover Your Calling—The Life's Task

Embrace Your Weirdness

The most courageous act is still to think for yourself.

—COCO CHANEL

What do we say about masters? "They're one of a kind." There's never been a Steve Jobs ever before. There's never been a Warren Buffett. There's never been an Albert Einstein. They're unique. They embraced what made them different. Yes, it comes with some pain. With my books, particularly *The 48 Laws of Power*, you might hate it, you might think it's satanic, but I can guarantee you've never read or seen a book that looks like it. The sections I created, the opening paragraphs, the quotes on the sides, the shapes—the book reflects me and my weirdness. The publisher was frightened by it. They wanted a more conventional book. And I said, "No. I know I've never published anything before, but I'm sticking to what I have here." I stuck to what was weird and strange about me.

Daily Law: Always stick to what makes you weird, odd, strange, different. That's your source of power.

Podcast Interview. *Curious with Josh Peck*. December 4, 2018

What Makes You Feel More Alive?

Sometimes an inclination becomes clear through a particular activity that brings with it a feeling of heightened power. As a child, Martha Graham felt intensely frustrated by her inability to make others understand her in a deep way; words seemed inadequate. Then one day, she saw her first dance performance. The lead dancer had a way of expressing certain emotions through movement; it was visceral, not verbal. She started dance lessons soon thereafter and immediately understood her vocation. Only when dancing could she feel alive and expressive. Years later she would go on to invent a whole new form of dance and revolutionize the genre.

Daily Law: Do something that makes you feel at the peak of your being today.

Mastery, I: Discover Your Calling—The Life's Task

The Obstacle Is the Way

Some people do not become aware of inclinations or future career paths in their childhood, but instead are made painfully aware of their limitations. They are not good at what others seem to find easy or manageable. The idea of a calling in life is alien to them. In some cases, they internalize the judgments and criticisms of others, and come to see themselves as essentially deficient. If they are not careful, this can become a self-fulfilling prophecy. Nobody faced this fate more powerfully than Temple Grandin. In 1950, at the age of three, Temple Grandin was diagnosed with autism. A doctor had suggested she be institutionalized for the rest of her life. Through the help of speech therapists, she was able to avoid such a fate and attend regular school. She slowly developed an intense interest in animals and in autism itself. This led to a career in the sciences. With her exceptional reasoning powers, she has been able to throw light on the phenomenon of autism and explain it in a way no one else has been able to. Somehow, she had managed to overcome all of the seemingly insurmountable obstructions in her path and find her way to the Life's Task that suited her to perfection. When you confront your limitations, you are moved to respond in some way that is creative. And as it was for Temple Grandin, it may be in a way that no one else has done or even thought of before.

Daily Law: Confront one of your limitations—one of the obstructions in your path—today. Break beyond it, climb over it, think your way around it. Don't run from it. It was created for you.

Mastery, I: Discover Your Calling—The Life's Task

Master the Small Things

When you are faced with deficiencies instead of strengths and inclinations, this is the strategy you must assume: Ignore your weaknesses and resist the temptation to be more like others. Instead, direct yourself toward the small things you are good at. Do not dream or make grand plans for the future, but instead concentrate on becoming proficient at these simple and immediate skills. This will bring you confidence and become a base from which you can expand to other pursuits. Proceeding in this way, step by step, you will hit upon your Life's Task. Your Life's Task does not always appear to you through some grand or promising inclination. It can appear in the guise of your deficiencies, making you focus on the one or two things that you are inevitably good at. Working at these skills, you learn the value of discipline and see the rewards you get from your efforts. Like a lotus flower, your skills will expand outward from a center of strength and confidence. Do not envy those who seem to be naturally gifted; it is often a curse, as such types rarely learn the value of diligence and focus, and they pay for this later in life. This strategy applies as well to any setbacks and difficulties we may experience. In such moments, it is generally wise to stick to the few things we know and do well, and to reestablish our confidence.

Daily Law: When in doubt, focus on the things you know you do well. Expand outward from the center.

Mastery, I: Discover Your Calling—The Life's Task

Avoid the False Path

At the center of your being you have the answer;
you know who you are and you know what you want.

—LAO TZU

A false path in life is generally something we are attracted to for the wrong reasons—money, fame, attention, and so on. If it is attention we need, we often experience a kind of emptiness inside that we are hoping to fill with the false love of public approval. Because the field we choose does not correspond with our deepest inclinations, we rarely find the fulfillment that we crave. Our work suffers for this, and the attention we may have gotten in the beginning starts to fade—a painful process. If it is money and comfort that dominate our decision, we are most often acting out of anxiety and the need to please our parents. They may steer us toward something lucrative out of care and concern, but lurking underneath this can be something else—perhaps a bit of envy that we have more freedom than they had when they were young. Your strategy must be twofold: First, to realize as early as possible that you have chosen your career for the wrong reasons, before your confidence takes a hit. And second, to actively rebel against those forces that have pushed you away from your true path. Scoff at the need for attention and approval—they will lead you astray. Feel some anger and resentment at the parental forces that want to foist upon you an alien vocation. It is a healthy part of your development to follow a path independent of your parents and to establish your own identity. Let your sense of rebellion fill you with energy and purpose.

Daily Law: If you're on the false path, get off. Find energy in rebellion.

Mastery, I: Discover Your Calling—The Life's Task

Let a Sense of Purpose Guide You

Just as a well-filled day brings blessed sleep,
so a well-employed life brings blessed death.

—LEONARDO DA VINCI

What we lack most in the modern world is a sense of a larger purpose to our lives. In the past, it was organized religion that often supplied this. But most of us now live in a secularized world. We human animals are unique—we must build our own world. We do not simply react to events out of biological scripting. But without a sense of direction provided to us, we tend to flounder. We don't know how to fill up and structure our time. There seems to be no defining purpose to our lives. We are perhaps not conscious of this emptiness, but it infects us in all kinds of ways. Feeling that we are called to accomplish something is the most positive way for us to supply this sense of purpose and direction. It is a religious-like quest for each of us. This quest should not be seen as selfish or antisocial. It is in fact connected to something much larger than our individual lives. Our evolution as a species has depended on the creation of a tremendous diversity of skills and ways of thinking.

Daily Law: Think back on the moments when you felt deeply and personally connected to an activity. Think about the pleasure it brought you. In such activities are signs of your true purpose.

Mastery, I: Discover Your Calling—The Life's Task

There Are No Superior Callings

Keep in mind that your contribution to the culture can come in many forms. You don't have to become an entrepreneur or figure largely on the world's stage. You can do just as well operating as one person in a group or organization, as long as you retain a strong point of view that is your own and use this to gently exert your influence. Your path can involve physical labor and craft—you take pride in the excellence of the work, leaving your particular stamp on the quality. It can be raising a family in the best way possible. In any event, you will want to go as far as you can in cultivating your uniqueness and the originality that goes with it. In a world full of people who seem largely interchangeable, you cannot be replaced. You are one of a kind. Your combination of skills and experience is not replicable. That represents true freedom and the ultimate power we humans can possess.

Daily Law: No calling is superior to another. What matters is that it be tied to a personal need and inclination, and that your energy moves you toward improvement and continuous learning from experience.

The Laws of Human Nature, 13: Advance with a Sense of Purpose—The Law of Aimlessness

The True Source of Creativity

You must alter your very concept of creativity and try to see it from a new angle. Most often, people associate creativity with something intellectual, a particular way of thinking. The truth is that creative activity is one that involves the entire self—our emotions, our levels of energy, our characters, and our minds. To make a discovery, to invent something that connects with the public, to fashion a work of art that is meaningful, inevitably requires time and effort. This often entails years of experimentation, various setbacks and failures, and the need to maintain a high level of focus. You must have patience and faith that what you are doing will yield something important. You could have the most brilliant mind, teeming with knowledge and ideas, but if you choose the wrong subject or problem to attack, you can run out of energy and interest. In such a case all of your intellectual brilliance will lead to nothing.

Daily Law: Work at what connects to you emotionally and ideas will come to you.

Mastery, V: Awaken the Dimensional Mind—The Creative-Active

Stop Being So Nice

*Everyone carries a shadow, and the less it is embodied in the
individual's conscious life, the blacker and denser it is.*

—CARL JUNG

You pay a greater price for being so nice and deferential than for consciously showing your Shadow. First, to follow the latter path you must
begin by respecting your own opinions more and those of others less,
particularly when it comes to your areas of expertise, to the field you have
immersed yourself in. Trust your native genius and the ideas you have
come up with. Second, get into the habit in your daily life of asserting yourself more and compromising less. Do this under control and at opportune
moments. Third, start caring less what people think of you. You will feel
a tremendous sense of liberation. Fourth, realize that at times you must
offend and even hurt people who block your path, who have ugly values,
who unjustly criticize you. Use such moments of clear injustice to bring
out your Shadow and show it proudly. Fifth, feel free to play the impu-
dent, willful child who mocks the stupidity and hypocrisy of others. Finally, flout the very conventions that others follow so scrupulously.

Daily Law: Keep in mind that power lies in asserting your uniqueness,
even if that offends some people along the way. Study your Shadow
side today.

The Laws of Human Nature, 9: Confront Your Dark Side—The Law of Repression

Listen to Your Inner Authority

You are here not merely to gratify your impulses and consume what others have made but to make and contribute as well, to serve a higher purpose. To serve this higher purpose, you must cultivate what is unique about you. Stop listening so much to the words and opinions of others, telling you who you are and what you should like and dislike. Judge things and people for yourself. Question what you think and why you feel a certain way. Know yourself thoroughly—your innate tastes and inclinations, the fields that naturally attract you. Work every day on improving those skills that mesh with your unique spirit and purpose. Add to the needed diversity of culture by creating something that reflects your uniqueness. Embrace what makes you different. Not following this course is the real reason you feel depressed at times. Moments of depression are a call to listen again to your inner authority.

> **Daily Law:** Reflect on those moments in life when you were active (followed your own path) and those moments when you were passive (followed what others wanted). Compare the emotions you experienced.

The Laws of Human Nature, 15: Make Them Want to Follow You—The Law of Fickleness

JANUARY 20

See Mastery as Salvation

The misery that oppresses you lies not in your profession but in
yourself! What man in the world would not find his situation
intolerable if he chooses a craft, an art, indeed any form of life,
without experiencing an inner calling?

—JOHANN WOLFGANG VON GOETHE

The world is teeming with problems, many of them of our own creation.
To solve them will require a tremendous amount of effort and creativity.
Relying on genetics, technology, magic, or being nice and natural will not
save us. We require the energy not only to address practical matters, but
also to forge new institutions and orders that fit our changed circumstances. We must create our own world or we will die from inaction. We
need to find our way back to the concept of mastery that defined us as a
species so many millions of years ago. This is not mastery for the purpose
of dominating nature or other people, but for determining our fate. The
passive-ironic attitude is not cool or romantic, but pathetic and destructive. You are setting an example of what can be achieved as a Master in
the modern world. You are contributing to the most important cause of
all—the survival and prosperity of the human race, in a time of stagna-
tion. And you must convince yourself of the following: people get the
mind and quality of brain that they deserve through their actions in life.

Daily Law: You must see your attempt at attaining mastery as something extremely necessary and positive.

Mastery, I: Discover Your Calling—The Life's Task

Depending on Others Is Misery

There is nothing worse than feeling dependent on other people. Dependency makes you vulnerable to all kinds of emotions—betrayal, disappointment, frustration—that play havoc with your mental balance. Being self-reliant is critical. To make yourself less dependent on others and so-called experts, you need to expand your repertoire of skills. And you need to feel more confident in your own judgment. Understand: we tend to overestimate other people's abilities—after all, they're trying hard to make it look as if they knew what they were doing—and we tend to underestimate our own. You must compensate for this by trusting yourself more and others less. It is important to remember, though, that being self-reliant does not mean burdening yourself with petty details. You must be able to distinguish between small matters that are best left to others and larger issues that require your attention and care.

Daily Law: It is simple: depending on others is misery; depending on yourself is power.

The 33 Strategies of War, Strategy 3: Amidst the Turmoil of Events, Do Not Lose Your Presence of Mind—The Counterbalance Strategy

Use Resistance and Negative Spurs

Every negative is a positive. The bad things that happen to me,
I somehow make them good.

—50 CENT

The key to success in any field is first developing skills in various areas, which you can later combine in unique and creative ways. But the process of doing so can be tedious and painful, as you become aware of your limitations and relative lack of skill. Most people, consciously or unconsciously, seek to avoid tedium, pain, and any form of adversity. They try to put themselves in places where they will face less criticism and minimize their chances of failure. You must choose to move in the opposite direction. You want to embrace negative experiences, limitations, and even pain as the perfect means of building up your skill levels and sharpening your sense of purpose.

Daily Law: Embrace negative experiences. When was the last time you failed, felt embarrassed, got criticized? What were you doing? What did the experience teach you?

The Laws of Human Nature, 13: Advance with a Sense of Purpose—The Law of Aimlessness

Create a Ladder of Descending Goals

Operating with long-term goals will bring you tremendous clarity and resolve. These goals—a project or business to create, for instance—can be relatively ambitious, enough to bring out the best in you. The problem, however, is that they will also tend to generate anxiety as you look at all you have to do to reach them from the present vantage point. To manage such anxiety, you must create a ladder of smaller goals along the way, reaching down to the present. Such objectives are simpler the further down the ladder you go, and you can realize them in relatively short time frames, giving you moments of satisfaction and a sense of progress. Always break tasks into smaller bites. Each day or week you must have microgoals. This will help you focus and avoid entanglements or detours that will waste your energy. At the same time, you want to continually remind yourself of the larger goal, to avoid losing track of it or getting too mired in details. Periodically return to your original vision and imagine the immense satisfaction you will have when it comes to fruition. This will give you clarity and inspire you forward. You will also want a degree of flexibility built into the process. At certain moments you reassess your progress and adjust the various goals as necessary, constantly learning from experience and adapting and improving your original objective.

> Daily Law: Remember that what you are after is a series of practical results and accomplishments, not a list of unrealized dreams and aborted projects. Working with smaller, embedded goals will keep you moving in such a direction.

The Laws of Human Nature, 13: Advance with a Sense of Purpose—The Law of Aimlessness

Combine Your Fascinations

If you are young and just starting out in your career, you will want to explore a relatively wide field related to your inclinations—for instance, if your affinity is words and writing, try all the different types of writing until you hit upon the right fit. If you are older and have more experience, you will want to take the skills you have already developed and find a way to adapt them more in the direction of your true calling. Steve Jobs, as one example, merged his two great fascinations: technology and design.

> Daily Law: Keep in mind that your calling could be combining several fields that fascinate you. Keep the process open ended; your experience will instruct you as to the way.

The Laws of Human Nature, 13: Advance with a Sense of Purpose—The Law of Aimlessness

Change Yourself from within, Little by Little

We humans tend to fixate on what we can see with our eyes. It is the most animal part of our nature. When we look at the changes in other people's lives, we see the good luck that someone had in meeting a person with all of the right connections and the funding. We see the project that brings the money and the attention. In other words, we see the visible signs of opportunity and success in our own lives but we are grasping at an illusion. What really allows for such dramatic changes are the things that occur inside a person. The slow accumulation of knowledge and skills, the incremental improvements in work habits, and the ability to withstand criticism. Any change in people's fortunes is merely the visible manifestation of all of that deep preparation over time. By essentially ignoring this internal invisible aspect, we fail to change anything fundamental within ourselves. And so in a few years' time we reach our limits. Yet again we grow frustrated, we crave change, we grab at something quick and superficial and we remain prisoners forever of these recurring patterns in our lives. The answer is to reverse this perspective: Stop fixating on what other people are saying and doing. Stop fixating on the money, the connections, the outward appearance of things. Instead look inward, focus on the smaller internal changes that lay the groundwork for a much larger change in fortune. It is the difference between grasping at an illusion and immersing yourself in reality. And reality is what will liberate and transform you.

Daily Law: What would you work on if no one was looking? If money were no object?

TED Talk, "The Key to Transforming Yourself," October 23, 2013

Avoid the Counterforces to Mastery

What weakens that force within us, what makes you not feel it or even doubt its existence, is the degree to which you have succumbed to another force in life—social pressures to conform. These counterforces can be very powerful. You want to fit into a group. Unconsciously, you might feel that what makes you different is embarrassing or painful. Your parents often act as a counterforce as well. They may seek to direct you to a career path that is lucrative and comfortable. If these counterforces become strong enough, you can lose complete contact with your uniqueness, with who you really are. Your inclinations and desires become modeled on those of others. This can set you off on a very dangerous path. You end up choosing a career that does not really suit you. Your desire and interest slowly wane and your work suffers for it. You come to see pleasure and fulfillment as something that comes from outside your work. Because you are increasingly less engaged in your career, you fail to pay attention to changes going on in the field—you fall behind the times and pay a price for this. At moments when you must make important decisions, you flounder or follow what others are doing because you have no sense of inner direction or radar to guide you. You have broken contact with your destiny as formed at birth. At all cost you must avoid such a fate.

Daily Law: The process of following your Life's Task all the way to mastery can essentially begin at any point in life. The hidden force within you is always there and ready to be engaged, but only if you can silence the noise from others.

Mastery, I: Discover Your Calling—The Life's Task

The Real Secret

The hunger for the magical shortcuts and simple formulas for success has been a constant throughout history. But in the end all of this searching is centered on something that doesn't exist. And while you lose yourself in these endless fantasies, you ignore the one real power that you actually possess. And unlike magic or simplistic formulas, we can see the material effects of this power in history—the great discoveries and inventions, the magnificent buildings and works of art, the technological prowess we possess, all works of the masterful mind. This power brings to those who possess it the kind of connection to reality and the ability to alter the world that the mystics and magicians of the past could only dream of. Over the centuries, people have placed a wall around mastery. They have called it genius and have thought of it as inaccessible. They have seen it as the product of privilege, inborn talent, or just the right alignment of the stars. They have made it seem as if it were as elusive as magic. But that wall is imaginary. This is the real secret: the brain that we possess is the work of six million years of development, and more than anything else, this evolution of the brain was designed to lead us to mastery, the latent power within us all.

Daily Law: Work to create the kind of mind you desire. Unleashing the masterful mind within, you will be at the vanguard of those who are exploring the extended limits of human willpower.

Mastery, Introduction

The Path Is Not Linear

You begin by choosing a field or position that roughly corresponds to your inclinations. This initial position offers you room to maneuver and important skills to learn. You don't want to start with something too lofty, too ambitious—you need to make a living and establish some confidence. Once on this path you discover certain side routes that attract you, while other aspects of this field leave you cold. You adjust and perhaps move to a related field, continuing to learn more about yourself, but always expanding off your skill base. You take what you do for others and make it your own. Eventually, you will hit upon a particular field, niche, or opportunity that suits you perfectly. You will recognize it when you find it because it will spark that childlike sense of wonder and excitement; it will feel right. Once found, everything will fall into place. You will learn more quickly and more deeply. Your skill level will reach a point where you will be able to claim your independence from within the group you work for and move out on your own. In a world in which there is so much we cannot control, this will bring you the ultimate form of power. You will determine your circumstances. As your own Master, you will no longer be subject to the whims of tyrannical bosses or scheming peers.

Daily Law: You must see your career or vocational path more as a journey with twists and turns rather than a straight line.

Mastery, I: Discover Your Calling—The Life's Task

Become Who You Are

Some 2,600 years ago the ancient Greek poet Pindar wrote, "Become who you are by learning who you are." What he meant is the following: You are born with a particular makeup and tendencies that mark you as a piece of fate. It is who you are to the core. Some people never become who they are; they stop trusting in themselves; they conform to the tastes of others, and they end up wearing a mask that hides their true nature.

Daily Law: If you allow yourself to learn who you really are by paying attention to that voice and force within you, then you can become what you were fated to become—an individual, a Master.

Mastery, I: Discover Your Calling—The Life's Task

Trust the Process

Let us say we are learning the piano. In the beginning, we are outsiders. When we first study the piano, the keyboard looks rather intimidating— we don't understand the relationships between the keys, the chords, the pedals, and everything else that goes into creating music. Although we might enter with excitement about what we can learn, we quickly realize how much hard work there is ahead of us. The great danger is that we give in to feelings of boredom, impatience, fear, and confusion. We stop observing and learning. The process comes to a halt. If, on the other hand, we manage these emotions and allow time to take its course, something remarkable begins to take shape. As we continue to observe and follow the lead of others, we gain clarity, learning the rules and seeing how things work and fit together. If we keep practicing, we gain fluency; basic skills are mastered, allowing us to take on newer and more exciting challenges. We begin to see connections that were invisible to us before. We slowly gain confidence in our ability to solve problems or overcome weaknesses through sheer persistence. At a certain point, we move from student to practitioner. Instead of just learning how others do things, we bring our own style and individuality into play. As years go by and we remain faithful to this process, yet another leap takes place—to mastery. The keyboard is no longer something outside of us; it is internalized and becomes part of our nervous system, our fingertips. We have learned the rules so well that we can now be the ones to break or rewrite them.

Daily Law: Trust the process—time is the essential ingredient of mastery. Use it to your advantage.

Mastery, Introduction

The Source of All Power

Do not try to bypass the work of discovering your Life's Task or imagine that it will simply come to you naturally. Although it may come to a few people early in life or in a lightning-bolt moment, for most of us it requires continual introspection and effort. Experimenting with the skills and options related to your personality and inclinations is not only the single most essential step in developing a high sense of purpose and attaining mastery, it is perhaps the most important step in life in general.

Daily Law: Knowing in a deep way who you are, your uniqueness, will make it that much easier to avoid all of life's other pitfalls.

The Laws of Human Nature, 13: Advance with a Sense of Purpose—The Law of Aimlessness

February

The Ideal Apprenticeship

TRANSFORMING YOURSELF

≈

In the stories of the greatest masters, past and present, we can inevitably detect a phase in their lives in which all of their future powers were in development, like the chrysalis of a butterfly. This part of their lives—a largely self-directed apprenticeship that lasts some five to ten years—receives little attention because it does not contain stories of great achievement or discovery. Often in their Apprenticeship Phase, these types are not yet much different from anyone else. Under the surface, however, their minds are transforming in ways we cannot see but contain all of the seeds of their future success. A close examination of their lives reveals a pattern that transcends their various fields, indicating a kind of Ideal Apprenticeship for mastery. You must see yourself as following in their footsteps. You are on a voyage in which you will craft your own future. It is the time of youth and adventure—of exploring the world with an open mind and spirit. In fact, whenever you must learn a new skill or alter your career path later in life, you reconnect with that youthful, adventurous part of yourself. You constantly look for challenges, pushing yourself past your comfort zone. You use difficulty as a way to measure your progress. This is the spirit you must adopt and see your apprenticeship as a kind of journey in which you will transform yourself, rather than as a drab indoctrination into the work world. The month of February will help you transform yourself through the Ideal Apprenticeship.

When I was twenty-two years old, I had an experience that taught me lessons that I've applied throughout my life. I had just graduated from university, and I decided that I was going to wander around Europe for a while and practice the languages that I had learned in school. I was eager to show off my language skills (French, German, Spanish, Italian). I traveled all over the continent, and then ended up in Paris. I fell in love with the place. I decided I wanted to try and stay for a while. But there was a problem: the French that I had learned over several years in university was woefully inadequate. The Parisians spoke so quickly I could barely understand a word. And when I tried to mutter something and bungled the French, they were actually quite unfriendly.

In all those years of studying French, I had not learned basic expressions for the simple things that one needed when one traveled, like how to order food in restaurants, etc. All of these problems made me rather shy and made me want to stay in my hotel room or keep to myself. But then I made a key decision. I was lonely and really wanted to stay in Paris, and to do so it was critical that I learned the language at a high level. So, I forced myself out of the hotel room. I made myself speak every single day with Parisians for several hours. As much as I could, I spoke no English and did not hang out with other Americans. Every time I interacted with Parisians, I listened to them carefully and noticed any words or expressions I did not understand. I asked questions. I took notes. I absorbed very deeply all of their phrases and their intonations and their gestures. I met a French girl that I wanted to date, and now I had to try even harder to master the language.

Soon my hard work at the language was paying off. I got a job working in a hotel as a receptionist. I was becoming more fluent by the day. I could converse with everyday people; I was meeting Parisians and my circle of acquaintances was expanding. I learned in this way that the Parisians were not unfriendly at all. I was invited into their homes and could feel what it was like to have grown up in that magical city.

Sometimes I would make mistakes and people would make fun of me or laugh. I decided never to take this personally. Even when I made a mistake, I would actually make fun of myself in the process. The Parisians appreciated my self-deprecating humor and my effort and my love of their language. After a year and a half in Paris, I emerged with a solid command of French, which I still have, and some very memorable adventures.

It was an immensely satisfying experience. And it taught me several lessons. The first is that when you want to learn something, motivation is absolutely key. At the university, during those two or three years of studying French, the stakes were not high enough for me to learn. The only thing was to get a good grade, but my life or my happiness or my work did not depend on it. There in Paris, it was sink or swim. I had to learn. I had to get a job and meet people. Because of this high motivation factor, my brain absorbed information at a much higher rate. I learned more in one month than in two or three years of university French because I was so excited.

I also learned the importance of the intensity of your focus, of being immersed in something. Practicing every single day for hours upon hours, having the language ringing in my ear, dreaming in French, my attention was intense and focused. And because of that, I learned rapidly.

But the most important lesson of all was that you really learn in this world by doing things, by practice. Not by reading books or taking tutorials. You need to be out on the street, interacting with people, trying things out, learning from your mistakes, not being afraid to make mistakes or be ridiculed.

This lesson has served me well in everything I've attempted. It gave me confidence that I could master anything with this basic pattern. When I had to write my first book, I was under a lot of stress to make it a success, but my experience in Paris helped guide me. I had learned the importance of going at it every day, being disciplined and excited at the same time. I had learned the value of intense focus, and that the more books I wrote the easier it would become. I applied the same thing to doing interviews. You learn by doing, over and over, practicing and practicing. And from this, you slowly get a pleasure, a joy from the process itself and from mastering something. And that joy and that pleasure stays with you for your whole life. It is embedded in your brain.

If you want to write a book, write it. If you want to be a musician, make music. If you want to start a business, go ahead and start it. Don't be afraid of making mistakes or failing; you learn best through failures. Find someone who is a master at music or at business and attach yourself to them. Get an education at their feet, doing whatever tasks they assign you. Immerse yourself in the world or the industry that you wish to master. This is better than all the books or courses you could read or take in the world—learning by doing.

Submit to Reality

*We receive three educations, one from our parents,
one from our school masters, and one from the world.
The third contradicts all that the first two teach us.*

—BARON DE MONTESQUIEU

After your formal education, you enter the most critical phase in your life—a practical education known as The Apprenticeship. Every time you change careers or acquire new skills, you reenter this phase of life. The goal of The Apprenticeship is not to make money. It's not to get fame or to get attention or to get some cushy position with a nice title. The goal of an apprenticeship is to literally transform yourself. You enter the apprenticeship as someone who's essentially naive. We all do. You're someone who doesn't yet have the skills that are necessary. You're probably someone who's a little bit impatient. And in the end, you are going to transform yourself into someone who's skilled, who's realistic, who understands the political nature of people, and who learns the rules that govern your field. You're going to develop patience and a solid work ethic. I call it reality. The reality is: in your field, for hundreds of years, people have been devising rules, procedures, and practices that have been passed through tradition. Medicine would be an easy example, but it pertains to every field. These rules and procedures represent reality, and you don't have any connection to it when you first enter the field. Your goal is literally to submit. In the deepest sense of the word, you submit to this reality. You recognize that you're starting over and you're going to immerse yourself in it, so that eventually you're going to be the one who actually rewrites those rules—like all masters do.

Daily Law: Learning how to learn is the most important skill to acquire.

Robert Greene, full address on Mastery to the Oxford Union Society, December 12, 2012

What the Mentor Needs

In 2006, I met a nineteen-year-old named Ryan Holiday. He was a fan of my books and offered to be my research assistant. I had the worst luck hiring researchers before him. The problem was they did not understand how I thought. One of the first things that became clear with Ryan was that he understood my way of thinking, the kind of books I like, the kind of stories I look for. Long before he met me, he put in the time. Just wanting to figure out my process, he had read the books that I cited in the bibliography to find the original sources I used. He reverse engineered how my books were made. He understood what I was looking for. Ryan put in the work to know what would actually help me. He saved me time. Then, I had a problem with my internet presence. Ryan said he could improve it. He helped me create my website. He had real internet skills. For me, as someone who was in his late forties at the time, I didn't know the internet that well. He took a problem off my hands. And because Ryan knew he wanted to be a writer, I could help him hone his researching and writing skills. I taught him how a book was made soup to nuts. I taught him the notecard method I created and mastered, which he used to eventually become a highly successful writer himself.

The mentor-apprentice relationship is a very mutually beneficial relationship. When you are in the inferior position and you are looking for a favor from someone who is powerful, you have to get outside of yourself and think of their needs. Obviously, mentors have a lot to give you. But, more important, you have to have something to give them.

Daily Law: Find a master to apprentice under, but instead of thinking about how much they can give you, think about how you can help them with their work.

Podcast interview, *Curious with Josh Peck*, December 4, 2018

You Have One Goal

Wisdom is not a product of schooling but of the
lifelong attempt to acquire it.

—ALBERT EINSTEIN

The principle is simple and must be engraved deeply in your mind: the goal of an apprenticeship is not money, a good position, a title, or a diploma, but rather the transformation of your mind and character—the first transformation on the way to mastery. You must choose places of work and positions that offer the greatest possibilities for learning. Practical knowledge is the ultimate commodity and is what will pay you dividends for decades to come—far more than the paltry increase in pay you might receive at some seemingly lucrative position that offers fewer learning opportunities. This means that you move toward challenges that will toughen and improve you, where you will get the most objective feedback on your performance and progress. You do not choose apprenticeships that seem easy and comfortable.

Daily Law: Practical knowledge is the ultimate commodity. Evaluate opportunities using one criterion: the greatest possibility for learning.

Mastery, II: Submit to Reality—The Ideal Apprenticeship

Value Learning above Everything Else

As you progress in life, you will become addicted to the fat paycheck and it will determine where you go, how you think, and what you do. Eventually, the time that was not spent on learning skills will catch up with you, and the fall will be painful. Instead, you must value learning above everything else. This will lead you to all of the right choices. You will opt for the situation that will give you the most opportunities to learn, particularly with hands-on work. You will choose a place that has people and mentors who can inspire and teach you. A job with mediocre pay has the added benefit of training you to get by with less—a valuable life skill. You must never disdain an apprenticeship with no pay. In fact, it is often the height of wisdom to find the perfect mentor and offer your services as an assistant for free. Happy to exploit your cheap and eager spirit, such mentors will often divulge more than the usual trade secrets. In the end, by valuing learning above all else, you will set the stage for your creative expansion, and the money will soon come to you.

Daily Law: Get one good piece of advice or guidance today from a master of your profession or of life.

Mastery, II: Submit to Reality—The Ideal Apprenticeship

Accumulate Skills

There is much to be known, life is short, and
life is not life without knowledge.

—BALTASAR GRACIÁN

Your main goal in the Apprenticeship Phase must be to learn and accumulate as many real-life skills as possible, particularly in areas that personally excite and stimulate you. If, later in life, your career path changes or your skills are less relevant, you will know how to adapt, adjusting the skills you have and knowing how to learn more. Mastery was once an arduous process because the necessary information to attain skills was not something that was shared. If your interest was in the sciences your only hope was to be in the right social class that would allow you to attend the only universities that trained scientists. Now, with the internet, these walls around information have been shattered. You must take supreme advantage of the opportunities the internet now offers for accumulating skills, through various online resources.

Daily Law: Acquiring a set of skills is the key to navigating a turbulent work world. The ability to later combine these skills is the best path to mastery.

Robert Greene, "Five Key Elements for a New Model of Apprenticeship,"
The New York Times, February 26, 2013

Consider Yourself a Builder

No matter your field, you must think of yourself as a builder, using actual materials and ideas. You are producing something tangible in your work, something that affects people in some direct, concrete way. To build anything well—a house, a political organization, a business, or a film—you must understand the building process and possess the necessary skills. For all of this, you must go through a careful apprenticeship. You cannot make anything worthwhile in this world unless you have first developed and transformed yourself.

Daily Law: Like a builder, develop the highest standards, and the patience for the step-by-step process.

Mastery, II: Submit to Reality—The Ideal Apprenticeship

The Only Shortcut to Mastery

Freedom consists not in refusing to recognize anything above us,
but in respecting something which is above us; for, by respecting it,
we raise ourselves to it, and, by our very acknowledgement,
prove that we bear within ourselves what is higher,
and are worthy to be on a level with it.

—JOHANN WOLFGANG VON GOETHE

Life is short, and your time for learning and creativity is limited. Without any guidance, you can waste valuable years trying to gain knowledge and practice from various sources. Instead, you must follow the example set by Masters throughout the ages and find the proper mentor. The mentor-protégé relationship is the most efficient and productive form of learning. The right mentors know where to focus your attention and how to challenge you. Their knowledge and experience become yours. They provide immediate and realistic feedback on your work, so you can improve more rapidly. Through an intense person-to-person interaction, you absorb a way of thinking that contains great power and can be adapted to your individual spirit. Choose the mentor who best fits your needs and connects to your Life's Task. Once you have internalized their knowledge, you must move on and never remain in their shadow. Your goal is always to surpass your mentors in mastery and brilliance.

Daily Law: Choosing the right mentor is like being able to choose your own parents; the wrong choice is fatal.

Mastery, III: Absorb the Master's Power—The Mentor Dynamic

The Perfect Mentor

Sometime in the late 1960s, V. S. Ramachandran, a medical student at a college in Madras, came upon a book called *Eye and Brain,* written by an eminent professor of neuropsychology, Richard Gregory. The book excited him—the style of writing, the anecdotes, the provocative experiments he recounted. Inspired by the book, Ramachandran did his own experiments on optics, and soon realized that he was better suited for the field than medicine. In 1974 he was admitted into the PhD Program at Cambridge University, in visual perception. He began to feel gloomy and alone in a strange country. Then one day Richard Gregory himself, a professor at Bristol University, came to Cambridge to give a lecture. Ramachandran was mesmerized. Gregory performed thought-provoking demonstrations of his ideas on stage; he had a flair for drama and a great sense of humor. "This is what science should be like," Ramachandran thought. He went up after the talk and introduced himself. They had an instant rapport. He mentioned to Gregory an optical experiment he had been pondering, and the professor was intrigued. He invited Ramachandran to visit Bristol and to stay in his home, where they could try out his idea together. Ramachandran took up the offer, and from the moment he saw Gregory's house he knew he had found his mentor—it was like something out of Sherlock Holmes, full of Victorian instruments, fossils, and skeletons. Gregory was precisely the kind of eccentric Ramachandran could identify with. Soon he was commuting to Bristol regularly for experiments. He had found a lifelong mentor to inspire and guide him, and over the years he would come to adapt much of Gregory's style of speculation and experiment.

Daily Law: What to look for: Whose work inspires you? Whose style excites you? Who do you want to be like in ten years?

Mastery, III: Absorb the Master's Power—The Mentor Dynamic

Redefine Pleasure

One can have no smaller or greater mastery than mastery of oneself.
—LEONARDO DA VINCI

When you practice and develop any skill you transform yourself in the process. You reveal to yourself new capabilities that were previously latent, that are exposed as you progress. You develop emotionally. Your sense of pleasure becomes redefined. What offers immediate pleasure comes to seem like a distraction, an empty entertainment to help pass the time. Real pleasure comes from overcoming challenges, feeling confidence in your abilities, gaining fluency in skills, and experiencing the power this brings. You develop patience. Boredom no longer signals the need for distraction, but rather the need for new challenges to conquer.

Daily Law: See the fruits of discipline and skill as the richest pleasures of all.

Mastery, II: Submit to Reality—The Ideal Apprenticeship

Learn from Everything

*A person of sharp observation and sound judgment rules over things,
not they him. . . . There is nothing he cannot discover,
notice, grasp, understand.*

—BALTASAR GRACIÁN

Every task you are given, no matter how menial, offers opportunities to observe this world at work. No detail about the people within it is too trivial. Everything you see or hear is a sign for you to decode. Over time, you will begin to see and understand more of the reality that eluded you at first. For instance, a person whom you initially thought had great power ended up being someone with more bark than bite. Slowly, you begin to see behind the appearances. As you amass more information about the rules and power dynamics of your new environment, you can begin to analyze why they exist, and how they relate to larger trends in the field. You move from observation to analysis, honing your reasoning skills, but only after months of careful attention.

Daily Law: Approach every task, even the most menial, the same: as an opportunity to observe and amass information about your environment.

Mastery, II: Submit to Reality—The Ideal Apprenticeship

Enter the Cycle of Accelerated Returns

That which we persist in doing becomes easier to do,
not that the nature of the thing has changed but that
our power to do has increased.

—RALPH WALDO EMERSON

In an activity such as riding a bicycle, we all know that it is easier to watch someone and follow their lead than to listen to or read instructions. The more we do it, the easier it becomes. Even with skills that are primarily mental, such as computer programming or speaking a foreign language, it remains the case that we learn best through practice and repetition—the natural learning process. We learn a foreign language by actually speaking it as much as possible, not by reading books and absorbing theories. The more we speak and practice, the more fluent we become. Once you take this far enough, you enter a cycle of accelerated returns in which the practice becomes easier and more interesting, leading to the ability to practice for longer hours, which increases your skill level, which in turn makes practice even more interesting. Reaching this cycle is the goal you must set for yourself.

Daily Law: Everything worth doing has a learning curve. When it gets hard, remember the goal: reaching the cycle of accelerated returns.

Mastery, II: Submit to Reality—The Ideal Apprenticeship

Learn by Doing

The problem with formal education is that it instills in us a passive approach to learning. We read books, take tests, or maybe write essays. Much of the process involves absorbing information. But in the real world, you learn best by doing, by actively trying your hand at the task. The great sushi master chef Eiji Ichimura began his work in restaurants as a dishwasher some forty-two years ago. His desire was to become a sushi chef, but nobody would tell him how it was done or give him direct instruction—it was a jealously guarded secret. He had to develop his skills by watching carefully, and then practicing the same techniques over and over. He would practice in off hours, going over the most intricate motions of the knife. Through such endless labor he turned himself into a master chef.

Daily Law: The brain is designed to learn through constant repetition and active, hands-on involvement. Through such practice and persistence, any skill can be mastered. Pick a skill to acquire and begin to practice.

Robert Greene, "Five Key Elements for a New Model of Apprenticeship,"
The New York Times, February 26, 2013

How to Learn Quickly and Deeply

People who cling to their delusions find it difficult, if not impossible, to learn anything worth learning: A people under the necessity of creating themselves must examine everything, and soak up learning the way the roots of a tree soak up water.

—JAMES BALDWIN

When you enter a new environment, your task is to learn and absorb as much as possible. For that purpose you must try to revert to a childlike feeling of inferiority—the feeling that others know much more than you and that you are dependent upon them to learn and safely navigate your apprenticeship. You drop all of your preconceptions about an environment or field, any lingering feelings of smugness. You have no fears. You interact with people and participate in the culture as deeply as possible. You are full of curiosity. Assuming this sensation of inferiority, your mind will open up and you will have a hunger to learn. This position is of course only temporary. You are reverting to a feeling of dependence, so that within five to ten years you can learn enough to finally declare your independence and enter full adulthood.

Daily Law: Revert to a childlike dependence. Today, act like those you interact with know much more than you.

Mastery, II: Submit to Reality—The Ideal Apprenticeship

Move Toward Resistance

By nature, we humans shrink from anything that seems possibly painful or overtly difficult. We bring this natural tendency to our practice of any skill. Once we grow adept at some aspect of this skill, generally one that comes more easily to us, we prefer to practice this element over and over. Our skill becomes lopsided as we avoid our weaknesses. This is the path of amateurs. To attain mastery, you must adopt what we shall call Resistance Practice. The principle is simple—you go in the opposite direction of all of your natural tendencies when it comes to practice. First, you resist the temptation to be nice to yourself. You become your own worst critic; you see your work as if through the eyes of others. You recognize your weaknesses, precisely the elements you are not good at. Those are the aspects you give precedence to in your practice. You find a kind of perverse pleasure in moving past the pain this might bring. Second, you resist the lure of easing up on your focus. You train yourself to concentrate in practice with double the intensity, as if it were the real thing times two. In devising your own routines, you become as creative as possible. In this way, you develop your own standards for excellence, generally higher than those of others. Soon enough you will see the results of such practice, and others will marvel at the apparent ease in which you accomplish your deeds.

Daily Law: Invent exercises that work upon your weaknesses. Give yourself arbitrary deadlines to meet certain standards, constantly pushing yourself past perceived limits.

Mastery, II: Submit to Reality—The Ideal Apprenticeship

Concentrated Practice Cannot Fail

For the things we have to learn before we can do them, we learn
by doing them. . . . Men become builders by building
and lyreplayers by playing the lyre.

—ARISTOTLE

Although it might seem that the time necessary to master the requisite skills and attain a level of expertise would depend on the field and your own talent level, those who have researched the subject repeatedly come up with the number of 10,000 hours. This seems to be the amount of quality practice time that is needed for someone to reach a high level of skill and it applies to composers, chess players, writers, and athletes, among others. This number has an almost magical or mystical resonance to it. It means that so much practice time—no matter the person or the field—leads to a qualitative change in the human brain. The mind has learned to organize and structure large amounts of information. With all of this tacit knowledge, it can now become creative and playful with it. Although the number of hours might seem high, it generally adds up to seven to ten years of sustained, solid practice—roughly the period of a traditional apprenticeship. In other words, concentrated practice over time cannot fail but produce results.

Daily Law: Put in an hour of concentrated practice today, and tomorrow, and the next day, and the day after that.

Mastery, III: Absorb the Master's Power—The Mentor Dynamic

Love the Detailed Work

Aaron Rodgers, the quarterback for the Green Bay Packers, had to spend his first three years as an understudy to one of the best, Brett Favre. It meant little or no opportunities to showcase himself during a real game. For those years, all he did was practice and watch. He'd later say, "Those first three years were critical to my success." It taught him patience and humility. He spent that time honing every possible skill a quarterback could need—hand-eye coordination, finger dexterity, footwork, throwing mechanics. Not exciting stuff. He taught himself to watch from the sidelines with complete attention, absorbing as many lessons as possible. All of this not only elevated his skill level but also caught the attention of his coaches, who were very impressed by his work ethic and his ability to learn. Through those years, he was able to master his impatience and elevate his game. In essence, Rodgers had taught himself to love the detailed work itself, and once you develop that there is no stopping you.

Daily Law: Master the details and the rest will fall into place.

Robert Greene, "Five Key Elements for a New Model of Apprenticeship,"
The New York Times, February 26, 2013

The Painful Truth

*It's like chopping down a huge tree of immense girth. You won't
accomplish it with one swing of your axe. If you keep chopping away
at it, though, and do not let up, eventually, whether it wants to or not,
it will suddenly topple down.*

—ZEN MASTER HAKUIN EKAKU

Einstein began his serious thought experiments at the age of sixteen. Ten years later he came up with his first revolutionary theory of relativity. It is impossible to quantify the time he spent honing his theoretical skills in those ten years but is not hard to imagine him working three hours a day on this particular problem, which would yield more than 10,000 hours after a decade. There are no shortcuts or ways to bypass the Apprenticeship Phase. It is the nature of the human brain to require such lengthy exposure to a field, which allows for complex skills to become deeply embedded and frees the mind up for real creative activity. The very desire to find shortcuts makes you eminently unsuited for any kind of mastery. There is no possible reversal to this process.

Daily Law: There's no bypassing the Apprenticeship Phase. Rid yourself of the desire to find shortcuts.

Mastery, II: Submit to Reality—The Ideal Apprenticeship

Two Kinds of Failure

A thinker sees his own actions as experiments and questions—
as attempts to find out something. Success and failure are
for him answers above all.

—FRIEDRICH NIETZSCHE, THE GAY SCIENCE

There are two kinds of failure. The first comes from never trying out your ideas because you are afraid, or because you are waiting for the perfect time. This kind of failure you can never learn from, and such timidity will destroy you. The second kind comes from a bold and venturesome spirit. If you fail in this way, the hit that you take to your reputation is greatly outweighed by what you learn. Repeated failure will toughen your spirit and show you with absolute clarity how things must be done. In fact, it is a curse to have everything go right on your first attempt. You will fail to question the element of luck, making you think that you have the golden touch. When you do inevitably fail, it will confuse and demoralize you past the point of learning. In any case, to apprentice as an entrepreneur you must act on your ideas as early as possible, exposing them to the public, a part of you even hoping that you'll fail. You have everything to gain.

Daily Law: Act boldly on one of your ideas today.

Mastery, III: Absorb the Master's Power—The Mentor Dynamic

Choose Time

After graduating from the Zurich Polytechnic in 1900, twenty-one-year-old Albert Einstein found his job prospects extremely meager. He had graduated near the bottom of the class, almost certainly nullifying any chance to obtain a teaching position. Happy to be away from the university, he now planned to investigate, on his own, certain problems in physics that had haunted him for several years. It would be a self-apprenticeship in theorizing and thought experiments. But in the meantime, he would have to make a living. He had been offered a job in his father's dynamo business in Milan as an engineer, but such work would not leave him any free time. A friend could land him a well-paid position in an insurance company, but that would stultify his brain and sap his energy for thinking. Then, a year later, another friend mentioned a job opening up in the Swiss Patent Office in Bern. The pay was not great, the position was at the bottom, the hours were long, and the work consisted of the rather mundane task of looking over patent applications, but Einstein leaped at the chance. It was everything he wanted. His task would be to analyze the validity of patent applications, many of which involved aspects of science that interested him. The applications would be like little puzzles or thought experiments; he could try to visualize how the ideas would actually translate into inventions. Working on them would sharpen his reasoning powers. After several months on the job, he became so good at this mental game that he could finish his work in two or three hours, leaving him the rest of the day to engage in his own thought experiments. In 1905 he published his first theory of relativity, much of the work having been done while he was at his desk in the patent office.

Daily Law: Time is the critical variable. Take one thing off your plate today to make more time for your Life's Task.

Mastery, II: Submit to Reality—The Ideal Apprenticeship

Understand How the Brain Works

To the extent that we believe we can skip steps, avoid the process, magically gain power through political connections or easy formulas, or depend on our natural talents, we move against this grain and reverse our natural powers. We become slaves to time—as it passes we grow weaker, less capable, trapped in some dead-end career. We become captive to the opinions and fears of others. Rather than the mind connecting us to reality, we become disconnected and locked in a narrow chamber of thought. The human that depended on focused attention for its survival now becomes the distracted scanning animal, unable to think in depth, yet unable to depend on instincts. It is the height of stupidity to believe that in the course of your short life, your few decades of consciousness, you can somehow rewire the configurations of your brain through technology and wishful thinking, overcoming the effect of six million years of development. To go against the grain might bring temporary distraction, but time will mercilessly expose your weakness and impatience.

Daily Law: Put your faith in learning, not technology.

Mastery, Introduction: The Evolution of Mastery

Create the Need for You

Make people depend on you. More is to be gained from such
dependence than courtesy. He who has slaked his thirst, immediately
turns his back on the well, no longer needing it.

—BALTASAR GRACIÁN

Many of the great condottieri of Renaissance Italy suffered the same fate:
they won battle after battle for their employers only to find themselves
banished, imprisoned, or executed. The problem was not ingratitude; it
was that there were so many other condottieri as able and valiant as they
were. They were replaceable. Nothing was lost by killing them. Meanwhile, the older among them had grown powerful themselves, and wanted
more and more money for their services. How much better, then, to do
away with them and hire a younger, cheaper mercenary. Such is the fate
(to a less violent degree, one hopes) of those who do not make others dependent on them. Sooner or later someone comes along who can do the
job as well as they can—someone younger, fresher, less expensive, less
threatening. Necessity rules the world. People rarely act unless compelled
to. If you create no need for yourself, then you will be done away with at
the first opportunity.

> Daily Law: Strive to be the only one who can do what you do and make
> the fate of those who hire you so entwined with yours that they cannot
> possibly get rid of you.

The 48 Laws of Power, Law 11: Learn to Keep People Dependent on You

Absorb Purposeful Energy

Coco Chanel began life from a position of great weakness—an orphan with little or no resources in life. She realized in her early twenties that her calling was to design clothes and to start her own apparel line. She desperately needed guidance, however, particularly when it came to the business side. She looked for people who could help her find her way. At the age of twenty-five she met the perfect target, a wealthy older English businessman named Arthur "Boy" Capel. She latched on to him with great vehemence. He was able to instill in her the confidence that she could become a famous designer. He taught her about business in general. He offered her tough criticisms that she could accept because of her deep respect for him. He helped guide her in her first important decisions in setting up her business. From him she developed a very honed sense of purpose that she retained her entire life. Without his influence, her path would have been too confusing and difficult. Later in life, she kept returning to this strategy. She found other men and women who had skills she lacked or needed to strengthen—social graciousness, marketing, a nose for cultural trends—and developed relationships that allowed her to learn from them. In this case, you want to find people who are pragmatic and not merely those who are charismatic or visionaries. You want their practical advice, and to absorb their spirit of getting things done. If possible, collect around you a group of people from different fields, as friends or associates, who have similar energy. You will help elevate one another's sense of purpose. Do not settle for virtual associations or mentors.

Daily Law: Make a list of the people in your life who live with purpose. Prioritize spending more time with them.

The Laws of Human Nature, 13: Advance with a Sense of Purpose—The Law of Aimlessness

Never Enough Knowledge

As a child, Napoleon Bonaparte found himself drawn to games of strategy and to books that presented examples of leadership in action. Entering a military academy, he was not focused on a military career and fitting into the system. Instead, he had an obsessive need to learn as much as he could about all aspects of the military arts. He read voraciously. The extent of his knowledge impressed his superiors. At a very early age he was given an unusual amount of responsibility. He learned quickly how to keep his cool, derive the right lessons from his experiences, and recover from mistakes. By the time he was given greater responsibilities on the battlefield, he had gone through an apprenticeship that was double or triple the intensity of his peers. Being so young, ambitious, and disdainful of authority, when he was given leadership positions he proceeded to effect the greatest revolution in military history, changing the size and shape of armies, singlehandedly introducing maneuver into battle, and so on. At the endpoint of his development, he came to possess a remarkable feel for battle and the overall shape of a campaign. In his case, this became known as his infamous coup d'oeil, his ability to assess a situation with a glance of his eye. This made his lieutenants and rivals imagine that he possessed mystical powers.

Daily Law: Find the deepest pleasure in absorbing knowledge and information. Feel like you never have enough.

powerseductionandwar.com, October 1, 2012

Surpass Your Master

Poor is the apprentice who does not surpass his Master.

—LEONARDO DA VINCI

It is often a curse to learn under someone so brilliant and accomplished— your own confidence becomes crushed as you struggle to follow all of their great ideas. Many apprentices become lost in the shadow of their illustrious mentors and never amount to anything. Because of his ambition, the pianist Glenn Gould found his way to the only real solution to this dilemma. He would listen to all of his mentor Alberto Guerrero's ideas about music and try them out. In the course of playing, he would subtly alter these ideas to suit his inclinations. This would make him feel that he had his own voice. As the years went by, he made this differentiation between himself and his instructor more pronounced. Because he was so impressionable, over the course of the apprenticeship he had unconsciously internalized all of the important ideas of his mentor, but through his own active engagement he had managed to adapt them to his individuality. In this way, he could learn and yet incubate a creative spirit that would help set him apart from everyone else once he left Guerrero.

Daily Law: Beware the illustrious mentor's shadow. Try out their ideas but always transfigure them and differentiate yourself. Your goal is to surpass them.

Mastery, III: Absorb the Master's Power—The Mentor Dynamic

Keep Expanding Your Horizons

The reality of the Apprenticeship Phase is no one is really going to help you or give you direction. In fact, the odds are against you. If you desire an apprenticeship, if you want to learn and set yourself up for mastery, you have to do it yourself, and with great energy. When you enter this phase, you generally begin at the lowest position. Your access to knowledge and people is limited by your status. If you are not careful, you will accept this status and become defined by it, particularly if you come from a disadvantaged background. Instead, you must struggle against any limitations and continually work to expand your horizons. (In each learning situation you will submit to reality, but that reality does not mean you must stay in one place.) Reading books and materials that go beyond what is required is always a good starting point. Being exposed to ideas in the wide world, you will tend to develop a hunger for more and more knowledge; you will find it harder to remain satisfied in any narrow corner, which is precisely the point. The people in your field, in your immediate circle, are like worlds unto themselves—their stories and viewpoints will naturally expand your horizons and build up your social skills. Mingle with as many different types of people as possible. Those circles will slowly widen. Any kind of outside schooling will add to the dynamic.

Daily Law: Be relentless in your pursuit for expansion. Whenever you feel like you are settling into some circle, force yourself to shake things up and look for new challenges.

Mastery, II: Submit to Reality—The Ideal Apprenticeship

Venture Outside Your Comfort Zone

Our vanity, our passions, our spirit of imitation, our abstract
intelligence, our habits have long been at work, and it is the task
of art to undo this work of theirs, making us travel back in the
direction from which we have come to the depths where
what has really existed lies unknown within us.

—MARCEL PROUST

As Leonardo da Vinci progressed in his studio work for Verrocchio, he
began to experiment and to assert his own style. He found to his surprise
that the Master was impressed with his inventiveness. For Leonardo, this
indicated that he was near the end of his apprenticeship. Most people wait
too long to take this step, generally out of fear. It is always easier to learn
the rules and stay within your comfort zone. Often you must force yourself to initiate such actions or experiments before you think you are ready.
You are testing your character, moving past your fears, and developing a
sense of detachment to your work—looking at it through the eyes of others. You are getting a taste for the next phase in which what you produce
will be under constant scrutiny.

Daily Law: Try the thing you don't think you're quite ready for.

Mastery, II: Submit to Reality—The Ideal Apprenticeship

Establish Your Own Style

The distance you establish from your predecessor often demands some symbolism, a way of advertising itself publicly. Louis XIV, for example, created such symbolism when he rejected the traditional palace of the French kings and built his own palace of Versailles. King Philip II of Spain did the same when he created his center of power, the palace of El Escorial, in what was then the middle of nowhere. But Louis carried the game further: He would not be a king like his father or earlier ancestors. He would not wear a crown or carry a scepter or sit on a throne. He would establish a new kind of imposing authority with symbols and rituals of its own. Louis made his ancestors' rituals into laughable relics of the past. Follow his example: Never let yourself be seen as following your predecessor's path. If you do you will never surpass him. You must physically demonstrate your difference, by establishing a style and symbolism that sets you apart.

Daily Law: Follow the master's example, not his path. Demonstrate your difference. Establish your own style.

The 48 Laws of Power, Law 41: Avoid Stepping into a Great Man's Shoes

To the Master Goes the Knife

One repays a teacher badly if one remains only a pupil.
—FRIEDRICH NIETZSCHE

In Spanish they say *al maestro cuchillada*—"to the Master goes the knife."
It is a fencing expression, referring to the moment when the young and
agile pupil becomes skillful enough to cut his Master. But this also refers
to the fate of most mentors who inevitably experience the rebellion of
their protégés, like the cut from a sword. In our culture, we tend to ven-
erate those who seem rebellious or at least strike the pose. But rebellion
has no meaning or power if it occurs without something solid and real to
rebel against. The mentor, or father figure, gives you just such a standard
from which you can deviate and establish your own identity. You internalize the important and relevant parts of their knowledge, and you apply
the knife to what has no bearing on your life. It is the dynamic of changing generations, and sometimes the father figure has to be killed in order
for the sons and daughters to have space to discover themselves. You will
probably have several mentors in your life, like stepping-stones along the
way to mastery. At each phase of life you must find the appropriate teachers, getting what you want out of them, moving on, and feeling no shame
for this. It is the path your own mentor probably took and it is the way of
the world.

Daily Law: Internalize the important and relevant parts of the Master's
knowledge. Apply the knife to everything else.

Mastery, III: Absorb the Master's Power—The Mentor Dynamic

Take the Hacker Approach

Each age tends to create a model of apprenticeship that is suited to the system of production that prevails at the time. We are now in the computer age, and it is the hacker approach to programming that may offer the most promising model for this new age. The model goes like this: You want to learn as many skills as possible, following the direction that circumstances lead you to, but only if they are related to your deepest interests. Like a hacker, you value the process of self-discovery. You avoid the trap of following one set career path. You are not sure where this will all lead, but you are taking full advantage of the openness of information, all of the knowledge about skills now at our disposal. You see what kind of work suits you and what you want to avoid at all cost. You move by trial and error. You are not wandering about because you are afraid of commitment, but because you are expanding your skill base and your possibilities. At a certain point, when you are ready to settle on something, ideas and opportunities will inevitably present themselves to you. When that happens, all of the skills you have accumulated will prove invaluable. You will be the master at combining them in ways that are unique and suited to your individuality.

Daily Law: In this new age, those who follow a rigid, singular path in their youth often find themselves in a career dead end in their forties or overwhelmed with boredom. The wide-ranging apprenticeship will yield the opposite—expanding possibilities.

Mastery, II: Submit to Reality—The Ideal Apprenticeship

March

The Master at Work

ACTIVATING SKILLS AND ATTAINING MASTERY

≈

In moving toward mastery, you are bringing your mind closer to reality and to life itself. Anything that is alive is in a continual state of change and movement. The moment that you rest, thinking that you have attained the level you desire, a part of your mind enters a phase of decay. You lose your hard-earned creativity and others begin to sense it. This is a power and intelligence that must be continually renewed or it will die. Your whole life, therefore, must be treated as a kind of apprenticeship to which you continually apply your learning skills. The month of March will teach you how to activate your skills and internalize the knowledge necessary for a life of mastery.

When I began writing my fifth book, *Mastery*, several years ago, something very strange and exciting occurred. This was a particularly difficult and complicated book to write. First of all, I had done my usual research: reading several hundred books, taking thousands of note cards on them, structuring them into various chapters, etc. But in addition, I had read a lot of books on science, which I had never done before—books examining the nature of the human brain—to give *Mastery* more of a scientific foundation. And that added yet another layer of difficulty to the writing. Furthermore, I had also interviewed six or seven contemporary masters to give the book a more up-to-date feel. Incorporating the science and the interviews into *Mastery* made it a particularly challenging project. And so, when I began the actual writing process, it was very slow going with the first couple of chapters; it took longer than usual to get into a flow.

And then chapter by chapter, week by week, month by month, I started to gain a little bit of momentum. And then by the fifth chapter, something unexpected happened. The fifth chapter is about the creative process itself. And the idea is that once you do enough work on a project, enough preparation, and you've had all of these months of experience delving into the subject, you often reach a state of creativity where ideas come to you out of nowhere. And suddenly this was happening to me. After all my research and all the preparation, by the time I had reached chapter five, ideas for that chapter were coming to me while I was taking a shower, while I was taking a walk. I was even dreaming about the book and ideas were coming to me in my sleep, confirming what I was writing about.

And this made me very surprised and very inspired. And then I came to chapter six, which is about mastery itself—the final chapter. The idea is that even further along in the process, you start to have a very intuitive feel for the subject. It's almost as if the book or the project is living inside of you. You can compare it to a chess master where the chessboard feels like it is inside his brain, inside his body, and he can feel what comes next.

I felt that the book was living inside of me and that I had what I call a fingertip feel for what I should be writing. There was this sort of fast-paced, intuitive series of ideas that would come to me out of nowhere. And this was an incredible experience, an incredible feeling—a feeling of great power.

I'm not claiming that I'm special, that I'm some sort of genius, or particularly gifted or talented. In fact, the whole point of the book is to demythologize our concept of genius and creativity. We tend to think that it is something you were born with, something in your DNA, some special way that you're wired. And I wanted to prove that it was actually a product of hard work and discipline, that when you practice something for so many months or years, you can reach this high level of creativity and mastery. And the writing of the book literally confirmed my idea. And because it is a function of relentless dedication, boring into a problem, it is an exhilarating experience that almost anyone can have, if they follow the pattern I have laid out.

It doesn't mean that if you spend years studying something, creative powers will inevitably come to you. You must have a certain intensity to your focus, as well as a love for the work itself that animates the final product. And it also depends on years of prior labor in the Apprenticeship Phase, which I had gone through in writing four other books.

There are no shortcuts to the creative process; drugs and alcohol are more of a hindrance. The very impatience that drives you to desire shortcuts makes you unsuited for mastery. But if you trust the process and take it as far as you can, you will be amazed at the results.

Awaken the Dimensional Mind

Learning never exhausts the mind.

—LEONARDO DA VINCI

As you accumulate more skills and internalize the rules that govern your field, your mind will want to become more active, seeking to use this knowledge in ways that are more suited to your inclinations. What will impede this natural creative dynamic from flourishing is not a lack of talent, but your attitude. Feeling anxious and insecure, you will tend to turn conservative with your knowledge, preferring to fit into the group and sticking to the procedures you have learned. Instead, you must force yourself in the opposite direction. As you emerge from your apprenticeship, you must become increasingly bold. Instead of feeling complacent about what you know, you must expand your knowledge to related fields, giving your mind fuel to make new associations between different ideas. You must experiment and look at problems from all possible angles. As your thinking grows more fluid, your mind will become increasingly dimensional, seeing more and more aspects of reality. In the end, you will turn against the very rules you have internalized, shaping and reforming them to suit your spirit. Such originality will bring you to the heights of power.

Daily Law: Expand your knowledge to related fields. Pick an auxiliary skill and start practicing.

Mastery, V: Awaken the Dimensional Mind—The Creative-Active

Get to the Inside

When I'm asked how I define mastery or what phrase guides me in my own life or in writing a book, I say, "It's getting to the inside." I'm always trying to move to the inside of things. On the outside, things look a certain way—kind of dead, because you're just seeing the appearances. When you get to the inside, you see the heart beating, you understand it, you get the reality. When you start learning to play chess or the piano, for instance, you're on the outside. You just see the exterior, visual, surfaces of things. And you're learning the rules or the basics. And it's very slow and tedious. You don't really have an understanding. It's all kind of confusing, a blur. Eventually, though, if you stick with it, you worm your way to the inside of it. And you're feeling the thing come alive. The chessboard or the piano is no longer a physical object, it's in you. You've internalized it. You no longer have to think of the keys; the keys are in your head. That is mastery. Sports are a great example. We say of the masters in soccer, "It's as if they have eyes in the back of their head." No, they are on the inside of the game itself. Or great quarterbacks talk about with each year of experience, "It's as if the game slows down." No, they are moving closer and closer to the inside. You could say the same thing of scientists, writers, actresses, et cetera—the masters know the thing from the inside out, not the outside in.

Daily Law: If you work hard, you will make your way to the inner circle of knowledge. That is the end goal of mastery: an inside-out understanding.

"Robert Greene: Mastery and Research," *Finding Mastery: Conversations with Michael Gervais*, January 25, 2017

Cultivate the Craftsman Ethic

The great masters, including contemporary ones, all manage to retain the craftsman spirit. What motivates them is not money, fame, or a high position, but making the perfect work of art, designing the best building, discovering some new scientific law, mastering their craft. This helps them to not get too caught up in the ups and downs of their career. It is the work that matters. And in the end, these masters end up making more money and become more famous by cultivating this spirit. Steve Jobs personified this craftsman ethic. He inherited it from his father, a man who loved to build things with his hands, and the love of perfection, for making something just right, is an attitude he transferred to the design of products for Apple. That's the master's goal: to make things well and to feel pride in it.

Daily Law: Retain the craftsman spirit. Keep in mind: the work is the only thing that matters.

Robert Greene, "Five Key Elements for a New Model of Apprenticeship,"
The New York Times, February 26, 2013

The Creative Process

Because the creative process is an elusive subject and one for which we receive no training, we often go quite wrong. From masters throughout the ages, we can discern an elemental pattern and principles that have wide application. First, it is essential to build into the creative process an initial period that is open-ended. You give yourself time to dream and wander, to start out in a loose and unfocused manner. In this period, you allow the project to associate itself with certain powerful emotions, ones that naturally come out of you as you focus on your ideas. It is always easy to tighten up your ideas later, and to make your project increasingly realistic and rational. Second, it is best to have wide knowledge of your field and other fields, giving your brain more possible associations and connections. Third, to keep this process alive, you must never settle into complacency, as if your initial vision represents the endpoint. You must cultivate profound dissatisfaction with your work and the need to constantly improve your ideas, along with a sense of uncertainty—you are not exactly sure where to go next, and this uncertainty drives the creative urge and keeps it fresh. Finally, you must come to embrace slowness as a virtue in itself. When it comes to creative endeavors, time is always relative. Whether your project takes months or years to complete, you will always experience a sense of impatience and a desire to get to the end. The single greatest action you can take for acquiring creative power is to reverse this natural impatience.

Daily Law: Imagine yourself years in the future looking back at the work you have done. From that future vantage point, the extra months and years you devoted to the process will not seem painful or laborious at all. Time is your greatest ally.

Mastery, V: Awaken the Dimensional Mind—The Creative-Active

Look Wider and Think Further Ahead

In any competitive environment in which there are winners or losers, the person who has the wider, more global perspective will inevitably prevail. The reason is simple: such a person will be able to think beyond the moment and control the overall dynamic through careful strategizing. Most people are perpetually locked in the present. Their decisions are overly influenced by the most immediate event; they easily become emotional and ascribe greater significance to a problem than it should have in reality. Moving toward mastery will naturally bring you a more global outlook, but it is always wise to expedite the process by training yourself early on to continually enlarge your perspective. You can do so by always reminding yourself of the overall purpose of the work you are presently engaged in and how this meshes with your long-term goals. In dealing with any problem, you must train yourself to look at how it inevitably connects to a larger picture. If your work is not having the desired effect, you must look at it from all angles until you find the source of the problem. You must not merely observe the rivals in your field but dissect and uncover their weaknesses. "Look wider and think further ahead" must be your motto. Through such mental training, you will smooth the path to mastery while separating yourself ever further from the competition.

Daily Law: The person with the more global perspective wins. Expand your gaze.

Mastery, VI: Fuse the Intuitive with the Rational—Mastery

The Gift of Our Original Mind

We all possess an inborn creative force that wants to become active. This is the gift of our Original Mind, which reveals such potential. The human mind is naturally creative, constantly looking to make associations and connections between things and ideas. It wants to explore, to discover new aspects of the world, and to invent. To express this creative force is our greatest desire, and the stifling of it the source of our misery. What kills the creative force is not age or a lack of talent, but our own spirit, our own attitude. We become too comfortable with the knowledge we have gained. We grow afraid of entertaining new ideas and the effort that this requires. To think more flexibly entails a risk—we could fail and be ridiculed. We prefer to live with familiar ideas and habits of thinking, but we pay a steep price for this: our minds go dead from the lack of challenge and novelty; we reach a limit in our field and lose control over our fate because we become replaceable.

Daily Law: Do what the mind wants to do—explore, entertain, and embrace new ideas.

Mastery, V: Awaken the Dimensional Mind—The Creative-Active

Keep the Mind Moving

When we were children, our minds never stopped. We were open to new experiences and absorbed as much of them as possible. We learned fast, because the world around us excited us. When we felt frustrated or upset, we would find some creative way to get what we wanted and then quickly forget the problem as something new crossed our path. Our minds were always moving, and they are always excited and curious. The Greek thinker Aristotle thought that life was defined by movement. What does not move is dead. What has speed and mobility has more possibilities, more life. We all start off with the mobile mind, but as we get older, the mind gets more and more immobile. You may think that what you'd like to recapture from your youth is your looks, your physical fitness, your simple pleasures, but what you really need is the fluidity of mind you once possessed. Whenever you find your thoughts revolving around a particular subject or idea—an obsession, a resentment—force them past it. Distract yourself with something else. Like a child, find something new to be absorbed by, something worthy of concentrated attention. Do not waste time on things you cannot change or influence. Just keep moving.

Daily Law: Respond to the moment. Thought to thought, task to task, topic to topic—let the mind be fluid.

The 33 Strategies of War, Strategy 2: Do Not Fight the Last War—The Guerrilla-War-of-the-Mind Strategy

Retain Your Sense of Wonder

Youth is happy because it has the capacity to see beauty. Anyone who
keeps the ability to see beauty never grows old.

—FRANZ KAFKA

After we pass through a rigorous apprenticeship and begin to flex our
creative muscles, we cannot help but feel satisfaction in what we have
learned and how far we have progressed. We naturally begin to take for
granted certain ideas we have learned and developed. Slowly, we stop asking the same kinds of questions that plagued us earlier on. We already
know the answers. We feel ever so superior. Unknown to ourselves, the
mind slowly narrows and tightens as complacency creeps into the soul,
and although we may have achieved public acclaim for our past work, we
stifle our own creativity and never get it back. Fight this downhill tendency as much as you can by upholding the value of active wonder. Constantly remind yourself of how little you truly know, and of how
mysterious the world remains.

Daily Law: Reality is infinitely mysterious. Let it continually fill you
with awe. Remind yourself of how much more you still can learn.

Mastery, V: Awaken the Dimensional Mind—The Creative-Active

Impatience Is Your Enemy

Patience is bitter, but its fruit is sweet.

—ARISTOTLE

The greatest impediment to creativity is your impatience, the almost inevitable desire to hurry up the process, express something, and make a splash. What happens in such a case is that you do not master the basics; you have no real vocabulary at your disposal. What you mistake for being creative and distinctive is more likely an imitation of other people's style, or personal rantings that do not really express anything. Audiences, however, are hard to fool. They feel the lack of rigor, the imitative quality, the urge to get attention, and they turn their backs, or give the mildest praise that quickly passes. The best route is to love learning for its own sake. Anyone who would spend ten years absorbing the techniques and conventions of their field, trying them out, mastering them, exploring and personalizing them, would inevitably find their authentic voice and give birth to something unique and expressive.

Daily Law: Take the long view. By being patient and following the process, individual expression will flow out of you naturally.

Mastery, V: Awaken the Dimensional Mind—The Creative-Active

Knowledge Is Your Superior

What makes the difference between an outstandingly creative person
and a less creative one is not any special power, but greater knowledge
(in the form of practiced expertise) and the motivation to acquire
and use it. This motivation endures for long periods, perhaps
shaping and inspiring a whole lifetime.

—MARGARET A. BODEN

To negate the ego you must adopt a kind of humility toward knowledge.
The great scientist Michael Faraday expressed this attitude in the following way: Scientific knowledge is constantly progressing. The greatest theories of the time are eventually disproven or altered at some future point.
The human mind is simply too weak to have a clear and perfect vision of
reality. The idea or theory that you are currently formulating, that seems
so fresh and alive and truthful, will almost certainly be shot down or
ridiculed in a few decades or centuries. (We tend to laugh at people prior
to the twentieth century who did not yet believe in evolution and who
saw the world as only 6,000 years old, but imagine how people will be
laughing at us for the naive beliefs we hold in the twenty-first century!)
And so it is best to keep this in mind and not grow too fond of your ideas
or too certain of their truth.

Daily Law: Knowledge is always progressing. Don't let your ego fool
you. You are always knowledge's inferior.

Mastery, V: Awaken the Dimensional Mind—The Creative-Active

Intensity of Focus

To many of those who knew Marcel Proust as a young man, he seemed the least likely person ever to attain mastery, because on the surface he appeared to waste so much valuable time. All he ever seemed to do was read books, take walks, write interminable letters, attend parties, sleep during the day, and publish frothy society articles. But under the surface was an intensity of attention. He did not simply read books—he took them apart, rigorously analyzed them, and learned valuable lessons to apply to his own life. All of this reading implanted in his brain various styles that would enrich his own writing style. He did not merely socialize—he strained to understand people at their core and to uncover their secret motivations. He did not just analyze his own psychology but went so deeply into the various levels of consciousness he found within himself that he developed insights about the functioning of memory that foreshadowed many discoveries in neuroscience. He even used the death of his mother to intensify his development. With her gone, he would have to write himself out of his depression and find a way to re-create the feelings between them in the book he was to write. As he later described it, all of these experiences were like seeds, and once he had started his great novel *In Search of Lost Time*, he was like a gardener tending and cultivating the plants that had taken root so many years before.

Daily Law: It is not your studies that will bear fruit but the intensity of your attention.

Mastery, VI: Fuse the Intuitive with the Rational—Mastery

Perfect Yourself through Failure

Henry Ford had one of those minds that was naturally attuned to the mechanical. He had the power of most great inventors—the ability to visualize the parts and how they functioned together. If he had to describe how something worked, Ford would inevitably take a napkin and sketch out a diagram rather than use words. With this type of intelligence, his apprenticeships on machines were easy and fast. But when it came to mass-producing his inventions, he had to confront the fact that he did not have the requisite knowledge. He needed an additional apprenticeship in becoming a businessman and entrepreneur. Fortunately, working on machines had developed in him a kind of practical intelligence, patience, and way of solving problems that could be applied to anything. When a machine malfunctions, you do not take it personally or grow despondent. It is in fact a blessing in disguise. Such malfunctions generally show you inherent flaws and means of improvement. You simply keep tinkering until you get it right. The same should apply to an entrepreneurial venture. Mistakes and failures are precisely your means of education. They tell you about your own inadequacies. It is hard to find out such things from people, as they are often political with their praise and criticisms. Your failures also permit you to see the flaws of your ideas, which are only revealed in the execution of them. You learn what your audience really wants, the discrepancy between your ideas and how they affect the public.

Daily Law: Malfunctions are a means of education. They are trying to tell you something. You must listen.

Mastery, II: Submit to Reality—The Ideal Apprenticeship

Creative Endurance

In contemplating work on *Mastery*, I realized it presented quite a challenge. I had known from previous books that near the end of the writing process I could often become so exhausted that the writing could suffer. I believe many writers tend to peter out halfway through their projects, overwhelmed by the complexity and the lack of organization of their material. I decided to treat it like a marathon and to find a way to build up endurance for the long slog. So I decided to up my exercise routine. I normally exercise every day, but I would increase the times and distances ever so slightly. At a certain point I knew I would reach a plateau in which I did not feel any more tired with these increases. I would stay at the plateau level for the entire length of the project. In sports such as long-distance cycling, this kind of training helps build up endurance levels. It is better to stay at the plateau for a period of time rather than keep increasing the workout. I wanted to see if this would translate to more consistent energy levels in my work.

In the last few months, when the looming deadline made me work even harder than before, I noticed that I was considerably calmer, better able to handle the stress, and that I had reservoirs of energy to draw upon for the long hours. I came to the conclusion that the mind and the body are so intertwined that it is impossible to separate out their effects on us. Feeling energized influences our mood, which influences our work in very direct ways. And feeling confused or disorganized in our work can have a terrible effect on us physically as well.

Daily Law: Creating anything worthwhile is like a marathon, and you must train for it.

HuffPost, November 15, 2012

Immerse Yourself in the Details

When Leonardo da Vinci wanted to create a whole new style of painting, one that was more lifelike and emotional, he engaged in an obsessive study of details. He spent endless hours experimenting with forms of light hitting various geometrical solids, to test how light could alter the appearance of objects. He devoted hundreds of pages in his notebooks to exploring the various gradations of shadows in every possible combination. He gave this same attention to the folds of a gown, the patterns in hair, the various minute changes in the expression of a human face. When we look at his work we are not consciously aware of these efforts on his part, but we feel how much more alive and realistic his paintings are, as if he had captured reality.

In general, try approaching a problem or idea with a much more open mind. Let your study of the details guide your thinking and shape your theories. Think of everything in nature, or in the world, as a kind of hologram—the smallest part reflecting something essential about the whole. Immersing yourself in details will combat the generalizing tendencies of the brain and bring you closer to reality.

Daily Law: Uncover the secret to any reality by uncovering the details.

Mastery, V: Awaken the Dimensional Mind—The Creative-Active

Make Your Work Come to Life

Leonardo da Vinci's hunger to get at the core of life by exploring its details drove him into elaborate research on human and animal anatomy. He wanted to be able to draw a human or a cat from the inside out. He personally dissected cadavers, sawing through bones and skulls, and he religiously attended autopsies so that he could see as closely as possible the structure of muscles and nerves. His anatomical drawings were far in advance of anything of his time for their realism and accuracy. In your own work you must follow the Leonardo path. Most people don't have the patience to absorb their minds in the fine points and minutiae that are intrinsically part of their work. They are in a hurry to create effects and make a splash; they think in large brush strokes. Their work inevitably reveals their lack of attention to detail—it doesn't connect deeply with the public, and it feels flimsy. You must see whatever you produce as something that has a life and presence of its own. Seeing your work as something alive, your path to mastery is to study and absorb these details in a universal fashion, to the point at which you feel the life force and can express it effortlessly in your work.

Daily Law: See your work as a living thing. Your task is to bring it alive and make others feel this.

Mastery, VI: Fuse the Intuitive with the Rational—Mastery

MARCH 16

Alter Your Perspective

The lesson is simple—what constitutes true creativity is the openness and adaptability of our spirit. When we see or experience something we must be able to look at it from several angles, to see other possibilities beyond the obvious ones. We imagine that the objects around us can be used and co-opted for different purposes. We do not hold on to our original idea out of sheer stubbornness, or because our ego is tied up with its rightness. Instead, we move with what presents itself to us in the moment, exploring and exploiting different branches and contingencies. We thus manage to turn feathers into flying material. The difference then is not in some initial creative power of the brain, but in how we look at the world and the fluidity with which we can reframe what we see.

Daily Law: Creativity and adaptability are inseparable. Look at things today from every possible angle.

Mastery, V: Awaken the Dimensional Mind—The Creative-Active

These Powers Can't Come Cheaply

To create a meaningful work of art or to make a discovery or invention requires great discipline, self-control, and emotional stability. It requires mastering the forms of your field. Drugs and madness only destroy such powers. Do not fall for the romantic myths and clichés that abound in culture about creativity—offering us the excuse or panacea that such powers can come cheaply. When you look at the exceptionally creative work of Masters, you must not ignore the years of practice, the endless routines, the hours of doubt, and the tenacious overcoming of obstacles these people endured.

Daily Law: Creative energy is the fruit of the Master's efforts and nothing else. Do not fall for the romantic myths.

Mastery, V: Awaken the Dimensional Mind—The Creative-Active

The Power of Desire and Determination

When I was younger, I worked at a publisher's house in New York. One of the people we published was Toni Morrison. It was her first novel. I'll never forget the story. Toni Morrison worked as an editor at this publication house. She worked until 6 or 7 p.m. then took the train home to where she lived in Connecticut. She was raising two children. She would go home, cook them meals, put them to bed, and at 11 p.m. she would sit down and write. And that's how she wrote her first novel. That's the kind of energy and determination you have to have. I always thought that was superhuman. I know I could never do that, but look at who she became. It's because she wanted it so badly.

Daily Law: To rise to the level of mastery requires intense dedication. You have to really want it. What would make you have such commitment and dedication?

Robert Greene in conversation at Live Talks Los Angeles, February 11, 2019

The Deadening Dynamic

Perhaps the greatest impediment to human creativity is the natural decay that sets in over time in any kind of medium or profession. In the sciences or in business, a certain way of thinking or acting that once had success quickly becomes a paradigm, an established procedure. As the years go by, people forget the initial reason for this paradigm and simply follow a lifeless set of techniques. In the arts, someone establishes a style that is new and vibrant, speaking to the particular spirit of the times. It has an edge because it is so different. Soon imitators pop up everywhere. It becomes a fashion, something to conform to, even if the conformity appears to be rebellious and edgy. This can drag on for ten, twenty years; it eventually becomes a cliché, pure style without any real emotion or need. Nothing in culture escapes this deadening dynamic. This problem, however, sets up a tremendous opportunity for creative types. The process goes as follows: You begin by looking inward. You have something you want to express that is unique to yourself and related to your inclinations. You must be sure it is not something that is sparked by some trend or fashion, but that it comes from you and is real. Perhaps it is a sound you are not hearing in music, a type of story not being told, a type of book that does not fit into the usual tidy categories. Let the idea, the sound, the image take root in you. Sensing the possibility of a new language or way of doing things, you must make the conscious decision to play against the very conventions that you find dead and want to get rid of.

> Daily Law: People are dying for the new, for what expresses the spirit of the time in an original way. By creating something new you will create your own audience and attain the ultimate position of power in culture.
>
> *Mastery*, V: Awaken the Dimensional Mind—The Creative-Active

The Master's Brain

We can now say with confidence that the brain is an extraordinarily
plastic biological system that is in a state of dynamic equilibrium with
the external world. Even its basic connections are being constantly
updated in response to changing sensory demands.

—V. S. RAMACHANDRAN

Something happens neurologically to the brain that is important for you
to understand. When you start something new, a large number of neurons in the frontal cortex (the higher, more conscious command area of
the brain) are recruited and become active, helping you in the learning
process. The brain has to deal with a large amount of new information,
and this would be stressful and overwhelming if only a limited part of the
brain were used to handle it. The frontal cortex even expands in size in
this initial phase, as we focus hard on the task. But once something is
repeated often enough, it becomes hardwired and automatic, and the neu-
ral pathways for this skill are delegated to other parts of the brain, farther
down the cortex. Those neurons in the frontal cortex that we needed in
the initial stages are now freed up to help in learning something else, and
the area goes back to its normal size. In the end, an entire network of
neurons is developed to remember this single task, which accounts for the
fact that we can still ride a bicycle years after we first learned how to do
so. If we were to take a look at the frontal cortex of those who have mastered something through repetition, it would be remarkably still and in-
active as they performed the skill. All of their brain activity is occurring
in areas that are lower down and require much less conscious control.

Daily Law: The more skills you learn, the richer the landscape of the
brain. It's up to you.

Mastery, II: Submit to Reality—The Ideal Apprenticeship

The Universal Master

Johann Wolfgang von Goethe's mastery was not over this subject or that one, but in the connections between them, based on decades of deep observation and thinking. Goethe epitomized what was known in the Renaissance as the Ideal of the Universal Man—a person so steeped in all forms of knowledge that his mind grows closer to the reality of nature itself and sees secrets that are invisible to most people. Today some might see a person such as Goethe as a quaint relic of the eighteenth century, and his ideal of unifying knowledge as a Romantic dream, but in fact the opposite is the case, and for one simple reason: the design of the human brain—its inherent need to make connections and associations—gives it a will of its own. Although this evolution might take various twists and turns in history, the desire to connect will win out in the end because it is so powerfully a part of our nature and inclination. Aspects of technology now offer unprecedented means to build connections between fields and ideas. In any way possible, you should strive to be a part of this universalizing process, extending your own knowledge to other branches, further and further out. The rich ideas that will come from such a quest will be their own reward.

Daily Law: Extend your knowledge further and further, leading to wide-ranging connections.

Mastery, VI: Fuse the Intuitive with the Rational—Mastery

On Meditation

All of humanity's problems stem from man's
inability to sit quietly in a room alone.

—BLAISE PASCAL

Often, writers begin with an exciting idea, which is reflected in the energy of the first chapters. Then, they get somewhat lost in the material. The organization of the book falls apart. They start to repeat the same ideas. The last few chapters do not have the same verve of the opening ones. It is hard to maintain one's enthusiasm, energy, and freshness over the course of months and years that a book requires. To help me avoid such a fate, I practice forty minutes of Zen meditation (known as *zazen*) every morning. In this form of meditation (referred to as *shikantaza*) the main goal is to learn how to empty the mind, develop superior powers of focus (*joriki*), and gain access to more unconscious, intuitive forms of thinking. Meditation has significantly improved my ability to concentrate when reading or taking notes. The nuisances that years ago used to get under my skin are now largely ignored or forgotten. I have developed patience in dealing with the drudgery of practice and am better able to handle petty criticisms. From early on I could see how this routine was helping me in several ways and I have since meditated every day in the morning. If you are feeling restless on your path to mastery or find that little things often aggravate and distract you from your life's work, I recommend you take up meditation.

Daily Law: The Master's mind must be able to concentrate on one thing for a long period of time. Develop such habits.

powerseductionandwar.com, September 4, 2014

Listen to Your Frustration

The composer Richard Wagner had worked so hard on his opera *Das Rheingold* that he became completely blocked. Beyond frustration, he took a long walk in the woods, lay down, and fell asleep. In a sort of half dream, he felt himself sinking in swiftly flowing water. The rushing sounds formed into musical chords. He awoke, terrified by a feeling of drowning. He hurried home and noted down the chords of his dream, which seemed to perfectly conjure up the sound of rushing water. These chords became the prelude of the opera, a leitmotif that runs throughout it, and one of the most astonishing pieces he had ever written. Similar stories are so common as to indicate something essential about the brain and how it reaches certain peaks of creativity. We can explain this pattern in the following way: If we remained as excited as we were in the beginning of our project, maintaining that intuitive feel that sparked it all, we would never be able to take the necessary distance to look at our work objectively and improve upon it. Losing that initial verve causes us to work and rework the idea. It forces us to not settle too early on an easy solution. The mounting frustration and tightness that comes from single-minded devotion to one problem or idea will naturally lead to a breaking point. We realize we are getting nowhere. Such moments are signals from the brain to let go, for however long a period necessary, and most creative people consciously or unconsciously accept this.

Daily Law: Walk away when you're blocked. Do something else. The brain will eventually lead you back.

Mastery, V: Awaken the Dimensional Mind—The Creative-Active

The Mind as a Muscle

Think of the mind as a muscle that naturally tightens up over time unless it is consciously worked upon. What causes this tightening is twofold. First, we generally prefer to entertain the same thoughts and ways of thinking because they provide us with a sense of consistency and familiarity. Sticking with the same methods also saves us a lot of effort. We are creatures of habit. Second, whenever we work hard at a problem or idea, our minds naturally narrow their focus because of the strain and effort involved. This means that the further we progress on our creative task, the fewer alternative possibilities or viewpoints we tend to consider. This tightening process afflicts all of us, and it is best to admit that you share in this flaw. The only antidote is to enact strategies to loosen up the mind and let in alternative ways of thinking. This is not only essential for the creative process but is also immensely therapeutic for our psyches. Stimulating your brain and senses from all directions will help unlock your natural creativity and help revive your original mind.

Daily Law: Don't get comfortable. Take risks. Change. Try learning about a field you don't know anything about. Or stepping into a viewpoint you've never considered.

Mastery, V: Awaken the Dimensional Mind—The Creative-Active

Cultivate Negative Capability

The ability to endure and even embrace mysteries and uncertainties is what the poet John Keats called "negative capability." All Masters possess this Negative Capability, and it is the source of their creative power. This quality allows them to entertain a broader range of ideas and experiment with them, which in turn makes their work richer and more inventive. Throughout his career, Mozart never asserted any particular opinions about music. Instead, he absorbed the styles he heard around himself and incorporated them into his own voice. Late in his career, he encountered for the first time the music of Johann Sebastian Bach—a kind of music very different from his own, and in some ways more complex. Most artists would grow defensive and dismissive of something that challenged their own principles. Instead, Mozart opened his mind up to new possibilities, studying Bach's use of counterpoint for nearly a year and absorbing it into his own vocabulary. This gave his music a new and surprising quality. This might seem like some kind of poetic conceit, but in fact cultivating Negative Capability will be the single most important factor in your success as a creative thinker. The need for certainty is the greatest disease the mind faces.

Daily Law: Develop the habit of suspending the need to judge everything that crosses your path. Consider and even momentarily entertain viewpoints opposite to your own, seeing how they feel. Do anything to break up your normal train of thinking and your sense that you already know the truth.

Mastery, V: Awaken the Dimensional Mind—The Creative-Active

Pay Attention to Negative Cues

In the Arthur Conan Doyle story "Silver Blaze," Sherlock Holmes solves a crime by paying attention to what did not happen—the family dog had not barked. This meant that the murderer must have been someone the dog knew. What this story illustrates is how the average person does not generally pay attention to what we shall call "negative cues": what should have happened but did not. It is our natural tendency to fixate on positive information, to notice only what we can see and hear. It takes a creative type such as Holmes to think more broadly and rigorously, pondering the missing information in an event, visualizing this absence as easily as we see the presence of something. For centuries, doctors considered diseases exclusively as something stemming from outside the body attacking it—a contagious germ, a draft of cold air, miasmic vapors, and so on. Treatment depended on finding drugs of some sort that could counteract the harmful effects of these environmental agents of disease. Then, in the early twentieth century, the biochemist Frederick Gowland Hopkins, studying the effects of scurvy, had the idea to reverse this perspective. What caused the problem in this particular disease, he speculated, was not what was attacking from the outside, but what was missing from within the body itself—in this case what came to be known as vitamin C. Thinking creatively, he did not look at what was present but precisely at what was absent in order to solve the problem. This led to his groundbreaking work on vitamins, and completely altered our concept of health.

> Daily Law: The ability to loosen our mind, to alter our perspective, is a function of our imagination. Learn to imagine more possibilities than you generally consider. Avoid fixating only on what is present. Ponder what is absent.

> *Mastery*, V: Awaken the Dimensional Mind—The Creative-Active

The Power of Peak Experiences

The person in peak-experiences feels himself, more than other times, to be the responsible, active, creating center of his activities and of his perceptions. He feels more like a prime-mover, more self-determined (rather than caused, determined, helpless, dependent, passive, weak, bossed). He feels himself to be his own boss, fully responsible, fully volitional, with more free-will than at other times, master of his fate, an agent.

—ABRAHAM MASLOW

Perhaps the greatest difficulty you will face in maintaining a high and consistent sense of purpose is the level of commitment that is required over time and the sacrifices that go with this. You have to handle many moments of frustration, boredom, and failure, and the endless temptations in our culture for more immediate pleasures. Benefits are often not immediately apparent. And as the years pile up, you can face burnout. To offset this tedium, you need to have moments of flow in which your mind becomes so deeply immersed in the work that you are transported beyond your ego. You experience feelings of profound calmness and joy. The psychologist Abraham Maslow called these "peak experiences"—once you have them, you are forever changed. You will feel the compulsion to repeat them. The more immediate pleasures the world offers will pale in comparison. And when you feel rewarded for your dedication and sacrifices, your sense of purpose will be intensified.

Daily Law: Get into a flow state today. Rid yourself of the distractions and cheap pleasures. Lose yourself in the work.

The Laws of Human Nature, 8: Change Your Circumstances by Changing Your Attitude—The Law of Self-sabotage

Move Beyond Intellect

Through intense absorption in a particular field over a long period of time, masters come to understand all of the parts involved in what they are studying. They reach a point where all of this has become internalized and they are no longer seeing the parts, but gain an intuitive feel for the whole. They literally see or sense the dynamic. In the living sciences, we have the example of Jane Goodall, who studied chimpanzees in the wilds of East Africa for years as she lived among them. Interacting with them constantly, she reached a point where she began to think like a chimpanzee and could see elements of their social life that no other scientist had come close to fathoming. She gained an intuitive feel for not only how they functioned as individuals but as a group, which is an inseparable part of their lives. She made discoveries about the social life of chimpanzees that forever altered our conception of the animal, and that are no less scientific for depending on this deep level of intuition.

Daily Law: Over time, Masters gain an intuitive feel for the whole of their field. It's an excitement and joy that awaits you if you are patient.

Mastery, VI: Fuse the Intuitive with the Rational—Mastery

Fuse the Intuitive with the Rational, A

Albert Einstein called the intuitive or metaphoric mind a sacred gift.
He added that the rational mind was a faithful servant. It is
paradoxical that in the context of modern life we have begun
to worship the servant and defile the divine.

—BOB SAMPLES, *The Metaphoric Mind*

All of us have access to a higher form of intelligence, one that can allow us to see more of the world, to anticipate trends, to respond with speed and accuracy to any circumstance. This intelligence is cultivated by deeply immersing ourselves in a field of study and staying true to our inclinations, no matter how unconventional our approach might seem to others. Through such intense immersion over many years we come to internalize and gain an intuitive feel for the complicated components of our field. When we fuse this intuitive feel with rational processes, we expand our minds to the outer limits of our potential and are able to see into the secret core of life itself. We then come to have powers that approximate the instinctive force and speed of animals, but with the added reach that our human consciousness brings us.

Daily Law: This power is what our brains were designed to attain, and we will be naturally led to this type of intelligence if we follow our inclinations to their ultimate ends.

Mastery, VI: Fuse the Intuitive with the Rational—Mastery

Fuse the Intuitive with the Rational, B

The great chess master Bobby Fischer spoke of being able to think beyond the various moves of his pieces on the chessboard; after a while he could see "fields of forces" that allowed him to anticipate the entire direction of the match. For the pianist Glenn Gould, he no longer had to focus on notes or parts of the music he was playing, but instead saw the entire architecture of the piece and could express it. Albert Einstein suddenly was able to realize not just the answer to a problem, but a whole new way of looking at the universe, contained in a visual image he intuited. In all of these instances, these practitioners of various skills described a sensation of seeing more. All of us have access to this higher form of intelligence, one that can allow us to see more of the world, to anticipate trends, to respond with speed and accuracy to any circumstance. In moving through these various steps, with an intense energy, you must have faith that these intuitive powers will come to you over time. The ability to sense the overall dynamic in any situation, to foresee problems and solutions before anyone else will bring you to the heights of power.

Daily Law: If you keep to the path, these powers of mastery will come to you.

Mastery, VI: Fuse the Intuitive with the Rational—Mastery

Connect to Your Destiny

Do not talk about giftedness, inborn talents! One can name great men
of all kinds who were very little gifted. They acquired greatness,
became "geniuses". . . . [T]hey allowed themselves time for it.

—FRIEDRICH NIETZSCHE

As you must know by now, mastery is not a question of genetics or luck,
but of following your natural inclinations and the deep desire that stirs
you from within. Everyone has such inclinations. This desire within you
is not motivated by egotism or sheer ambition for power, both of which
are emotions that get in the way of mastery. It is instead a deep expression
of something natural, something that marked you at birth as unique. In
following your inclinations and moving toward mastery, you make a great
contribution to society, enriching it with discoveries and insights, and
making the most of the diversity in nature and among human society. It
is in fact the height of selfishness to merely consume what others create
and to retreat into a shell of limited goals and immediate pleasures.
Alienating yourself from your inclinations can only lead to pain and disappointment in the long run, and a sense that you have wasted something
unique. This pain will be expressed in bitterness and envy, and you will
not recognize the true source of your depression. Your true self does not
speak in words or banal phrases. Its voice comes from deep within you,
from the substrata of your psyche, from something embedded physically
within you. It emanates from your uniqueness, and it communicates
through sensations and powerful desires that seem to transcend you. You
cannot ultimately understand why you are drawn to certain activities or
forms of knowledge. This cannot really be verbalized or explained. It is
simply a fact of nature.

Daily Law: In following this voice you realize your own potential and satisfy your deepest longings to create and express your uniqueness. It exists for a purpose, and it is your Life's Task to bring it to fruition.

Mastery, VI: Fuse the Intuitive with the Rational—Mastery

April

The Perfect Courtier

PLAYING THE GAME OF POWER

≈

The game of power is a game of constant duplicity most resembling the power dynamic that existed in the scheming world of the old aristocratic court. Throughout history, a court has always formed itself around the person in power—king, queen, emperor, leader. The courtiers who filled this court were in an especially delicate position: They had to serve their masters, but if they seemed to fawn, if they curried favor too obviously, the other courtiers around them would notice and would act against them. Meanwhile, the court was supposed to represent the height of civilization and refinement. This was the courtier's dilemma: While appearing the very paragon of elegance, they had to outwit and thwart their own opponents in the subtlest of ways. Life in the court was a never-ending game that required constant vigilance and tactical thinking. It was civilized war. Today we face a peculiarly similar paradox to that of the courtier: Everything must appear civilized, decent, democratic, and fair. But if we play by those rules too strictly, if we take them too literally, we are crushed by those around us who are not so foolish. As the great Renaissance diplomat and courtier Niccolò Machiavelli wrote, "Any man who tries to be good all the time is bound to come to ruin among the great number who are not good." The court imagined itself the pinnacle of refinement, but underneath its glittering surface a cauldron of dark emotions—greed, envy, lust, hatred—boiled and simmered. Our world today similarly imagines itself the pinnacle of fairness, yet the same ugly emotions still stir within us, as they have forever. The game is the same. The month of April will teach you how to play the game of power as the perfect courtier.

When you enter the real world, you are suddenly blindsided by this whole realm that exists. It is like our dirty little secret. People will talk about their sex lives. But nobody talks about all the power games that are constantly going on in the world. So, I want to interject my own personal story from when I got out of college and was suddenly confronted with this real world.

I had graduated with a background in Classics, ancient Greek and Latin. I was immersed in studying philosophy and literature and languages. And so, when I started working, essentially in magazines, with my first job at *Esquire*, I had no idea of how things operated in the real world, and I was very much shocked by all the egos, the insecurities, the game playing, and the political stuff. It really kind of disturbed and upset me. I can remember, when I was about twenty-six or twenty-seven years old, one particular job that affected me deeply.

I am not going to tell you which job this was. I don't want you googling it and figuring out who I'm talking about. But, basically, the job was that I had to find stories that would then be put into a documentary series, and I was judged on how many good stories I found. I am a very competitive person, and I was doing better than anybody else there at the job. I was finding more stories that ended up getting produced, and I told myself, "Isn't that the whole point?" We are trying to produce a show. We are trying to get work done, and I was more than holding up my fair share.

Suddenly I found that my superior made it very clear that she wasn't happy with me. I was doing something wrong, she was displeased, and yet I couldn't figure out what it was.

I tried to put myself in her shoes. And I'm thinking, "What is it that I'm doing that might be displeasing her? I am clearly producing in my work." And I figured out, well, maybe it is because I'm not involving her in what I'm doing, in my ideas. Maybe I need to run them by her. I need to involve her more so she feels like she is a part of the research that I am doing.

I would then go into her office and I would tell her where my ideas were coming from. I was trying to engage with her, assuming that was the problem. Well, that didn't seem to work. She was still clearly unhappy with me. Maybe she simply didn't like me. So, I thought, going further, "Well, maybe I'm not being friendly enough with her. Maybe I need to be nice to her. Maybe I need to go in and not talk about work, but just talk, and be nice."

Okay. So that was strategy number two. I started doing that. She still seemed really cold. I figured, all right, she hates me. That's just life. Not everybody can love you. That must be it. I'll just continue doing my job. Then one day we are having a meeting in which we are discussing our ideas, and my mind was elsewhere, and she suddenly interrupts and says, "Robert, you have an attitude problem."

"What?"

"You're not listening to people here."

"I'm listening." I got a little defensive. I produce. I work hard, I said. You are going to judge me about how wide my eyes are open and how I'm listening to people? She goes, "No. You have a problem here."

"I'm sorry. I don't think I do."

Anyway, over the course of the next few weeks she just started torturing me about my supposed attitude. And, of course, naturally, I developed an attitude. I started resenting her. A couple weeks later I quit, because I just hated it. I probably quit a week before they were going to fire me anyway. I went home, and over the course of several weeks I thought really deeply about it. What happened here? What did I do wrong? I mean, she just didn't like me? I think I'm a likable person.

Finally, after much analysis, I came to the conclusion that I had violated a law of power ten years before I ever wrote the book. Law 1: Never Outshine the Master. I had gone into this environment thinking that what mattered was doing a great job and showing how talented I was. But, in doing that, I had made this woman, my superior, insecure that maybe I was after her job or that I was better than she was. And I would make her look bad because the great ideas were coming from me and not from her. It wasn't really her fault. I had violated Law 1. And when you violate Law 1, you are going to suffer for it, because you are touching on a person's ego and their insecurities. That is the worst thing you can do, and that is what had happened.

In reflecting on this, it became a turning point in my life. I said, "I'm never going to let this happen again. And I'm never going to take things personally and get emotional." Because that is what happened. I basically reacted emotionally to her coldness and antagonism and developed an attitude. Never again. I'm a writer. I'm going to look at these jobs that I get with some distance. I am going to become a master observer of the game of power. I am going to watch these people as if they were mice in a laboratory, and I'm the scientist.

This suddenly allowed me to not only observe the power games going on in the many different kinds of jobs I've had, but also, in having this distance and looking at the world like this, suddenly I had power. I wasn't emotionally entangled, and I could deal with things much more easily. Out of such a perspective, I developed *The 48 Laws of Power*. What I decided in *The 48 Laws* is that this is the reality we must all deal with—we are social creatures, we live in environments where there are all kinds of complicated networks, and we are, in a way, defined by how we handle these environments, this reality.

Never Outshine the Master

*Avoid outshining the master. All superiority is odious, but the
superiority of a subject over his prince is not only stupid, it is fatal.*
—BALTASAR GRACIÁN

In your desire to please and impress, do not go too far in displaying your
talents or you might accomplish the opposite—inspire fear and insecurity. Everyone has insecurities. When you show yourself in the world and
display your talents, you naturally stir up all kinds of resentment, envy,
and other manifestations of insecurity. This is to be expected. You cannot
spend your life worrying about the petty feelings of others. With those
above you, however, you must take a different approach: When it comes
to power, outshining the master is perhaps the worst mistake of all. Make
your masters appear more brilliant than they are, and you will attain the
heights of power. If your ideas are more creative than your master's, ascribe them to him, in as public a manner as possible. Make it clear that
your advice is merely an echo of his advice. If you surpass your master in
wit, it is okay to play the role of the court jester, but do not make him
appear cold and surly by comparison. If you are naturally more sociable
and generous than your master, be careful not to be the cloud that blocks
his radiance from others. He must appear as the sun around which everyone revolves, radiating power and brilliance, the center of attention.

Daily Law: Always make those above you feel comfortably superior.

The 48 Laws of Power, Law 1: Never Outshine the Master

Make the Master Feel Glorious and Superior

Like all Renaissance scientists, Galileo depended on the generosity of great rulers to support his research. No matter how great the discovery, however, his patrons usually paid him with gifts, not cash. This made for a life of constant insecurity and dependence. In 1610, he hit on a new strategy when he discovered the moons of Jupiter. Galileo turned his discovery into a cosmic event honoring the Medicis' greatness. The Medicis made Galileo their official court philosopher and mathematician, with a full salary. Scientists are not spared the vagaries of court life and patronage. They too must serve masters who hold the purse strings. And their great intellectual powers can make the master feel insecure, as if he were only there to supply the funds—an ugly, ignoble job. The producer of a great work wants to feel he is more than just the provider of the financing. He wants to appear creative and powerful, and also more important than the work produced in his name. Instead of insecurity you must give him glory. Galileo did not challenge the intellectual authority of the Medicis with his discovery or make them feel inferior in any way; by literally aligning them with the stars, he made them shine brilliantly among the courts of Italy. He did not outshine the master, he made the master outshine all others.

Daily Law: Not only don't outshine the master but make those above you shine brilliantly.

The 48 Laws of Power, Law 1: Never Outshine the Master

Find Out Who Holds the Strings

Power always exists in concentrated forms. In any organization it is inevitable for a small group to hold the strings. And often it is not those with the titles. In the game of power, only the fool flails about without fixing his target. You must find out who controls the operations, who is the real director behind the scenes. As Richelieu discovered at the beginning of his rise to the top of the French political scene during the early seventeenth century, it was not King Louis XIII who decided things, it was the king's mother. And so he attached himself to her, and catapulted through the ranks of the courtiers, all the way to the top. It is enough to strike oil once—your wealth and power are assured for a lifetime.

> Daily Law: When looking for sources of power to elevate you, look for those who really control the operations. They are not always who you think. Once identified, attach yourself to them.

The 48 Laws of Power, Law 23: Concentrate Your Forces

Know When to Take and Give Credit

Be sure you know when letting other people share the credit serves your purpose. It is especially important to not be greedy when you have a master above you. President Richard Nixon's historic visit to the People's Republic of China was originally his idea, but it might never have come off but for the deft diplomacy of Henry Kissinger. Nor would it have been as successful without Kissinger's skills. Still, when the time came to take credit, Kissinger adroitly let Nixon take the lion's share. Knowing that the truth would come out later, he was careful not to jeopardize his standing in the short term by hogging the limelight. Kissinger played the game expertly: He took credit for the work of those below him while graciously giving credit for his own labors to those above. That is the way to play the game.

Daily Law: Take credit from those below you. Give credit to those above.

The 48 Laws of Power, Law 7: Get Others to Do the Work for You,
but Always Take the Credit

Remake Yourself into a Character of Power

In 1832 a publisher accepted Aurore Dupin Dudevant's first major novel, *Indiana*. She had chosen to publish it under a pseudonym, "George Sand," and all of Paris assumed this impressive new writer was male. Dudevant had sometimes worn men's clothes before creating "George Sand"; now, as a public figure, she exaggerated the image. She added long men's coats, gray hats, heavy boots, and dandyish cravats to her wardrobe. She smoked cigars and in conversation expressed herself like a man, unafraid to dominate the conversation or to use a saucy word. This strange "male/female" writer fascinated the public. But those who knew Sand well understood that her male persona protected her from the public's prying eyes. Out in the world, she enjoyed playing the part to the extreme; in private she remained herself. She also realized that the character of "George Sand" could grow stale or predictable, and to avoid this she would every now and then dramatically alter the character she had created; she began meddling in politics, leading demonstrations, inspiring student rebellions. No one would dictate to her the limits of the character she had created. Long after she died, and after most people had stopped reading her novels, the larger-than-life theatricality of that character has continued to fascinate and inspire. Understand: The character you seem to have been born with is not necessarily who you are; beyond the characteristics you have inherited, your parents, your friends, and your peers have helped to shape your personality. The Promethean task of the powerful is to take control of the process, to stop allowing others that ability to limit and mold them.

Daily Law: Remake yourself into a character of power. Working on yourself like clay should be one of your greatest and most pleasurable life tasks. It makes you, in essence, an artist—an artist creating yourself.

The 48 Laws of Power, Law 25: Re-create Yourself

APRIL 6

Seem Dumber Than Your Mark

Know how to make use of stupidity: The wisest man plays
this card at times. There are occasions when the highest wisdom
consists in appearing not to know—you must not
be ignorant but capable of playing it.

—BALTASAR GRACIÁN

If you are ambitious yet find yourself low in the hierarchy, this trick can
be useful: Appearing less intelligent than you are, even a bit of a fool, is
the perfect disguise. Look like a harmless pig and no one will believe you
harbor dangerous ambitions. They may even promote you since you seem
so likable and subservient. Intelligence is the obvious quality to down-
play, but why stop there? Taste and sophistication rank close to intelligence on the vanity scale; make people feel they are more sophisticated
than you are and their guard will come down. An air of complete naiveté
can work wonders.

> Daily Law: In general, always make people believe they are smarter
> and more sophisticated than you are. They will keep you around be-
> cause you make them feel better about themselves, and the longer you
> are around, the more opportunities you will have to deceive them.

The 48 Laws of Power, Law 21: Play a Sucker to Catch a Sucker—
Seem Dumber Than Your Mark

Do Not Be the Court Cynic

Wax, a substance naturally hard and brittle, can be made soft by the
application of a little warmth, so that it will take any shape you please.
In the same way, by being polite and friendly, you can make people
pliable and obliging, even though they are apt to be crabbed and
malevolent. Hence politeness is to human nature what warmth is to wax.

—ARTHUR SCHOPENHAUER

Express admiration for the good work of others. If you constantly criticize
your equals or subordinates, some of that criticism will rub off on you,
hovering over you like a gray cloud wherever you go. People will groan at
each new cynical comment, and you will irritate them. By expressing
modest admiration for other people's achievements, you paradoxically call
attention to your own.

Daily Law: The ability to express wonder and amazement, and seem
like you mean it, is a rare and dying talent, but one still greatly valued.

The 48 Laws of Power, Law 24: Play the Perfect Courtier

APRIL 8

Master Your Emotional Responses

A sovereign should never launch an army out of anger,
a leader should never start a war out of wrath.

—SUN TZU

Angry people usually end up looking ridiculous, for their response seems out of proportion to what occasioned it. They have taken things too seriously, exaggerating the hurt or insult that has been done to them. They are so sensitive to slight that it becomes comical how much they take personally. More comical still is their belief that their outbursts signify power. The truth is the opposite: Petulance is not power, it is a sign of helplessness. People may temporarily be cowed by your tantrums, but in the end they lose respect for you. They also realize they can easily undermine a person with so little self-control.

Daily Law: Displaying anger and emotion are signs of weakness; you cannot control yourself, so how can you control anything?

The 48 Laws of Power, Law 39: Stir Up Waters to Catch Fish

So Much Depends on Reputation

In the social realm, appearances are the barometer of almost all our judgments, and you must never be misled into believing otherwise. One false slip, one awkward or sudden change in your appearance, can prove disastrous. This is the reason for the supreme importance of making and maintaining a reputation that is of your own creation. That reputation will protect you in the dangerous game of appearances, distracting the probing eyes of others from knowing what you are really like, and giving you a degree of control over how the world judges you—a powerful position to be in. Reputation has a power like magic: With one stroke of its wand, it can double your strength. It can also send people scurrying away from you. Whether the exact same deeds appear brilliant or dreadful can depend entirely on the reputation of the doer. Reputation therefore is a treasure to be carefully collected and hoarded. Especially when you are first establishing it, you must protect it strictly, anticipating all attacks on it. Once it is solid, do not let yourself get angry or defensive at the slanderous comments of your enemies—that reveals insecurity, not confidence in your reputation. Take the high road instead, and never appear desperate in your self-defense.

> Daily Law: Reputation is the cornerstone of power. Through reputation alone you can intimidate and win; once it slips, however, you are vulnerable, and will be attacked on all sides. Never let others define it for you.

The 48 Laws of Power, Law 5: So Much Depends on Reputation—Guard It with Your Life

Always Say Less Than Necessary

Undutiful words of a subject do often take deeper root
than the memory of ill deeds.
— SIR WALTER RALEIGH

When you are trying to impress people with words, the more you say, the more common you appear, and the less in control. Even if you are saying something banal, it will seem original if you make it vague, open-ended, and sphinxlike. Powerful people impress and intimidate by saying less. The more you say, the more likely you are to say something foolish.

Daily Law: By saying less than necessary you create the appearance of meaning and power. Also, the less you say, the less risk you run of saying something foolish, even dangerous.

The 48 Laws of Power, Law 4: Always Say Less Than Necessary

Appeal to People's Self-Interest

The shortest and best way to make your fortune is to let people
see clearly that it is in their interests to promote yours.

—JEAN DE LA BRUYÈRE

In your quest for power, you will constantly find yourself in the position
of asking for help from those more powerful than you. There is an art to
asking for help, an art that depends on your ability to understand the
person you are dealing with, and to not confuse your needs with theirs.
Most people never succeed at this, because they are completely trapped in
their own wants and desires. They start from the assumption that the
people they are appealing to have a selfless interest in helping them. They
talk as if their needs mattered to these people—who probably couldn't
care less. Sometimes they refer to larger issues: a great cause, or grand
emotions such as love and gratitude. They go for the big picture when
simple, everyday realities would have much more appeal. What they do
not realize is that even the most powerful person is locked inside needs of
his own, and that if you make no appeal to his self-interest, he merely sees
you as desperate or, at best, a waste of time.

**Daily Law: When asking for anything, uncover something in your re-
quest that will benefit the person you are asking, and emphasize it out
of all proportion. They will respond enthusiastically when they see
something to be gained for themselves.**

The 48 Laws of Power, Law 13: When Asking for Help, Appeal to People's Self-Interest,
Never to Their Mercy or Gratitude

Use Your Enemies

Men are more ready to repay an injury than a benefit, because gratitude is a burden and revenge a pleasure.

—TACITUS

In 1971, during the Vietnam War, Henry Kissinger was the target of an unsuccessful kidnapping attempt, a conspiracy involving, among others, the renowned antiwar activist priests the Berrigan brothers, four more Catholic priests, and four nuns. In private, without informing the Secret Service or the Justice Department, Kissinger arranged a Saturday-morning meeting with three of the alleged kidnappers. Explaining to his guests that he would have most American soldiers out of Vietnam by mid-1972, he completely charmed them. They gave him some "Kidnap Kissinger" buttons and one of them remained a friend of his for years, visiting him on several occasions. This was not just a one-time ploy: Kissinger made a policy of working with those who disagreed with him. Colleagues commented that he seemed to get along better with his enemies than with his friends. Whenever you can, bury the hatchet with an enemy, and make a point of putting him in your service.

Daily Law: As Lincoln said, you destroy an enemy when you make a friend of him.

The 48 Laws of Power, Law 2: Never Put Too Much Trust in Friends

Better to Be Attacked Than Ignored

Burning more brightly than those around you is a skill that no one is born with. You have to learn to attract attention, "as surely as the lodestone attracts iron." At the start of your career, you must attach your name and reputation to a quality, an image, that sets you apart from other people. This image can be something like a characteristic style of dress, or a personality quirk that amuses people and gets talked about. Once the image is established, you have an appearance, a place in the sky for your star. It is a common mistake to imagine that this peculiar appearance of yours should not be controversial, that to be attacked is somehow bad. Nothing could be further from the truth. To avoid being a flash in the pan, and having your notoriety eclipsed by another, you must not discriminate between different types of attention; in the end, every kind will work in your favor. Society craves larger-than-life figures, people who stand above the general mediocrity. Never be afraid, then, of the qualities that set you apart and draw attention to you. Court controversy, even scandal. It is better to be attacked, even slandered, than ignored. All professions are ruled by this law, and all professionals must have a bit of the showman about them.

Daily Law: Make no distinction between kinds of attention—notoriety of any sort will bring you power. Better to be slandered and attacked than ignored.

The 48 Laws of Power, Law 6: Court Attention at All Cost

View the World as a Vast Interconnected Palace

The world is dangerous and enemies are everywhere—everyone has to protect themselves. A fortress seems the safest. But isolation exposes you to more dangers than it protects you from—it cuts you off from valuable information, it makes you conspicuous and an easy target. Since power is a human creation, it is inevitably increased by contact with other people. Instead of falling into the fortress mentality, view the world in the following manner: It is like a vast palace of Versailles, with every room communicating with another. You need to be permeable, able to float in and out of different circles and mix with different types. That kind of mobility and social contact will protect you from plotters, who will be unable to keep secrets from you, and from your enemies, who will be unable to isolate you from your allies. Always on the move, you mix and mingle in the rooms of the palace, never sitting or settling in one place. No hunter can fix his aim on such a swift-moving creature.

Daily Law: Because humans are social creatures by nature, power depends on social interaction and circulation. To make yourself powerful, place yourself at the center of things, make yourself more accessible, seek out old allies and make new ones, force yourself into more and more different circles.

The 48 Laws of Power, Law 18: Do Not Build Fortresses to Protect Yourself—Isolation Is Dangerous

Create a Cultlike Following

Having a large following opens up all sorts of possibilities for deception; not only will your followers worship you, they will defend you from your enemies and will voluntarily take on the work of enticing others to join your fledgling cult. This kind of power will lift you to another realm: You will no longer have to struggle or use subterfuge to enforce your will. You are adored and can do no wrong. You might think it's a gargantuan task to create such a following, but in fact it is fairly simple. As humans, we have a desperate need to believe in something, anything. This makes us eminently gullible: We simply cannot endure long periods of doubt, or the emptiness that comes from a lack of something to believe in. Dangle in front of us some new cause, elixir, get-rich-quick scheme, or the latest technological trend or art movement, and we leap as one from the water to take the bait.

Daily Law: People have an overwhelming desire to believe in something. Become the focal point of such desire by offering them a cause, a new faith to follow. In the absence of organized religion and grand causes, your new belief system will bring you untold power.

The 48 Laws of Power, Law 27: Play on People's Need to
Believe to Create a Cultlike following

APRIL 16

Do Not Commit to Anyone

I would rather be a beggar and single than a queen and married.

—QUEEN ELIZABETH I

It is the fool who always rushes to take sides. Do not commit to any side or cause but yourself. By maintaining your independence, you become the master of others—playing people against one another, making them pursue you. If you allow people to feel they possess you to any degree, you lose all power over them. By not committing your affections, they will only try harder to win you over. Stay aloof and you gain the power that comes from their attention and frustrated desire.

Daily Law: Play the Virgin Queen: give them hope but never satisfaction.

The 48 Laws of Power, Law 20: Do Not Commit to Anyone

Stay Above the Fray

Regard it as more courageous not to become involved in an
engagement than to win in battle, and where there is already one
interfering fool, take care that there shall not be two.

—BALTASAR GRACIÁN

Do not let people drag you into their petty fights and squabbles. At the
same time, you cannot completely stand aside, for that would cause need-
less offense. To play the game properly, you must seem interested in other
people's problems, even sometimes appear to take their side. But while
you make outward gestures of support, you must maintain your inner
energy and sanity by keeping your emotions disengaged. No matter how
hard people try to pull you in, never let your interest in their affairs and
petty squabbles go beyond the surface. Give them gifts, listen with a
sympathetic look, even occasionally play the charmer—but inwardly keep
both the friendly kings and the perfidious tyrants at arm's length. By refusing to commit and thus maintaining your autonomy, you retain the
initiative: your moves stay matters of your own choosing, not defensive
reactions to the push-and-pull of those around you.

**Daily Law: Always try to inwardly maintain your independence and
avoid entanglements not of your choosing.**

The 48 Laws of Power, Law 20: Do Not Commit to Anyone

Startle the Snakes

You can sit back and read the signs or you can actively work to uncover your enemies. In the Bible we read of David's suspicion that his father-in-law, King Saul, secretly wanted him dead. How could David find out? He confided his suspicion to Saul's son Jonathan, his close friend. Jonathan refused to believe it, so David suggested a test. He was expected at court for a feast. He would not go; Jonathan would attend and pass along David's excuse, which would be adequate but not urgent. Sure enough, the excuse enraged Saul, who exclaimed, "Send at once and fetch him unto me—he deserves to die!" David's test succeeded because it was ambiguous. His excuse for missing the feast could be read in more than one way: if Saul meant well toward David, he would have seen his son-in-law's absence as no more than selfish at worst, but because he secretly hated David, he saw it as effrontery, and it pushed him over the edge. Follow David's example: say or do something that can be read in more than one way, that may be superficially polite but that could also indicate a slight coolness on your part or be seen as subtle insult. A friend may wonder but will let it pass. The secret enemy, though, will react with anger. Any strong emotion and you will know that there's something boiling under the surface.

Daily Law: As the Chinese say, beat the grass to startle the snakes.

The 33 Strategies of War, Strategy 1: Declare War on Your Enemies—The Polarity Strategy

Tailor Your Flattery

Courtiers have to gain the attention of leaders and ingratiate themselves in some way. The most immediate way to do this is through flattery, since leaders inevitably have large egos and a hunger to have their high self-opinion validated. Flattery can do wonders, but it comes with risks. If it is too obvious, the flatterer looks desperate, and it is easy to see through the strategy. The best courtiers know how to tailor their flattery to the particular insecurities of the leader and to make it less direct. They focus on flattering qualities in the leader that no one else has bothered to pay attention to but that need extra validation. If everyone praises the leader's business acumen but not his or her cultural refinement, you will want to aim at the latter. Mirroring the leader's ideas and values, without using their exact words, can be a highly effective form of indirect flattery.

Daily Law: Overt flattery can be effective but has its limits; it is too direct and obvious and looks bad to other courtiers. Discreet flattery, tailored to the insecurities of your target, is much more powerful.

The Laws of Human Nature, 14: Resist the Downward Pull
of the Group—The Law of Conformity

Be Royal in Your Own Fashion

*With all great deceivers there is a noteworthy occurrence to which
they owe their power. In the actual act of deception they are overcome
by belief in themselves: it is this which then speaks so miraculously
and compellingly to those around them.*

—FRIEDRICH NIETZSCHE

The way you carry yourself will often determine how you are treated: in
the long run, appearing vulgar or common will make people disrespect
you. For a king respects himself and inspires the same sentiment in others. It is up to you to set your own price. Ask for less and that is just what
you will get. Ask for more, however, and you send a signal that you are
worth a king's ransom. Even those who turn you down respect you for
your confidence, and that respect will eventually pay off in ways you cannot imagine.

**Daily Law: By acting regally and confident of your powers, you make
yourself seem destined to wear a crown.**

The 48 Laws of Power, Law 34: Be Royal in Your Own Fashion:
Act Like a King to Be Treated Like One

Be Merciless with Your Enemies

The remnants of an enemy can become active like those of a disease or
fire. Hence, these should be exterminated completely. One should
never ignore an enemy, knowing him to be weak. He becomes
dangerous in due course, like the spark of fire in a haystack.

—KAUTILYA, THIRD CENTURY BC.

"Crush the enemy" is a key strategic tenet of Sun Tzu, the fourth-century
BC author of *The Art of War*. The idea is simple: your enemies wish you
ill. There is nothing they want more than to eliminate you. If, in your
struggles with them, you stop halfway or even three-quarters of the way,
out of mercy or hope of reconciliation, you only make them more determined, more embittered, and they will someday take revenge. They may
act friendly for the time being, but this is only because you have defeated
them. They have no choice but to bide their time.

The solution: Have no mercy. Crush your enemies as totally as they
would crush you. Ultimately the only peace and security you can hope for
from your enemies is their disappearance. It is not, of course, a question
of murder, it is a question of banishment. Sufficiently weakened and then
exiled from your court forever, your enemies are rendered harmless. And
if they cannot be banished, at least understand that they are plotting
against you, and pay no heed to whatever friendliness they feign.

Daily Law: Judge your enemies carefully, looking at their past patterns.
Sometimes it is best to convert them into an ally and neutralize them.
But with others it only pays to be merciless and crush them totally.

The 48 Laws of Power, Law 15: Crush Your Enemy Totally—Learn to
Keep People Dependent on You

Sow the Seeds of Doubt

It is easier to cope with a bad conscience than with a bad reputation.

—FRIEDRICH NIETZSCHE

Doubt is a powerful weapon: Once you let it out of the bag with insidious rumors, your opponents are in a horrible dilemma. On the one hand, they can deny the rumors, even prove that you have slandered them. But a layer of suspicion will remain: Why are they defending themselves so desperately? Maybe the rumor has some truth to it? If, on the other hand, they take the high road and ignore you, the doubts, unrefuted, will be even stronger. If done correctly, the sowing of rumors can so infuriate and unsettle your rivals that in defending themselves they will make numerous mistakes. This is the perfect weapon for those who have no reputation of their own to work from.

Daily Law: Destroy your rivals with rumors.

The 48 Laws of Power, Law 5: So Much Depends on Reputation—Guard It with Your Life

Fear the Power of Infection

Those misfortunates among us who have been brought down by circumstances beyond their control deserve all the help and sympathy we can give them. But there are others who are not born to misfortune or unhappiness, but who draw it upon themselves by their destructive actions and unsettling effect on others. It would be a great thing if we could raise them up, change their patterns, but more often than not it is their patterns that end up getting inside and changing us. You can die from someone else's misery—emotional states are as infectious as diseases. You may feel you are helping the drowning man, but you are only precipitating your own disaster. Infectors can be recognized by the misfortune they draw on themselves, their turbulent past, their long line of broken relationships, their unstable careers, and the very force of their character, which sweeps you up and makes you lose your reason. Be forewarned by these signs of an infector; learn to see the discontent in their eye. Most important of all, do not take pity. Do not enmesh yourself in trying to help. The infector will remain unchanged, but you will be unhinged.

Daily Law: People sometimes draw misfortune on themselves; they will also draw it on you. Associate with the happy and fortunate instead.

The 48 Laws of Power, Law 10: Infection—Avoid the Unhappy and Unlucky

Avoid the False Alliance

No one can get far in life without allies. The trick, however, is to recognize the difference between false allies and real ones. A false alliance is created out of an immediate emotional need. It requires that you give up something essential about yourself and makes it impossible for you to make your own decisions. A true alliance is formed out of mutual self-interest, each side supplying what the other cannot get alone. It does not require you to fuse your own identity with that of a group or pay attention to everyone else's emotional needs. It allows you autonomy.

Daily Law: Cultivate real allies. Find those with mutual self-interests and make an alliance.

The 33 Strategies of War, Strategy 27: Seem to Work for the Interests of Others while Furthering Your Own—The Alliance Strategy

Enter Action with Boldness

Always set to work without misgivings on the score of imprudence.

—BALTASAR GRACIÁN

Most of us are timid. We want to avoid tension and conflict and we want to be liked by all. We may contemplate a bold action, but we rarely bring it to life. Although we may disguise our timidity as a concern for others, a desire not to hurt or offend them, in fact it is the opposite—we are really self-absorbed, worried about ourselves and how others perceive us. Boldness, on the other hand, is outer-directed, and often makes people feel more at ease, since it is less self-conscious and less repressed. And so we admire the bold, and prefer to be around them, because their self-confidence infects us and draws us outside our own realm of inwardness and reflection. But few are born bold. You must practice and develop your boldness. You will often find uses for it. The best place to begin is often the delicate world of negotiation, particularly those discussions in which you are asked to set your own price. How often we put ourselves down by asking for too little. Understand: If boldness is not natural, neither is timidity. It is an acquired habit, picked up out of a desire to avoid conflict. If timidity has taken hold of you, then root it out. Your fears of the consequences of a bold action are way out of proportion to reality, and in fact the consequences of timidity are worse. Your value is lowered and you create a self-fulfilling cycle of doubt and disaster.

Daily Law: Timidity is dangerous: Better to enter with boldness. Any mistakes you commit through audacity are easily corrected with more audacity.

The 48 Laws of Power, Law 28: Enter Action with Boldness

Make Your Accomplishments Seem Effortless

*A line [of poetry] will take us hours maybe; Yet if it does not seem
a moment's thought, Our stitching and unstitching has been naught.*
—"ADAM'S CURSE," WILLIAM BUTLER YEATS

In *The Book of the Courtier*, published in 1528, Baldassare Castiglione describes the highly elaborate and codified manners of the perfect court citizen. And yet, Castiglione explains, the courtier must execute these gestures with what he calls "sprezzatura," the capacity to make the difficult seem easy. He urges the courtier to "practice in all things a certain nonchalance which conceals all artistry and makes whatever one says or does seem uncontrived and effortless." We all admire the achievement of some unusual feat, but if it is accomplished naturally and gracefully, our admiration increases tenfold—"whereas . . . to labor at what one is doing and . . . to make bones over it, shows an extreme lack of grace and causes everything, whatever its worth, to be discounted." Much of the idea of sprezzatura came from the world of art. All the great Renaissance artists carefully kept their works under wraps. Only the finished masterpiece could be shown to the public. Michelangelo forbade even popes to view his work in process. A Renaissance artist was always careful to keep his studios shut to patrons and public alike, not out of fear of imitation, but because to see the making of the works would mar the magic of their effect, and their studied atmosphere of ease and natural beauty.

Daily Law: Your actions must seem natural and executed with ease. When you act, act as if you could do much more. Avoid the temptation of revealing how hard you work—it only raises questions.

The 48 Laws of Power, Law 30: Make Your Accomplishments Seem Effortless

Despise the Free Lunch

The powerful never forget that what is offered for free is inevitably a trick. Friends who offer favors without asking for payment will later want something far dearer than the money you would have paid them. The bargain has hidden problems, both material and psychological. What has worth is worth paying for. By paying your own way you stay clear of gratitude, guilt, and deceit. It is also often wise to pay the full price—there is no cutting corners with excellence.

Daily Law: Learn to pay and to pay well.

The 48 Laws of Power, Law 40: Despise the Free Lunch

There Is No Revenge Like Oblivion

There is no revenge like oblivion, for it is the entombment of the
unworthy in the dust of their own nothingness.

—BALTASAR GRACIÁN

It is tempting to want to fix our mistakes, but it is sometimes more politic to leave them alone. In 1971, when *The New York Times* published the Pentagon Papers, a group of government documents about the history of U.S. involvement in Indochina, Henry Kissinger erupted into a volcanic rage. Furious about the Nixon administration's vulnerability to this kind of damaging leak, he made recommendations that eventually led to the formation of a group called the Plumbers to plug the leaks. This was the unit that later broke into Democratic Party offices in the Watergate Hotel, setting off the chain of events that led to Nixon's downfall. In reality the publication of the Pentagon Papers was not a serious threat to the administration, but Kissinger's reaction made it a big deal. In trying to fix one problem, he created another: a paranoia for security that in the end was much more destructive to the government. Had he ignored the Pentagon Papers, the scandal they had created would eventually have blown over. Instead of inadvertently focusing attention on a problem, making it seem worse by publicizing how much concern and anxiety it is causing you, it is often far wiser to play the contemptuous aristocrat, not deigning to acknowledge the problem's existence.

Daily Law: The harder we try to fix our mistakes, the worse we often make them.

The 48 Laws of Power, Law 36: Disdain Things You Cannot Have—
Ignoring Them Is the Best Revenge

Cultivate an Air of Unpredictability

People are always trying to read the motives behind your actions and to use your predictability against you. Throw in a completely inexplicable move and you put them on the defensive. Because they do not understand you, they are unnerved, and in such a state you can easily intimidate them. Pablo Picasso once remarked, "The best calculation is the absence of calculation. Once you have attained a certain level of recognition, others generally figure that when you do something, it's for an intelligent reason. So it's really foolish to plot out your movements too carefully in advance. You're better off acting capriciously." Humans are creatures of habit with an insatiable need to see familiarity in other people's actions. Your predictability gives them a sense of control. Turn the tables: Be deliberately unpredictable. Behavior that seems to have no consistency or purpose will keep them off-balance. Scrambling your patterns on a day-to-day basis will cause a stir around you and stimulate interest. People will talk about you, ascribe motives and explanations that have nothing to do with the truth, but that keep you constantly in their minds.

Daily Law: In the end, the more capricious you appear, the more respect you will garner. Only the terminally subordinate act in a predictable manner. Strategically reveal your human side.

The 48 Laws of Power, Law 17: Keep Others in Suspended Terror—
Cultivate an Air of Unpredictability

Never Appear Too Perfect

It takes great talent and skill to conceal one's talent and skill.
—FRANÇOIS DE LA ROCHEFOUCAULD

Sir Walter Raleigh was one of the most brilliant men at the court of Queen Elizabeth of England. He had skills as a scientist, wrote poetry still recognized as among the most beautiful writing of the time, was a proven leader of men, an enterprising entrepreneur, a great sea captain, and on top of all this was a handsome, dashing courtier who charmed his way into becoming one of the queen's favorites. Wherever he went, however, people blocked his path. Eventually he suffered a terrific fall from grace, leading even to prison and finally the executioner's axe. Raleigh could not understand the stubborn opposition he faced from the other courtiers. He did not see that he had not only made no attempt to disguise the degree of his skills and qualities, but he had imposed them on one and all, making a show of his versatility, thinking it impressed people and won him friends. In fact it made him silent enemies, people who felt inferior to him and did all they could to ruin him the moment he tripped up or made the slightest mistake. In the end, the reason he was executed was treason, but envy will use any cover it finds to mask its destructiveness.

Daily Law: Appearing better than others is always dangerous, but most dangerous of all is to appear to have no faults or weaknesses. Envy creates silent enemies. Defuse it by occasionally downplaying your virtues.

The 48 Laws of Power, Law 46: Never Appear Too Perfect

May

The Supposed Nonplayers of Power

RECOGNIZING TOXIC TYPES AND DISGUISED POWER STRATEGIES

Power is a social game. To learn and master it, you must develop the ability to study and understand people. As the great seventeenth-century thinker and courtier Baltasar Gracián wrote: "Many people spend time studying the properties of animals or herbs; how much more important it would be to study those of people, with whom we must live or die!" To be a master player you must also be a master psychologist. You must recognize motivations and see through the cloud of dust with which people surround their actions. Some people, for instance, believe they can opt out of the game by behaving in ways that have nothing to do with power. You must beware of such people, for while they express such opinions outwardly, they are often among the most adept players at power. They are what I call "supposed nonplayers." They utilize strategies that cleverly disguise the nature of the manipulation involved. The month of May will teach you how to recognize the supposed nonplayers and other toxic types you'll want try to keep your distance from.

I once counted that I had some sixty different jobs before I wrote *The 48 Laws of Power*.

I tried a lot of different things and in those experiences I saw every kind of power-hungry person you could imagine. Every kind of manipulator that is out there. I saw them. I saw their maneuvers. I saw how they thought.

And then I began working in Hollywood as an assistant to various directors. That's where I started to see some particularly hardcore Machiavellian tactics used on actors and producers, and I'd think, "Wow, that reminds me of Cesare Borgia in the Renaissance. That reminds me of what Napoleon did. That reminds me of that line from Gracián."

I was building up this catalog of experiences. I didn't know what would come of it.

Then when I was thirty-six, I was working yet another new job in Italy, and one day one of my colleagues on this job, a book packager and designer named Joost Elffers, asked me out of the blue if I had any ideas for a book. Interested in the prospect, I improvised several ideas, one of which would turn into *The 48 Laws of Power*.

I told Joost that, in my experience, power has not changed. We live in a very politically correct world where film directors and producers project the image of being the nicest, most liberal, most progressive people on the planet. But behind closed doors, they turn into raging manipulators who will do anything to get exactly what they want.

Power is timeless. People may not be beheaded for making mistakes; instead they'll be summarily fired. Law 1 in *The 48 Laws of Power*, for instance, is "Never Outshine the Master"—in the old days, Nicolas Fouquet outshone Louis XIV, and he was thrown in prison for the rest of his life. Now, you're simply let go without knowing why. It's just a different form of punishment. The game is the same.

There are three types of people in this world in dealing with this game. There are, what I call, the deniers, the people who deny this reality exists.

They almost want to pretend that we are descended from angels and not from primates. They imagine that what I am talking about here is just cynical. These laws don't really exist. These hardcore tactics may be used, but only by the nastiest and least moral people out there.

Among these deniers, you will find two types. You will find people who are genuinely disturbed by the politicking aspect of human nature. They don't want any kind of job in which they have to do that. Because they refuse to understand the game, they find themselves slowly marginalized. They are fine with such a fate. They are never going to assume a position of great responsibility anyway because it involves all this game-playing, and that's okay.

The other branch of the deniers are the people that are the passive-aggressors—those who consciously don't want to admit that they ever engage in manipulation, but unconsciously are playing all kinds of games. In several of my books, I describe the many different varieties of these passive-aggressive warriors. These types, the supposed nonplayers, are often the most slippery and dangerous of all.

The second type of person besides the deniers are those who love this Machiavellian part of our nature and revel in it. They are master manipulators, con artists, and outright aggressors. They have no problem handling this part of the game. In fact, they love it. This type of person, which usually you will find one or two in any office or group, can get pretty far, but eventually they are tripped up in life because they are too Machiavellian. They don't understand that there is a whole other side to the game, which requires empathy, cooperation, and seducing people into working with you. They are too tied to their egos to see the limits of the games they are playing and so they inevitably go too far and experience a fall from power. There is a wall they can never get past.

The third type is what I call the radical realist. This is what I'm promulgating in my books, and it goes as follows.

The desire for power is part of our nature. It is a part of how we evolved over millions of years. There is no point in denying our nature. It is who we are. And not only are we not going to deny it, but we are going to accept that this is the human being that we are, the product of evolution.

There is nothing wrong with the fact that in this world people are playing political games. There is nothing wrong with the fact that there are seducers and con artists. It is the Human Comedy since the beginning of recorded history. It is just reality, the world as it is. Let's stop fighting it.

With such acceptance, it is not that we love it and want to go out in the world and play all these nasty games. It is that we understand they exist. If, occasionally, we have to use the laws in playing offense or defense, we're okay with that, within reason. Most often it is the case that other people are practicing them on us, and it is better to understand what they're up to than to live in the dream world of our angelic nature.

And so we understand the laws of power. We understand what people are up to, so they can't easily hurt us. We learn how to recognize in advance the truly toxic narcissists, aggressors, and passive aggressors, the nonplayers, before getting too emotionally enmeshed in their dramas. And armed with such an attitude and with such knowledge we are prepared to go to battle in the game of life. Instead of being blindsided by the manipulators, we have calmness, power, and the freedom that comes with awareness of the laws.

Everyone Is a Player in the Game

Courts are, unquestionably, the seats of politeness and good breeding;
were they not so, they would be the seats of slaughter and desolation.
Those who now smile upon and embrace, would affront and stab,
each other, if manners did not interpose.

—LORD CHESTERFIELD

You can recognize supposed nonplayers by the way they flaunt their moral qualities, their piety, their exquisite sense of justice. But since all of us hunger for power, and almost all of our actions are aimed at gaining it, the nonplayers are merely throwing dust in our eyes, distracting us from their power plays. If you observe them closely, you will see in fact that they are often the ones most skillful at indirect manipulation, even if some of them practice it unconsciously. And they greatly resent any publicizing of the tactics they use every day.

Daily Law: The world is like a giant scheming court and we are all trapped inside it. There is no opting out of the game. Everyone is playing.

The 48 Laws of Power, Preface

Take on the Toxic Types

Aggressive, envious, and manipulative people don't usually announce themselves as such. They have learned to appear charming in initial encounters, to use flattery and other means of disarming us. When they surprise us with their ugly behavior, we feel betrayed, angry, and helpless. They create constant pressure, knowing that in doing so they overwhelm our minds with their presence, making it doubly hard to think straight or strategize. Your greatest defense against them is to identify them in advance. Either you will steer clear of them or, foreseeing their manipulative actions, you will not be blindsided and thus will be better able to maintain your emotional balance. You will learn to mentally cut them down to size and focus on the glaring weaknesses and insecurities behind all of their bluster. You will not fall for their myth, and this will neutralize the intimidation they depend on. You will scoff at their cover stories and elaborate explanations for their selfish behavior. Your ability to stay calm will infuriate them and often push them into overreaching or making a mistake.

Daily Law: Come to appreciate these encounters as a chance to hone your skills of self-mastery. Outsmarting just one of these types will give you a great deal of confidence that you can handle the worst in human nature.

The Laws of Human Nature, Introduction

Judge Them on Their Behavior, Not on Their Words

Character is destiny.

—HERACLITUS

You need to train yourself to pay less attention to the words that people say and greater attention to their actions. People will say all kinds of things about their motives and intentions; they are used to dressing things up with words. Their actions, however, say much more about what is going on underneath the surface. If they present a harmless front but have acted aggressively on several occasions, give the knowledge of that aggression much greater weight than the surface they present. In a similar vein, you should take special note of how people respond to stressful situations—often the mask they wear in public falls off in the heat of the moment. When looking for cues to observe, be sensitive to any kind of extreme behavior on their part—for instance, a blustery front, an overly friendly manner, a constant penchant for jokes. You will often notice that they wear this like a mask to hide the opposite. They are blustery because they are inwardly very insecure; they are overly friendly because they are secretly ambitious and aggressive; or they joke to hide a mean-spiritedness. What might seem like small issues—chronically being late, insufficient attention to detail, not returning favors—are signs of something deeper about their character. Nothing is too small to notice.

Daily Law: What you want is a picture of a person's character over time. Restrain from the natural tendency to judge right away, and let the passage of time reveal more and more about who people are.

Mastery, IV: See People as They Are—Social Intelligence

The Appearance of Naiveté

He who poses as a fool is not a fool.

—BALTASAR GRACIÁN

Those who claim to be nonplayers may affect an air of naiveté, to protect them from the accusation that they are after power. Beware, however, for the appearance of naiveté can be an effective means of deceit. And even genuine naiveté is not free of the snares of power. Children may be naive in many ways, but they often act from an elemental need to gain control over those around them. Children suffer greatly from feeling powerless in the adult world, and they use any means available to get their way. Genuinely innocent people may still be playing for power, and are often horribly effective at the game, since they are not hindered by reflection.

Daily Law: Those who make a show or display of innocence are often the least innocent of all.

The 48 Laws of Power, Preface

Be Careful Whom You Offend

In the fifth-century BC, Ch'ung-erh, the prince of Ch'in (in present-day China), had been forced into exile. He lived modestly—even, sometimes, in poverty—waiting for the time when he could return home and resume his princely life. Once he was passing through the state of Cheng, where the ruler, not knowing who he was, treated him rudely. Years later, the prince was finally able to return home, his circumstances greatly changed. He did not forget who had been kind to him, and who had been insolent, during his years of poverty. Least of all did he forget his treatment at the hands of the ruler of Cheng. At his first opportunity he assembled a vast army and marched on Cheng, taking eight cities, destroying the kingdom, and sending the ruler into an exile of his own. Never assume that the person you are dealing with is weaker or less important than you are. A man who is of little importance and means today can be a person of power tomorrow. We forget a lot in our lives, but we rarely forget an insult.

Daily Law: Swallow the impulse to offend, even if the other person seems weak. The satisfaction is meager compared to the danger that someday he or she will be in a position to hurt you.

The 48 Laws of Power, Law 19: Know Who You're Dealing with—Do Not Offend the Wrong Person

See Through the False Front

One who is good at combating the enemy fools it with inscrutable
moves, confuses it with false intelligence, makes it relax by concealing
one's strength . . . deafens its ears by jumbling one's orders and
signals, blinds its eyes by converting one's banners and insignias, . . .
confounds its battle plan by providing
distorted facts.

—TOU BI FU TAN

The false front is the oldest form of military deception. It originally involved making the enemy believe that one was weaker than in fact was the case. A leader would feign a retreat, say, baiting a trap for the enemy to rush into, luring it into an ambush. This was a favorite tactic of Sun Tzu's. The appearance of weakness often brings out people's aggressive side, making them drop strategy and prudence for an emotional and violent attack. When Napoleon found himself outnumbered and in a vulnerable strategic position before the Battle of Austerlitz, he deliberately showed signs of being panicked, indecisive, and scared. The enemy armies abandoned their strong position to attack him and rushed into a trap. It was his greatest victory. In general, as advocated since the days of ancient China, nonplayers present a face to the world that promises the opposite of what they are actually planning.

Daily Law: Never take appearances for reality.

The 33 Strategies of War, Strategy 23: Weave a Seamless Blend of Fact and
Fiction—Misperception Strategies

The Subtle-Superiority Strategy

A friend, colleague, or employee is chronically late, but he or she always has a ready excuse that is logical, along with an apology that seems sincere. Or similarly, such individuals forget about meetings, important dates, and deadlines, always with impeccable excuses at hand. If this behavior repeats often enough, your irritation will increase, but if you try to confront them, they very well might try to turn the tables by making you seem uptight and unsympathetic. It is not their fault, they say—they have too much on their mind, people are pressuring them, they are temperamental artists who can't keep on top of so many irritating details, they are overwhelmed. They may even accuse you of adding to their stress. You must understand that at the root of this is the need to make it clear to themselves and to you that they are in some way superior. If they were to say in so many words that they felt superior to you, they would incur ridicule and shame. They want you to feel it in subtle ways, while they are able to deny what they are up to. Putting you in the inferior position is a form of control, in which they get to define the relationship. You must pay attention to the pattern more than the apologies. They are not really sorry.

Daily Law: If this is chronic behavior, you must not get angry or display overt irritation—passive aggressors thrive on getting a rise out of you. Instead, stay calm and subtly mirror their behavior, calling attention to what they are doing, and inducing some shame if possible.

The Laws of Human Nature, 16: See the Hostility Behind the Friendly Facade—The Law of Aggression

Look at Their Past

The most significant indicator of people's character comes through their actions over time. Despite what people say about the lessons they have learned, and how they have changed over the years, you will inevitably notice the same actions and decisions repeating in the course of their life. In these decisions they reveal their character. You must take notice of any salient forms of behavior—disappearing when there is too much stress, not completing an important piece of work, turning suddenly belligerent when challenged, or, conversely, suddenly rising to the occasion when given responsibility. With this fixed in your mind, you do some research into their past. You look at other actions you have observed that fit into this pattern, now in retrospect. You pay close attention to what they do in the present. You see their actions not as isolated incidents but as parts of a compulsive pattern. If you ignore the pattern it is your own fault.

Daily Law: When choosing people to work and associate with, do not be mesmerized by their reputation or taken in by the surface image they try to project. Instead, train yourself to look deep within them, to their past actions, to see their character.

The Laws of Human Nature, 4: Determine the Strength of People's
Character—The Law of Compulsive Behavior

See Through the Emotional Outburst

If a person explodes with anger at you (and it seems out of proportion to what you did to them), you must remind yourself that it is not exclusively directed at you—do not be so vain. The cause is much larger, goes way back in time, involves dozens of prior hurts, and is actually not worth the bother to understand. Instead of seeing it as a personal grudge, look at the emotional outburst as a disguised power move, an attempt to control or punish you cloaked in the form of hurt feelings and anger. This shift of perspective will let you play the game of power with more clarity and energy.

Daily Law: Instead of overreacting and becoming ensnared in people's emotions, turn their loss of control to your advantage: you keep your head while they are losing theirs.

The 48 Laws of Power, Law 3: Conceal Your Intentions

Don't Mistake Extra Conviction for Truth

We humans are by nature quite gullible. We want to believe in certain things—that we can get something for nothing; that we can easily regain or rejuvenate our health thanks to some new trick, perhaps even cheat death; that most people are essentially good and can be trusted. This propensity is what deceivers and manipulators thrive on. It would be immensely beneficial for the future of our species if we were all less gullible, but we cannot change human nature. Instead, the best we can do is to learn to recognize certain telltale signs of an attempt at deception and maintain our skepticism as we examine the evidence further. The most clear and common sign comes when people assume an extra-animated front. When they smile a lot, seem more than friendly, and even are quite entertaining, it is hard for us to not be drawn in and lower ever so slightly our resistance to their influence. Similarly, if people are trying to cover something up, they tend to become extra vehement, righteous, and chatty. They are playing on the conviction bias—if I deny or say something with so much gusto, with an air of being a victim, it is hard to doubt me. We tend to take extra conviction for truth.

Daily Law: When people try to explain their ideas with so much exaggerated energy, or defend themselves with an intense level of denial, that is precisely when you should raise your antennae.

The Laws of Human Nature, 3: See Through People's Masks—The Law of Role-Playing

The Pattern

The problem that Howard Hughes presented to all those who chose to work with him in some capacity was that he carefully constructed a public image that concealed the glaring weaknesses in his character. Instead of the irrational micromanager, he could present himself as the rugged individualist and the consummate American maverick. Most damaging of all was his ability to portray himself as a successful businessman leading a billion-dollar empire. In truth, he had inherited a highly profitable tool business from his father. Over the years, the only parts of his empire that ran substantial profits were the tool company and an earlier version of Hughes Aircraft that he had spun out of the tool company. The many other businesses he personally ran—his later aircraft division, his film ventures, his hotels and real estate in Las Vegas—all lost substantial amounts that were fortunately covered by the other two. In fact, Hughes was a terrible businessman, and the pattern of failures that revealed this was plain for everyone to see. But this is the blind spot in human nature: we are poorly equipped to gauge the character of the people we deal with. Their public image, the reputation that precedes them, easily mesmerizes us. We are captivated by appearances. If they surround themselves with some alluring myth, as Hughes did, we want to believe in it. Instead of determining people's character—their ability to work with others, to keep to their promises, to remain strong in adverse circumstances—we choose to work with or hire people based on their glittering résumé, their intelligence, and their charm. But even a positive trait such as intelligence is worthless if the person also happens to be of weak or dubious character. And so, because of our blind spot, we suffer under the irresolute leader, the micromanaging boss, the conniving partner. This is the source of endless tragedies in history, our pattern as a species.

Daily Law: Ignore the front that people display, the myth that surrounds them, and instead plumb their depths for signs of their character. This can be seen in the patterns they reveal from their past, the quality of their decisions, how they delegate authority and work with others, and countless other signs.

The Laws of Human Nature, 4: Determine the Strength of People's
Character—The Law of Compulsive Behavior

Be Wary of the Noble Gesture

It is a world not of angels but of angles, where men speak of moral principles but act on power principles; a world where we are always moral and our enemies always immoral.

—RULES FOR RADICALS, SAUL D. ALINSKY

The noble gesture is one of the most effective smoke screens—a favorite of the supposed nonplayer. The art dealer Joseph Duveen was once confronted with a terrible problem. The millionaires who had paid so dearly for Duveen's paintings were running out of wall space, and with inheritance taxes getting ever higher, it seemed unlikely that they would keep buying. The solution was the National Gallery of Art in Washington, D.C., which Duveen helped create in 1937 by getting Andrew Mellon to donate his collection to it. The National Gallery was the perfect front for Duveen. In one gesture, his clients avoided taxes, cleared wall space for new purchases, and reduced the number of paintings on the market, maintaining the upward pressure on their prices. All this while the donors created the appearance of being public benefactors.

Daily Law: People want to believe apparently noble gestures are genuine, for the belief is pleasant. They rarely notice how deceptive these gestures can be.

The 48 Laws of Power, Law 3: Conceal Your Intentions

Recognize Deep Narcissists before You Fall for Them

You can recognize deep narcissists by the following behavior patterns: If they are ever insulted or challenged, they have no defense, nothing internal to soothe them or validate their worth. They generally react with great rage, thirsting for vengeance, full of a sense of righteousness. This is the only way they know how to assuage their insecurities. In such battles, they will position themselves as the wounded victim, confusing others and even drawing sympathy. They are prickly and oversensitive. Almost everything is taken personally. They can become quite paranoid and have enemies in all directions to point to. You can see an impatient or distant look on their face whenever you talk about something that does not directly involve them in some way. They immediately turn the conversation back to themselves, with some story or anecdote to distract from the insecurity behind it. They can be prone to vicious bouts of envy if they see others getting the attention they feel they deserve. They frequently display extreme self-confidence. This always helps to gain attention, and it neatly covers up their gaping inner emptiness and their fragmented sense of self. But beware if this confidence is ever truly put to the test. When it comes to other people in their lives, deep narcissists have an unusual relationship that is hard for us to understand. They tend to see others as extensions of themselves, what is known as self-objects. People exist as instruments for attention and validation. Their desire is to control them like they control their own arm or leg. In a relationship, they will slowly make the partner cut off contact with friends—there must be no competition for attention.

Daily Law: In the end, deep narcissists must have everything revolve around them. The best solution is to get out of their way so as not to get entangled in their never-ending dramas, and you can do so by picking up on the warning signs.

The Laws of Human Nature, 2: Transform Self-Love into Empathy—The Law of Narcissism

The Grandiose Leader

The trick grandiose leaders play is to place the emphasis on their cultural tastes, not on the actual class they come from. They may fly first class and wear the most expensive suits, but they counteract this by seeming to have the same culinary tastes as the public, enjoy the same movies as others, and avoid at all costs the whiff of cultural elitism. In fact, they will go out of their way to ridicule the elites, even though they probably depend on such experts to guide them. They are simply just like the common folk out there, but with a lot more money and power. The public can now identify with them despite the obvious contradictions. But the grandiosity of this goes beyond merely gaining more attention. These leaders become vastly enlarged by this identification with the masses. They are not merely one man or woman but embody an entire nation or interest group. To follow them is to be loyal to the group itself. To criticize them is to want to crucify the leader and betray the cause. Even in the prosaic corporate world of business we find such religious-style identification. If you notice such paradoxes and primitive forms of popular association, stand back and analyze the reality of what is going on. You will find at the core something quasi-mystical, highly irrational, and quite dangerous in that the grandiose leader now feels licensed to do whatever he or she wants in the name of the public.

Daily Law: A simple fact about grandiose leaders: they depend on the attention they are given. Do not feed their egos by giving them what they crave.

The Laws of Human Nature, 11: Know Your Limits—The Law of Grandiosity

The Machiavellian Gift

The essence of a nonplayer's deception is distraction. Distracting the people they want to deceive gives them the time and space to do something their targets won't notice. An act of kindness, generosity, or honesty is often the most powerful form of distraction because it disarms other people's suspicions. It turns them into children, eagerly lapping up any kind of affectionate gesture. In ancient China this was called "giving before you take"—the giving makes it hard for the other person to notice the taking. Nonplayers know: it is a device with infinite practical uses. Perhaps the best, though, is one of generosity. Few people can resist a gift, even from the most hardened enemy, which is why it is often the perfect way to disarm people. A gift brings out the child in us, instantly lowering our defenses. When we are children, all kinds of complicated feelings about our parents center around gifts; we see the giving of a gift as a sign of love and approval. And that emotional element never goes away. The recipients of gifts, financial or otherwise, are suddenly as vulnerable as children, especially when the gift comes from someone in authority. They cannot help opening up; their will is loosened. Beware especially of the gift that comes out of the blue. The one that is remarkable for the fact that you have never been given a gift like it ever before. Most likely, the gift-giver is loosening the soil before planting their seeds.

Daily Law: Although we often view other people's actions in the most cynical light, we rarely see the Machiavellian element of a gift, which quite often hides ulterior motives.

The 48 Laws of Power, Law 12: Use Selective Honesty and Generosity to Disarm Your Victim

The Fake Traditionalist

He who desires or attempts to reform the government of a state,
and wishes to have it accepted, must at least retain the semblance
of the old forms; so that it may seem to the people that there
has been no change in the institutions, even though in
fact they are entirely different from the old ones.

—NICCOLÒ MACHIAVELLI

A strategy the clever nonplayer uses to disguise change: making a loud and public display of support for the values of the past. Renaissance Florence had a centuries-old republic and was suspicious of anyone who flouted its traditions. Cosimo de' Medici made a show of enthusiastic support for the republic, while in reality he worked to bring the city under the control of his wealthy family. In form, the Medicis retained the appearance of a republic; in substance, they rendered it powerless. They quietly enacted a radical change, while appearing to safeguard tradition.

Daily Law: Don't let the person who seems to be a zealot for tradition fool you. Notice how unconventional they really are.

The 48 Laws of Power, Law 45: Preach the Need for Change, but Never Reform Too Much at Once

Deciphering the Shadow

In the course of your life you will come upon people who have very emphatic traits that set them apart and seem to be the source of their strength—unusual confidence, exceptional niceness and affability, great moral rectitude and a saintly aura, toughness and rugged masculinity, an intimidating intellect. If you look closely at them, you may notice a slight exaggeration to these traits, as if they were performing or laying it on just a little too thick. As a student of human nature, you must understand the reality: the emphatic trait generally rests on top of the opposite trait, distracting and concealing it from public view. We can see two forms of this: Early on in life some people sense a softness, vulnerability, or insecurity that might prove embarrassing or uncomfortable. They unconsciously develop the opposite trait, a resilience or toughness that lies on the outside like a protective shell. The other scenario is that a person has a quality that they feel might be antisocial—for instance, too much ambition or an inclination to be selfish. They develop the opposite quality, something very prosocial. In both cases, over the years they hone and perfect this public image. The underlying weakness or antisocial trait is a key component of their Shadow—something denied and repressed. But as the laws of human nature dictate, the deeper the repression, the greater the volatility of the Shadow.

Daily Law: Be extra wary around people who display emphatic traits. It is very easy to get caught up in the appearance and first impression. Watch for the signs and emergence of the opposite over time.

The Laws of Human Nature, 9: Confront Your Dark Side—The Law of Repression

Look Beneath the Mask

Remember that people are generally trying to present the best possible front to the world. This means concealing their possible antagonistic feelings, their desires for power or superiority, their attempts at ingratiation, and their insecurities. They will use words to hide their feelings and distract you from the reality, playing on people's verbal fixation. They will also use certain facial expressions that are easy to put on and that people assume mean friendliness. Your task is to look past the distractions and become aware of those signs that leak out automatically, revealing something of the true emotion beneath the mask.

Daily Law: Train yourself to pay no attention to the front that people display.

The Laws of Human Nature, 3: See Through People's Masks—The Law of Role-Playing

Demanding Equality

Another strategy of the supposed nonplayer is to demand equality in every area of life. Everyone must be treated alike, whatever their status and strength. But if, to avoid the taint of power, you attempt to treat everyone equally and fairly, you will confront the problem that some people do certain things better than others. Treating everyone equally means ignoring their differences, elevating the less skillful and suppressing those who excel.

> Daily Law: Many of those who demand equality across the board are actually deploying another power strategy, redistributing people's rewards in a way that they determine. Judge and reward people on the quality of their work.//
>
> *The 48 Laws of Power*, Preface

The Unambitious Front

Of all the disorders of the soul, envy is the
only one no one confesses to.

—PLUTARCH

When Ivan the Terrible died, Boris Godunov knew he was the only one on the scene who could lead Russia. But if he sought the position eagerly, he would stir up envy and suspicion among the boyars, so he refused the crown, not once but several times. He made people insist that he take the throne. George Washington used the same strategy to great effect, first in refusing to keep the position of commander in chief of the American army, second in resisting the presidency. In both cases he made himself more popular than ever. People cannot envy the power that they themselves have given a person who does not seem to desire it.

Daily Law: Be most suspicious of those who seem unambitious.

The 48 Laws of Power, Law 46: Never Appear Too Perfect

The Aggressive Pleaser

In those days force and arms did prevail; but now the wit of the fox is everywhere on foot, so hardly a faithful or virtuous man may be found.
—QUEEN ELIZABETH I

There are people who are amazingly accommodating when you first meet them, so much so that you tend to let them into your life rather quickly. They smile a lot. They are upbeat and always willing to help. At some point, you may return the favor by hiring them for a job or helping them in their careers. You will detect along the way some cracks in the veneer—perhaps they make a somewhat critical comment out of the blue, or you hear from friends that they have been talking about you behind your back. Then something ugly occurs—a blowup, some act of sabotage or betrayal—so unlike that nice, charming person you first befriended. The truth is that these types realize early on in life that they have aggressive, envious tendencies that are hard to control. They want power. They intuit that such inclinations will make life hard for them. Over many years they cultivate the opposite facade—their niceness has an almost aggressive edge. Through this stratagem they are able to gain social power. But they secretly resent having to play such a role and be so deferential. They can't maintain it. Under stress or simply worn out by the effort, they will lash out and hurt you. They can do this well now that they know you and your weak spots. They will, of course, blame you for what ensues.

Daily Law: Your best defense is to be wary of people who are too quick to charm and befriend, too nice and accommodating at first. Such extreme niceness is never natural.

The Laws of Human Nature, 9: Confront Your Dark Side—The Law of Repression

Determine the Strength of
People's Character

Remember this: weak character will neutralize all of the other possible good qualities a person might possess. For instance, people of high intelligence but weak character may come up with good ideas and even do a job well, but they will crumble under pressure, or they will not take too kindly to criticism, or they will think first and foremost of their own agenda, or their arrogance and annoying qualities will cause others around them to quit, harming the general environment. There are hidden costs to working with them or hiring them. Someone less charming and intelligent but of strong character will prove more reliable and productive over the long run. People of real strength are as rare as gold, and if you find them, you should respond as if you had a discovered a treasure.

Daily Law: In gauging strength or weakness, look at how people handle stressful moments and responsibility. Look at their patterns: what have they actually completed or accomplished?

The Laws of Human Nature, 4: Determine the Strength of People's
Character—The Law of Compulsive Behavior

Don't Always Believe Your Eyes

The CBS News reporter Lesley Stahl had been covering the 1984 presidential campaign, and as Election Day neared, she had an uneasy feeling. It wasn't so much that Ronald Reagan had focused on emotions and moods rather than hard issues. It was more that the media was giving him a free ride; he and his election team, she felt, were playing the press like a fiddle. She decided to assemble a news piece that would show the public how Reagan used television to cover up the negative effects of his policies. A senior White House official telephoned her the evening it aired: "Great piece," he said. "What?" asked a stunned Stahl. "Great piece," he repeated. "Did you listen to what I said?" she asked. "Lesley, when you're showing four and a half minutes of great pictures of Ronald Reagan, no one listens to what you say. Don't you know that the pictures are overriding your message because they conflict with your message? The public sees those pictures and they block your message. They didn't even hear what you said. So, in our minds, it was a four-and-a-half-minute free ad for the Ronald Reagan campaign for reelection." Most of the men who worked on communications for Reagan had a background in marketing. They knew the importance of telling a story crisply, sharply, and with good visuals. Each morning they went over what the headline of the day should be, and how they could shape this into a short visual piece, getting the president into a video opportunity. They paid detailed attention to the backdrop behind the president in the Oval Office, to the way the camera framed him when he was with other world leaders, and to having him filmed in motion, with his confident walk. The visuals carried the message better than any words could do. As one Reagan official said, "What are you going to believe, the facts or your eyes?"

Daily Law: Nonplayers are masters at visual effects, to distract from their manipulations. Guard yourself by paying more attention to the content and the facts than the form of their message.

The Art of Seduction: Soft Seduction—How to Sell Anything to the Masses

Easy Money

*This desire to get something for nothing has been very costly
to many people who have dealt with me and with other con
men. . . . When people learn—as I doubt they will—that they
can't get something for nothing, crime will diminish and
we shall all live in greater harmony.*

—JOSEPH WEIL

Dangling the lure of a free lunch is the con artist's stock in trade. No man was better at this than the most successful con artist of our age, Joseph Weil, aka "The Yellow Kid." The Yellow Kid learned early that what made his swindles possible was his fellow humans' greed. Over the years Weil devised many ways to seduce people with the prospect of easy money. He would hand out "free" real estate—who could resist such an offer?—and then the suckers would learn they had to pay $25 to register the sale. Since the land was free, it seemed worth the high fee, and the Yellow Kid would make thousands of dollars on the phony registration. In exchange he would give his suckers a phony deed. Other times, he would tell suckers about a fixed horse race, or a stock that would earn 200 percent in a few weeks. As he spun his stories he would watch the sucker's eyes open wide at the thought of a free lunch. Don't let yourself get lured in by the prospect of easy money. As the Yellow Kid said himself: greed does not pay.

Daily Law: Be suspicious of anyone dangling the lure of something for nothing. Get-rich-quick schemes are scams. The lottery is really a tax on the mathematically illiterate. There are no shortcuts to power.

The 48 Laws of Power, Law 40: Despise the Free Lunch

Avoid the Drama Magnet

In anything, it is a mistake to think one can perform an action or
behave in a certain way once and no more.

—CESARE PAVESE

They will draw you in with their exciting presence. They have unusual
energy and stories to tell. Their features are animated and they can be
quite witty. They are fun to be around, until the drama turns ugly. As
children, they learned that the only way to get love and attention that
lasted was to enmesh their parents in their troubles and problems, which
had to be large enough to engage the parents emotionally over time. This
became a habit, their way of feeling alive and wanted. Most people shrink
from any kind of confrontation, but they seem to live for it. As you get to
know them better, you hear more stories of bickering and battles in their
life, but they manage to always position themselves as the victim. You
must realize that their greatest need is to get their hooks into you by any
means possible. They will embroil you in their drama to the point that
you will feel guilty for disengaging.

Daily Law: It is best to recognize them as early as possible, before you
become enmeshed and dragged down. Examine their past for evidence
of the pattern and run for the hills if you suspect you are dealing with
such a type.

The Laws of Human Nature, 4: Determine the Strength of People's
Character—The Law of Compulsive Behavior

The Sincerity Ploy

A trick to be aware of comes from La Rochefoucauld, who wrote, "Sincerity is found in very few men, and is often the cleverest of ruses—one is sincere in order to draw out the confidence and secrets of the other."

Daily Law: By pretending to bare their heart to you, clever nonplayers know they make it more likely that you will reveal your own secrets. They give you a false confession in hopes that you will give them a real one.

The 48 Laws of Power, Law 14: Pose as a Friend, Work as a Spy

Detect Their True Motives

Knowing any man's mainspring of motive, you have,
as it were, the key to his will.

—BALTASAR GRACIÁN

In the Machiavellian perspective, few events in public life are rarely what they seem to be. Power depends on appearances, on manipulating what the public sees. On seeming good, while doing what is necessary to gain and maintain power. Sometimes it is easy to see through the fog and pick out people's motives or intentions. But usually, it is quite complicated—what is really going on, we ask ourselves? In the new media environment, the ability to create fog and confusion has been greatly enhanced. Stories and rumors can be planted with virtually no source behind them. The story will spread virally. Before people begin to question the validity of story A, their attention is distracted by something else, story B or C; in the meantime, story A takes root in people's minds in subtle ways. It is an added layer of uncertainty and doubt that makes it quite easy for all kinds of insinuation games. To decipher events that seem hard to read, I sometimes rely on a strategy that comes from the Latin *Cui bono?* It was first used in this context by Cicero and it literally translates to, "For whose good, or benefit?" It means: when you are trying to figure out the motives behind some murky action, look to see whom it really benefits in the end, and then work backward. Self-interest rules the world.

Daily Law: Don't be fooled by appearances, by what happens, by what people do and say. Always ask: *Cui bono?*

powerseductionandwar.com, November 23, 2007

The Effective Truth

*For the great majority of mankind are satisfied with appearances,
as though they were realities.*

—NICCOLÒ MACHIAVELLI

Machiavelli calls this "the effective truth," and it is his most brilliant concept, in my opinion. It works like this: People will say almost anything to justify their actions, to give them a moral or sanctimonious veneer. The only thing that is clear, the only way we can judge people and cut away all this crap is by looking at their actions, the results of their actions. That is their effective truth. Take the Pope, for instance. He will sermonize forever about the poor, about morality, about peace, but in the meantime he presides over the most powerful organization in the world (in Machiavelli's time). And his actions are basically concerned with increasing this power. The effective truth is that the Pope is a political animal, and that his decisions inevitably involve maintaining the Catholic Church's preeminent place in the world. The religious verbiage is simply a part of his political gamesmanship, serving as a distracting device.

Daily Law: Judge people by the results of their actions and maneuvers, and not by the stories they tell.

powerseductionandwar.com, July 28, 2006

Nothing Personal

A lot of people in life have terrible problems dealing with politics, with disassociating their emotions from the work world or the realm of power. They take everything personally. I myself had a terrible problem working in offices, working in Hollywood, working in journalism, and so on. I'm a bit naive, and a lot of other people are too. And basically what happens in these situations is, because nobody trains you for these things, you get emotional—you take what people say and do personally. The moment you get wrapped up in the emotions of it, you're done. You have to be able to look at life as if it were moves on a chessboard. Marcus Aurelius has this great quote that I'll paraphrase: if you're in a boxing ring and the boxer punches you in the face, you don't whine about the unfairness or the cruelty. No, that's just part of the game. I want you to see life like this: If someone does something to you that is nasty, get control of your emotions. Don't react. Don't get upset. Look at it as moves on a chessboard. They are moving you. Don't listen to their words, because people will say anything. Look at their moves. Look at their maneuvers. Look at their past actions. Actions tell you who they are, not what they say. That kind of self-control is immensely liberating and empowering.

Daily Law: Judging people by their actions and not taking them personally will free you up, help you keep your emotional balance.

"Robert Greene: Mastery and Research," *Finding Mastery: Conversations with Michael Gervais*, January 25, 2017

Everyone Wants More Power

There's the famous line from Lord Acton that absolute power corrupts absolutely. People quote it a lot. But Malcolm X said the opposite is also true, namely that having power may corrupt, but having absolutely no power corrupts absolutely. I maintain in *The 48 Laws of Power* that the feeling of having no power over people and events is generally unbearable to us—when we feel helpless we feel miserable. No one wants less power; everyone wants more.

> **Daily Law:** When in doubt, assume that people are doing what they are doing and saying what they are saying because they want more power, not less.

"Robert Greene: The 48 Laws of Power," *Between the Lines with Barry Kibrick*, May 15, 2015

Know Who You're Dealing With

Be convinced, that there are no persons so insignificant
and inconsiderable, but may, some time or other, have it in
their power to be of use to you; which they certainly will not,
if you have once shown them contempt.

—LORD CHESTERFIELD

The ability to measure people is the most important skill of all in gathering and conserving power. Without it you are blind: not only will you offend the wrong people, you will choose the wrong types to work on and will think you are flattering people when you are actually insulting them. Before embarking on any move, take the measure of your mark or potential opponent. Otherwise you will waste time and make mistakes. Study people's weaknesses, the chinks in their armor, their areas of both pride and insecurity. Know their ins and outs before you even decide whether or not to deal with them. Two final words of caution: First, in judging and measuring your opponent, never rely on your instincts. You will make the greatest mistakes of all if you rely on such inexact indicators. Nothing can substitute for gathering concrete knowledge. Study and spy on your opponent for however long it takes; this will pay off in the long run. Second, never trust appearances. Anyone with a serpent's heart can use a show of kindness to cloak it; a person who is blustery on the outside is often really a coward. Never trust the version that people give of themselves—it is utterly unreliable.

Daily Law: What possible good can come from ignorance about other people? Learn to tell the lions from the lambs or pay the price.

The 48 Laws of Power, Law 19: Know Who You're Dealing
With—Do Not Offend the Wrong Person

June

The Divine Craft

MASTERING THE ARTS OF INDIRECTION
AND MANIPULATION

≈

In Greek myths, in India's Mahabharata cycle, in the Middle Eastern epic of *Gilgamesh*, it is the privilege of the gods to use deceptive arts; a great man, Odysseus for instance, was judged by his ability to rival the craftiness of the gods, stealing some of their divine power by matching them in wits and deception. Deception is a developed art of civilization and the most potent weapon in the game of power. Deception and masquerade should not be seen as ugly or immoral. All human interaction requires deception on many levels, and in some ways what separates humans from animals is our ability to lie and deceive. Outwardly, you must seem to respect the niceties, but inwardly, unless you are a fool, you learn quickly to be prudent, and to do as Napoleon advised: place your iron hand inside a velvet glove. If you can master the arts of deception and indirection, learning to seduce, charm, deceive, and subtly outmaneuver your opponents, you will attain the heights of power. The month of June will teach you how to make people bend to your will without their realizing what you have done. And if they do not realize what you have done, they will neither resent nor resist you.

A few years ago, to help my mind get over the grind of writing *The 33 Strategies of War*, I bought a pool table. After a hard day's work, I would settle into the game of pool and make myself completely focus on the green felt, the cue stick, the stripes and solids. It ended up being the perfect choice of a diversion. Pool, it became clear to me, is all about angles. First, there are simple angles, as you must hit the cue ball to either side when you are not straight on. This is often not as easy as it seems. Then, there are the angles you take when you bank the targeted ball off the sides, an entirely new game in and of itself. This goes further with the double bank shot.

There are the angles of the combination shots, and even more slippery combinations when you use a solid to slide off a stripe and knock in a solid. Then there is the whole language of angles that comes into play when you are thinking ahead and trying to keep the cue ball in solid position, working with the open spaces of the table.

Finally, there are the abstract angles in psychological space and time: Playing with your opponent's mind; letting him get ahead, but putting himself in a corner in relation to the final balls on the table; snookering him into impossible positions (the trick bag); or seeing the entire table and how you will run it in short order. In other words, there are layers of angles, all more subtle and artistic as you go up the ladder and improve your game. I am no longer a rank beginner, but I am certainly no hustler, not yet.

To play well, to raise your game, your focus must be total.

As in pool, so in life. Suckers and beginners are locked into the single-ball-at-a-time mentality and get all excited when they knock one in on a clever shot, but leave themselves nowhere to go. They never learn the angles above the angles above the angles.

Then there are people who raise their game a little, who give the appearance of knowing how to hustle, who can actually knock in a few shots in a row. In Hollywood, I worked for some people like that. They would let others do the work and take all the credit. One director I knew would constantly play the game of hiring someone else to direct the pet script he had written, someone young and eager and inexperienced. This person would inevitably fail rather early on in the process; the director would have to come in and rescue the situation, his goal all along. Better to set it up that way than for him to be seen as being overly ambitious and greedy, always insisting he direct all the projects on his plate. Similar to how Pat Riley engineered his whole return to coaching.

But these types do not really see the whole table, or have a good endgame mapped out. They have some angles, but not of a high order. They never really get that far. They stir up much resentment and resistance. They are low- to mid-level hustlers.

An acquaintance of mine who runs his own media business came to me a few years ago with a problem: a high-level employee had leaked something embarrassing about him to other employees. His angle in leaking this was to get the boss's attention and warn him about what else he might do. He was worried the boss was planning to fire him, and so this was his warning shot across the bow.

My advice to him was to be aware first of what the leaker was up to, and then to not indicate any kind of negative reaction on his part. He was to continue seeming friendly, as if nothing had happened. This was a front, a distraction. The employee would have to focus on this and figure out what it meant. Was the boss being coy? Did he not care? Was he trying to win him back over? Was he intimidated? This would buy the boss time.

As we then investigated the situation, we saw more of what was going on and a solution came to us. First, he fired two other employees who were allies of the leaker and obvious troublemakers. A third he got transferred to an office in a distant location. All of this was ostensibly done as a reaction to their lack of performance and had no apparent links to the leaker in question. The purpose was twofold: to isolate the target, make it harder for him to conspire and stir things up; and to send an indirect warning to him that the boss was not someone he could easily mess with.

His moves were not simple to figure out; they got the leaker's attention and froze him in place. As we considered the leaker's possible reactions to these moves and how he might ratchet it all up if he felt threatened, we worked on a higher angle to this reaction, so that we had as many bases as possible covered. We had mapped out a way to even checkmate him if he maneuvered to go public with his information.

Iceberg Slim is one of my favorite authors. To Iceberg, the world is divided between hustler and sucker. You are either one or the other. The sucker has no angles on life, no sense of the art of indirection, and can only make one stupid play at a time. The hustler always aims for the angles, learns how to play them, and becomes an artist in the game.

Wear the Appropriate Mask

You cannot succeed at deception unless you take a somewhat distanced approach to yourself—unless you can be many different people, wearing the mask that the day and the moment require. With such a flexible approach to all appearances, including your own, you lose a lot of the inward heaviness that holds people down. Make your face as malleable as the actor's, work to conceal your intentions from others, practice luring people into traps.

Daily Law: Playing with appearances and mastering arts of deception are among the aesthetic pleasures of life. They are also key components in the acquisition of power.

The 48 Laws of Power, Preface

Use Absence to Increase Respect

If I am often seen at the theater, people will cease to notice me.
—NAPOLEON

Today, in a world inundated with presence through the flood of images, the game of withdrawal is powerful. We rarely know when to withdraw anymore, and nothing seems private, so we are awed by anyone who is able to disappear by choice. In the science of economics, the law of scarcity gives us this truth: too much circulation makes the price go down. But by withdrawing something from the market, you create instant value. In seventeenth-century Holland, the upper classes wanted to make the tulip more than just a beautiful flower—they wanted it to be a kind of status symbol. Making the flower scarce, indeed almost impossible to obtain, they sparked what was later called tulipomania. A single flower was now worth more than its weight in gold. Extend the law of scarcity to your own skills. Make what you are offering the world rare and hard to find, and you instantly increase its value.

Daily Law: The more you are seen and heard from, the more common you appear. If you are already established in a group, temporary withdrawal from it will make you more talked about, even more admired. You must learn when to leave. Create value through scarcity.

The 48 Laws of Power, Law 16: Use Absence to Increase Respect and Honor

Take Control of Your Image

The man who intends to make his fortune in this ancient capital of
the world [Rome] must be a chameleon susceptible of reflecting
the colors of the atmosphere that surrounds him—a Proteus apt
to assume every form, every shape.

—GIOVANNI CASANOVA

People will tend to judge you based on your outward appearance. If you
are not careful and simply assume that it is best to be yourself, they will
begin to ascribe to you all kinds of qualities that have little to do with
who you are but correspond to what they want to see. All of this can confuse you, make you feel insecure, and consume your attention. Internaliz-
ing their judgments, you will find it hard to focus on your work. Your
only protection is to turn this dynamic around by consciously molding
these appearances, creating the image that suits you, and controlling people's judgments. At times you will find it appropriate to stand back and
create some mystery around you, heightening your presence. At other
times you will want to be more direct and impose a more specific appearance. In general, you never settle on one image or give people the power
to completely figure you out. You are always one step ahead of the public.

Daily Law: Never let people think they have you completely figured
out. Create some mystery around you.

Mastery, IV: See People as They Are—Social Intelligence

Play on People's Instinct to Trust Appearances

Appearance and intention inevitably ensnare people when
artfully used, even if people sense that there is an ulterior
intention behind the overt appearance

—YAGYŪ MUNENORI

Basic to an ability to deceive is a simple truth about human nature: our first instinct is to always trust appearances. We cannot go around doubting the reality of what we see and hear—constantly imagining that appearances concealed something else would exhaust and terrify us. This fact makes it relatively easy to deceive. Simply dangle an object you seem to desire, a goal you seem to aim for, in front of people's eyes and they will take the appearance for reality. Once their eyes focus on the decoy, they will fail to notice what you are really up to.

Daily Law: Hide your intentions behind a cloak of carefully constructed appearances.

The 48 Laws of Power, Law 3: Conceal Your Intentions

Create Dramatic Effects

At the time of Franklin Delano Roosevelt's 1932 presidential election, the United States was in the midst of a dire economic crisis. Banks were failing at an alarming rate. Shortly after winning the election, Roosevelt went into a kind of retreat. He said nothing about his plans or his cabinet appointments. He even refused to meet the sitting president, Herbert Hoover, to discuss the transition. By the time of Roosevelt's inauguration, the country was in a state of high anxiety. In his inaugural address, Roosevelt shifted gears. He made a powerful speech, making it clear that he intended to lead the country in a completely new direction, sweeping away the timid gestures of his predecessors. From then on the pace of his speeches and public decisions—cabinet appointments, bold legislation— unfolded at an incredibly rapid rate. The period after the inauguration became known as the "Hundred Days," and its success in altering the country's mood partly stemmed from Roosevelt's clever pacing and use of dramatic contrast. He held his audience in suspense, then hit them with a series of bold gestures that seemed all the more momentous because they came from nowhere.

> **Daily Law:** Use theatrical timing to surprise and divert. Learn to orchestrate events like Roosevelt, never revealing all your cards at once, but unfolding them in a way that heightens their dramatic effect.

The 48 Laws of Power, Law 25: Re-create Yourself

Play Your Role Well

In method acting you train yourself to be able to display the proper emotions on command. You feel sad when your part calls for it by recalling your own experiences that caused such emotions, or if necessary by simply imagining such experiences. The point is that you have control. In real life it is not possible to train ourselves to such a degree, but if you have no control, if you are continually emoting whatever comes to you in the moment, you will subtly signal weakness and an overall lack of self-mastery. Learn how to consciously put yourself in the right emotional mood by imagining how and why you should feel the emotion suitable to the occasion or performance you are about to give. Surrender to the feeling for the moment so that the face and body are naturally animated. Sometimes, by actually making yourself smile or frown, you will experience some of the emotions that go with these expressions. Just as important, train yourself to return to a more neutral expression at a natural moment, careful to not go too far with your emoting. Realize the following: the word *personality* comes from the Latin *persona*, which means "mask." In public, we all wear masks, and this has a positive function. If we displayed exactly who we are and spoke our minds truthfully, we would offend almost everyone and reveal qualities that are best concealed. Having a persona, playing a role well, actually protects us from people looking too closely at us, with all of the insecurities that would churn up.

Daily Law: We are all actors in the theater of life and the better you play your role and wear the proper mask, the more power you will accrue.

The Laws of Human Nature, 3: See Through People's Masks—The Law of Role-Playing

Never Impugn People's Intelligence

The best way to be well received by all is to clothe yourself
in the skin of the dumbest of brutes.

—BALTASAR GRACIÁN

The feeling that someone else is more intelligent than we are is almost intolerable. We usually try to justify it in different ways: "He only has book knowledge, whereas I have real knowledge." "Her parents paid for her to get a good education. If my parents had had as much money, if I had been as privileged . . . " "He's not as smart as he thinks." Last but not least: "She may know her narrow little field better than I do, but beyond that she's really not smart at all. Even Einstein was a boob outside physics." Given how important the idea of intelligence is to most people's vanity, it is critical never inadvertently to insult or impugn a person's brain power. That is an unforgivable sin. But if you can make this iron rule work for you, it opens up all sorts of avenues of deception. The feeling of intellectual superiority you give them will disarm their suspicion-muscles.

Daily Law: Subliminally reassure people that they are more intelligent than you are, or even that you are a bit of a moron, and you can run rings around them.

The 48 Laws of Power, Law 21: Play a Sucker to Catch a
Sucker—Seem Dumber Than Your Mark

Distract Them from Your Real Goal

During the War of the Spanish Succession in 1711, the Duke of Marlborough, head of the English army, wanted to destroy a key French fort, because it protected a vital thoroughfare into France. Yet he knew that if he destroyed it, the French would realize what he wanted—to advance down that road. Instead, then, he merely captured the fort, and garrisoned it with some of his troops, making it appear as if he wanted it for some purpose of his own. The French attacked the fort and the duke let them recapture it. Once they had it back, though, they destroyed it, figuring that the duke had wanted it for some important reason. Now that the fort was gone, the road was unprotected, and Marlborough could easily march into France. Use this tactic in the following manner: hide your intentions not by closing up (with the risk of appearing secretive and making people suspicious) but by talking endlessly about your desires and goals—just not your real ones. You will kill three birds with one stone: you appear friendly, open, and trusting; you conceal your intentions; and you send your rivals on time-consuming wild-goose chases.

Daily Law: Seem to want something in which you are actually not at all interested and your enemies will be thrown off the scent, making all kinds of errors in their calculations.

The 48 Laws of Power, Law 3: Conceal Your Intentions

Give People the Opportunity
to Feel Superior

Some people will see an appeal to their self-interest as ugly and ignoble. They actually prefer to be able to exercise charity, mercy, and justice, which are their ways of feeling superior to you: when you beg them for help, you emphasize their power and position. They are strong enough to need nothing from you except the chance to feel superior. This is the wine that intoxicates them. They are dying to fund your project, to introduce you to powerful people—provided, of course, that all this is done in public, and for a good cause (usually the more public, the better). Not everyone, then, can be approached through cynical self-interest. Some people will be put off by it, because they don't want to seem to be motivated by such things. They need opportunities to display their good heart. Do not be shy. Give them that opportunity. It's not as if you are conning them by asking for help—it is really their pleasure to give, and to be seen giving.

Daily Law: You must figure out what makes others tick. When they ooze greed, appeal to their greed. When they want to look charitable and noble, appeal to their charity.

The 48 Laws of Power, Law 13: When Asking for Help, Appeal to People's Self-Interest, Never to Their Mercy or Gratitude

Infect the Group with Productive Emotions

Infect the group with a sense of resolution that emanates from you. You are not upset by setbacks; you keep advancing and working on problems. You are persistent. The group senses this, and individuals feel embarrassed for becoming hysterical over the slightest shift in fortune. You can try to infect the group with confidence, but be careful that this does not slip into grandiosity. Your confidence and that of the group mostly stems from a successful track record. Periodically change up routines, surprise the group with something new or challenging. This will wake them up and stir them out of the complacency that can settle into any group that achieves success. Most important, showing a lack of fear and an overall openness to new ideas will have the most therapeutic effect of all. The members will become less defensive, which encourages them to think more on their own, and not operate as automatons.

Daily Law: People are naturally more emotional and permeable to the moods of others. Work with human nature and turn this into a positive by infecting the group with the proper set of emotions. People are more susceptible to the moods and attitudes of the leader than of anyone else.

The Laws of Human Nature, 14: Resist the Downward Pull of the
Group—The Law of Conformity

Strike the Shepherd

When the tree falls, the monkeys scatter.
—CHINESE SAYING

Within any group, trouble can most often be traced to a single source—the unhappy, chronically dissatisfied one who will always stir up dissension and infect the group with his or her ill ease. Before you know what hit you, the dissatisfaction spreads. Act before it becomes impossible to disentangle one strand of misery from another, or to see how the whole thing started. First, recognize troublemakers by their overbearing presence, or by their complaining nature. Once you spot them do not try to reform them or appease them—that will only make things worse. Do not attack them, whether directly or indirectly, for they are poisonous in nature and will work underground to destroy you. Do this instead: Banish them before it is too late. Separate them from the group before they become the eye of a whirlpool. Do not give them time to stir up anxieties and sow discontent; do not give them room to move. Let one person suffer so that the rest can live in peace.

Daily Law: When the leader is gone, the center of gravity is gone; there is nothing to revolve around and everything falls apart. Strike at the source of the trouble and the sheep will scatter.

The 48 Laws of Power, Law 42: Strike the Shepherd and the Sheep Will Scatter

Use the Surrender Tactic

When you are weaker, never fight for honor's sake; choose surrender instead. Surrender gives you time to recover, time to torment and irritate your conquerors, time to wait for their power to wane. Do not give them the satisfaction of fighting and defeating you—surrender first. By turning the other cheek you infuriate and unsettle them. Make surrender a tool of power. And keep in mind the following: people trying to make a show of their authority are easily deceived by the surrender tactic. Your outward sign of submission makes them feel important; satisfied that you respect them, they become easier targets for a later counterattack.

> **Daily Law: If you find yourself temporarily weakened, the surrender tactic is perfect for raising yourself up again—it disguises your ambition; it teaches you patience and self-control, key skills in the game.**

The 48 Laws of Power, Law 22: Use the Surrender Tactic—Transform Weakness into Power

Lead from the Front

Hannibal was the greatest general of antiquity by reason of his
admirable comprehension of the morale of combat. . . . His men were not
better than the Roman soldiers. They were not as well-armed, one-half
less in number. Yet he was always the conqueror. He understood the
value of morale. He had the absolute confidence of his people.

—COLONEL CHARLES ARDANT DU PICQ

Morale is contagious, and you, as leader, set the tone. Ask for sacrifices you won't make yourself (doing everything through assistants) and your troops grow lethargic and resentful; act too nice, show too much concern for their well-being, and you drain the tension from their souls and create spoiled children who whine at the slightest pressure or request for more work. Personal example is the best way to set the proper tone and build morale. When your people see your devotion to the cause, they ingest your spirit of energy and self-sacrifice. A few timely criticisms here and there and they will only try harder to please you, to live up to your high standards. Instead of having to push and pull your army, you will find them chasing after you.

> Daily Law: In commanding influence in the world, human beings—a devoted army of followers—are more valuable than money. They will do things for you that money cannot buy.

The 33 Strategies of War, Strategy 7: Transform Your War into a Crusade—Morale Strategies

Deter with a Threatening Presence

When opponents are unwilling to fight with you, it is because
they think it is contrary to their interests, or because you
have misled them into thinking so.

—SUN TZU

We all have to fit in, play politics, seem nice and accommodating. Most often this works fine, but in moments of danger and difficulty being seen as so nice will work against you: it says that you can be pushed around, discouraged, and obstructed. If you have never been willing to fight back before, no threatening gesture you make will be credible. Understand: there is great value in letting people know that when necessary you can let go of your niceness and be downright difficult and nasty. A few clear, violent demonstrations will suffice. Once people see you as a fighter, they will approach you with a little fear in their hearts. And as Machiavelli said, it is more useful to be feared than to be loved. Uncertainty is sometimes better than overt threat: if your opponents are never sure what messing with you will cost, they will not want to find out.

Daily Law: Build up a reputation: You're a little crazy. Fighting you is not worth it. Create this reputation and make it credible with a few impressive—impressively violent—acts.

The 33 Strategies of War, Strategy 10: Create a Threatening Presence—Deterrence Strategies

The Art of Presence and Absence

Absence diminishes minor passions and inflames great ones,
as the wind douses a candle and fans a fire.
—FRANÇOIS DE LA ROCHEFOUCAULD

Leaders must know how to balance presence and absence. In general, it is best to lean slightly more in the direction of absence, so that when you do appear before the group, you generate excitement and drama. If done right, in those moments when you are not available, people will be thinking of you. Today people have lost this art. They are far too present and familiar, their every move displayed on social media. That might make you relatable, but it also makes you seem just like everyone else, and it is impossible to project authority with such an ordinary presence. Keep in mind that talking too much is a type of overpresence that grates and reveals weakness. Silence is a form of absence and withdrawal that draws attention; it spells self-control and power; when you do talk, it has a greater effect. In a similar fashion, if you commit a mistake, do not overexplain and overapologize. You make it clear you accept responsibility and are accountable for any failures, and then you move on. Your contrition should be relatively quiet; your subsequent actions will show you have learned the lesson. Avoid appearing defensive and whiny if attacked. You are above that.

Daily Law: If you are too present and familiar, always available and visible, you seem too banal. You give people no room to idealize you. But if you are too aloof, people cannot identify with you.

The Laws of Human Nature, 15: Make Them Want to Follow You—The Law of Fickleness

Get Others to Play with the Cards You Deal

Words like "freedom," "options," and "choice" evoke a power of possibility far beyond the reality of the benefits they entail. When examined closely, the choices we have—in the marketplace, in elections, in our jobs—tend to have noticeable limitations: they are often a matter of a choice simply between A and B, with the rest of the alphabet out of the picture. Yet as long as the faintest mirage of choice flickers on, we rarely focus on the missing options. We "choose" to believe that the game is fair, and that we have our freedom. We prefer not to think too much about the depth of our liberty to choose.

This unwillingness to probe the smallness of our choices stems from the fact that too much freedom creates a kind of anxiety. The phrase "unlimited options" sounds infinitely promising, but unlimited options would actually paralyze us and cloud our ability to choose. Our limited range of choices comforts us. This supplies the clever and cunning with enormous opportunities for deception. For people who are choosing between alternatives find it hard to believe they are being manipulated or deceived; they cannot see that you are allowing them a small amount of free will in exchange for a much more powerful imposition of your own will. Setting up a narrow range of choices, then, should always be a part of your deceptions.

Daily Law: There is a saying: if you can get the bird to walk into the cage on its own, it will sing that much more prettily. Give people options that come out in your favor, whichever one they choose. Force them to make choices between the lesser of two evils, both of which serve your purpose.

The 48 Laws of Power, Law 31: Control the Options—Get Others
to Play with the Cards You Deal

The Seductive Visuals

The people are always impressed by the superficial
appearance of things.
—NICCOLÒ MACHIAVELLI

When the con artist Yellow Kid Weil created a newsletter touting the
phony stocks he was peddling, he called it the "Red Letter Newsletter"
and had it printed, at considerable expense, in red ink. The color created
a sense of urgency, power, and good fortune. Weil recognized details like
these as keys to deception—as do modern advertisers and mass-marketers.
If you use "gold" in the title of anything you are trying to sell, for example, print it in gold. Since the eye predominates, people will respond more
to the color than to the word.

Daily Law: Never neglect the way you arrange things visually. Factors
like color have enormous symbolic resonance.

The 48 Laws of Power, Law 37: Create Compelling Spectacles

Never Reform Too Much at Once

It must be considered that there is nothing more difficult to carry out,
nor more doubtful of success, nor more dangerous to handle, than
to initiate a new order of things.

—NICCOLÒ MACHIAVELLI

Human psychology contains many dualities, one of them being that even while people understand the need for change, knowing how important it is for institutions and individuals to be occasionally renewed, they are also irritated and upset by changes that affect them personally. They know that change is necessary, and that novelty provides relief from boredom, but deep inside they cling to the past. Change in the abstract, or superficial change, they desire, but a change that upsets core habits and routines is deeply disturbing to them. No revolution has gone without a powerful later reaction against it, for in the long run the void it creates proves too unsettling to the human animal, who unconsciously associates such voids with death and chaos. The opportunity for change and renewal seduces people to the side of the revolution, but once their enthusiasm fades, which it will, they are left with a certain emptiness. Yearning for the past, they create an opening for it to creep back in. It is far easier, and less bloody, to play a kind of con game. Preach change as much as you like, and even enact your reforms, but give them the comforting appearance of older events and traditions.

Daily Law: If you are new to a position of power, or trying to build a power base, make a show of respecting the old way of doing things. If change is necessary, make it feel like a gentle improvement on the past.

The 48 Laws of Power, Law 45: Preach the Need for Change, but Never Reform Too Much at Once

Make Others Come to You

Filippo Brunelleschi, the great Renaissance artist and architect, was a great practitioner of the art of making others come to him as a sign of his power. On one occasion he had been engaged to repair the dome of the Santa Maria del Fiore cathedral in Florence. The commission was important and prestigious. But when the city officials hired a second man, Lorenzo Ghiberti, to work with Brunelleschi, the great artist brooded in secret. He knew that Ghiberti had gotten the job through his connections, and that he would do none of the work and get half the credit. At a critical moment of the construction, then, Brunelleschi suddenly developed a mysterious illness. He had to stop work, but pointed out to city officials that they had hired Ghiberti, who should have been able to continue the work on his own. Soon it became clear that Ghiberti was useless and the officials came begging to Brunelleschi. He ignored them, insisting that Ghiberti should finish the project, until finally they realized the problem: they fired Ghiberti. By some miracle, Brunelleschi recovered within days. He did not have to throw a tantrum or make a fool of himself; he simply practiced the art of making others come to you.

> Daily Law: If on one occasion you make it a point of dignity that others must come to you and you succeed, they will continue to do so even after you stop trying.

The 48 Laws of Power, Law 8: Make Other People Come to You—Use Bait if Necessary

Display a Hint of Weakness

Learn to transform your vulnerabilities into power. The game is subtle: if you wallow in your weakness, overplay your hand, you will be seen as angling for sympathy, or, worse, as pathetic. No, what works best is to allow people an occasional glimpse into the soft, frail side of your character, and usually only after they have known you for a while. That glimpse will humanize you, lowering their suspicions, and preparing the ground for a deeper attachment. Normally strong and in control, at moments you let go, give in to your weakness, let them see it.

Daily Law: Do not struggle against your vulnerabilities, or try to repress them, but put them into play.

The Art of Seduction: Disarm Through Strategic Weakness and Vulnerability

---

The Slow Power Grab

Ambition can creep as well as soar.

—EDMUND BURKE

In almost every film Alfred Hitchcock made, he had to go through the same wars, gradually wresting control of the film from the producer, the actors, and the rest of the team. His struggles with screenwriters were a microcosm of the larger war. Hitchcock always wanted his vision for a film to be exactly reflected in the script, but too firm a hand on his writer's neck would get him nothing except resentment and mediocre work. So instead he moved slowly, starting out by giving the writer room to work loosely off his notes, then asking for revisions that shaped the script his way. His control became obvious only gradually, and by that time the writer was emotionally tied to the project and, however frustrated, was working for his approval. A very patient man, Hitchcock let his power plays unfold over time, so that producer, writer, and stars understood the completeness of his domination only when the film was finished. To gain control of any project, you must be willing to make time your ally. If you start out with complete control, you sap people's spirit and stir up envy and resentment. So begin by generating the illusion that you're all working together on a team effort; then slowly nibble away. If in the process you make people angry, do not worry. That's just a sign that their emotions are engaged, which means they can be manipulated.

Daily Law: Overt manipulation and power grabs are dangerous, creating envy, distrust, and suspicion. Often the best solution is to move slowly.

The 33 Strategies of War, Strategy 29: Take Small Bites—The Fait Accompli Strategy

Control What You Reveal

Never start moving your own lips and teeth before the subordinates
do. The longer I keep quiet, the sooner others move their lips and
teeth. As they move their lips and teeth, I can thereby understand
their real intentions. . . . If the sovereign is not mysterious, the
ministers will find opportunity to take and take.

—HAN FEI-TZU

Power is in many ways a game of appearances, and when you say less than
necessary, you inevitably appear greater and more powerful than you are.
Your silence will make other people uncomfortable. Humans are machines of interpretation and explanation; they have to know what you are
thinking. When you carefully control what you reveal, they cannot pierce
your intentions or your meaning. Your short answers will put them on the
defensive, and they will jump in, nervously filling the silence with all
kinds of comments that will reveal valuable information about them and
their weaknesses. They will leave a meeting with you feeling as if they
had been robbed, and they will go home and ponder your every word.
This extra attention to your brief comments will only add to your power.

Daily Law: Powerful people impress and intimidate by saying less.

The 48 Laws of Power, Law 4: Always Say Less Than Necessary

Play to Their High Self-Opinion

The true spirit of conversation consists more in bringing out the
cleverness of others than in showing a great deal of it yourself.
—JEAN DE LA BRUYÈRE

If you need a favor from people, do not remind them of what you have
done for them in the past, trying to stimulate feelings of gratitude. Gratitude is rare because it tends to remind us of our helplessness, our dependence on others. We like to feel independent. Instead, remind them of the
good things they have done for you in the past. This will help confirm
their self-opinion: "Yes, I am generous." And once reminded, they will
want to continue to live up to this image and do yet another good deed.
A similar effect can come from suddenly forgiving your enemies and forging a rapprochement. In the emotional turmoil this creates, they will feel
obligated to live up to the high opinion you have now shown toward them
and will be extra motivated to prove themselves worthy.

Daily Law: Stimulate feelings of a high self-opinion in your targets.

The Laws of Human Nature, 7: Soften People's Resistance by Confirming
Their Self-Opinion—The Law of Defensiveness

Demonic Language

Most people employ symbolic language—their words stand for something real, the feelings, ideas, and beliefs they really have. Or they stand for concrete things in the real world. (The origin of the word *symbolic* lies in a Greek word meaning "to bring things together"—in this case, a word and something real.) To master the art of indirection, you need to master the opposite: diabolic language. Your words do not stand for anything real; their sound, and the feelings they evoke, are more important than what they are supposed to stand for. (The word *diabolic* ultimately means to separate, to throw things apart—here, words and reality.) The more you make people focus on your sweet-sounding language, and on the illusions and fantasies it conjures, the more you diminish their contact with reality. You lead them into the clouds, where it is hard to distinguish truth from untruth, real from unreal.

Daily Law: Keep your words vague and ambiguous, so people are never quite sure what you mean. Envelop them in demonic, diabolical language and they will not be able to focus on your maneuvers, on the possible consequences of your manipulations.

The Art of Seduction: Use the Demonic Power of Words to Sow Confusion

Create an Air of Mystery

Mix a little mystery with everything, and the
very mystery stirs up veneration.

—BALTASAR GRACIÁN

Count Victor Lustig, the aristocrat of swindlers, played the game to perfection. He was always doing things that were different or seemed to make no sense. He would show up at the best hotels in a limo driven by a Japanese chauffeur; no one had ever seen a Japanese chauffeur before, so this seemed exotic and strange. Lustig would dress in the most expensive clothing, but always with something—a medal, a flower, an armband—out of place, at least in conventional terms. This was seen not as tasteless but as odd and intriguing. In hotels he would be seen receiving telegrams at all hours, one after the other, brought to him by his Japanese chauffeur—telegrams he would tear up with utter nonchalance. (In fact they were fakes, completely blank.) He would sit alone in the dining room, reading a large and impressive-looking book, smiling at people yet remaining aloof. Within a few days, of course, the entire hotel would be abuzz with interest in this strange man. All this attention allowed Lustig to lure suckers in with ease. They would beg for his confidence and his company. Everyone wanted to be seen with this mysterious aristocrat. And in the presence of this distracting enigma, they wouldn't even notice that they were being robbed blind.

Daily Law: People love mysteries and enigmas, so give them what they want.

The 48 Laws of Power, Law 6: Court Attention at All Cost

Never Conventional

No one is so brave that he is not disturbed by something unexpected.
—JULIUS CAESAR

The unconventional is generally the province of the young, who are not comfortable with conventions and take great pleasure in flouting them. The danger is that as we age, we need more comfort and predictability and lose our taste for the unorthodox. This is how Napoleon declined as a strategist: he came to rely more on the size of his army and on its superiority in weapons than on novel strategies and fluid maneuvers. He lost his taste for the spirit of strategy and succumbed to the growing weight of his accumulating years. You must fight the psychological aging process even more than the physical one, for a mind full of stratagems, tricks, and fluid maneuvers will keep you young. Keep the wheels turning and churning the soil so that nothing settles and clumps into the conventional.

Daily Law: Make a point of breaking the habits you have developed, of acting in a way that is contrary to how you have operated in the past; practice a kind of unconventional warfare on your own mind.

The 33 Strategies of War, Strategy 24: Take the Line of Least Expectation—The Ordinary-Extraordinary Strategy

Play to People's Fantasies

The most detested person in the world is the one who always tells the
truth, who never romances. . . . I found it far more interesting and
profitable to romance than to tell the truth.

JOSEPH WEIL, AKA "THE YELLOW KID"

The truth is often avoided because it is ugly and unpleasant. Never appeal
to truth and reality unless you are prepared for the anger that comes from
disenchantment. To gain power, you must be a source of pleasure for
those around you—and pleasure comes from playing to people's fantasies.
Never promise a gradual improvement through hard work; rather, promise the moon, the great and sudden transformation, the pot of gold.

> Daily Law: Life is so harsh and distressing that people who can manu-
> facture romance or conjure up fantasy are like oases in the desert: every-
> one flocks to them. There is great power in tapping into the fantasies of
> the masses.

The 48 Laws of Power, Law 32: Play to People's Fantasies

Renew Your Aura of Authority

Your authority will grow with each action that inspires trust and respect. It gives you the luxury to remain in power long enough to realize great projects. But as you get older, the authority you established can become rigid and stodgy. You become the father figure who starts to seem oppressive by how long he has monopolized power, no matter how deeply people admired him in the past. A new generation inevitably emerges that is immune to your charm, to the aura you have created. They see you as a relic. You also have the tendency as you get older to become ever so slightly intolerant and tyrannical, as you cannot help but expect people to follow you. Without being aware, you start to feel entitled, and people sense this. Besides, the public wants newness and fresh faces.

The first step in avoiding this danger is to maintain a kind of sensitivity, noting the moods behind people's words, gauging the effect you have on newcomers and young people. Losing that empathy should be your greatest fear, as you will begin to cocoon yourself in your great reputation. The second step is to look for new markets and audiences to appeal to, which will force you to adapt. If possible, expand the reach of your authority. Without making a fool of yourself by attempting to appeal to a younger crowd that you cannot really understand, try to alter your style somewhat with the passing years. In the arts, this has been the secret to success of people like Pablo Picasso, or Alfred Hitchcock, or Coco Chanel.

Daily Law: Flexibility and adaptability gives you a touch of the divine and immortal—your spirit remains alive and open, and your authority is renewed.

The Laws of Human Nature, 15: Make Them Want to Follow You—The Law of Fickleness

Mirror Their Values

Do not give dogs what is holy; and do not throw your pearls before swine, lest they trample them under foot and turn to attack you.
—JESUS CHRIST, MATTHEW 7:6

Wise and clever people learn early on that they can display conventional behavior and mouth conventional ideas without having to believe in them. The power these people gain from blending in is that of being left alone to have the thoughts they want to have, and to express them to the people they want to express them to, without suffering isolation or ostracism. The logical extension of this practice is the invaluable ability to be all things to all people. When you go into society, leave behind your own ideas and values, and put on the mask that is most appropriate for the group in which you find yourself. People will swallow the bait because it flatters them to believe that you share their ideas. They will not take you as a hypocrite if you are careful—for how can they accuse you of hypocrisy if you do not let them know exactly what you stand for? Nor will they see you as lacking in values. Of course you have values—the values you share with them, while in their company.

Daily Law: Complete free expression is a social impossibility. Conceal your thoughts, then, telling the prickly and insecure what you know they want to hear.

The 48 Laws of Power, Law 38: Think as You Like but Behave Like Others

Play the Honest Rogue

No smoke screen, red herring, false sincerity, or any other diversionary device will succeed in concealing your intentions if you already have an established reputation for deception. And as you get older and achieve success, it often becomes increasingly difficult to disguise your cunning. Everyone knows you practice deception; persist in playing naive and you run the risk of seeming the rankest hypocrite, which will severely limit your room to maneuver. In such cases it is better to own up, to appear the honest rogue, or, better, the repentant rogue. Not only will you be admired for your frankness, but, most wonderful and strange of all, you will be able to continue your stratagems. As P. T. Barnum, the nineteenth-century king of humbuggery, grew older, he learned to embrace his reputation as a grand deceiver. At one point he organized a buffalo hunt in New Jersey, complete with Indians and a few imported buffalo. He publicized the hunt as genuine, but it came off as so completely fake that the crowd, instead of getting angry and asking for their money back, was greatly amused. They knew Barnum pulled tricks all the time; that was the secret of his success, and they loved him for it. Learning a lesson from this affair, Barnum stopped concealing all of his devices, even revealing his deceptions in a tell-all autobiography. As Kierkegaard wrote, "The world wants to be deceived."

Daily Law: When you can no longer disguise your cunning, reveal your devices.

The 48 Laws of Power, Law 3: Conceal Your Intentions

July

The Seductive Character

PENETRATING HEARTS AND MINDS

≈

Most of us have known the power of having someone fall in love with us. Our actions, gestures, the things we say, all have positive effects on this person; we may not completely understand what we have done right, but this feeling of power is intoxicating. It gives us confidence, which makes us more seductive. We may also experience this in a social or work setting—one day we are in an elevated mood and people seem more responsive, more charmed by us. These moments of power are fleeting, but they resonate in the memory with great intensity. We want them back. Nobody likes to feel awkward or unable to reach people. The siren call of seduction is irresistible because power is irresistible, and nothing will bring you more power in the modern world than the ability to seduce. Repressing the desire to seduce is a kind of hysterical reaction, revealing your deep-down fascination with the process; you are only making your desires stronger. Some day they will come to the surface. To have such power does not require a total transformation in your character or any kind of physical improvement in your looks. Seduction is a game of psychology, not beauty, and it is within the grasp of any person to become a master at the game. The month of July will arm you with weapons of charm, so that those around you will slowly lose their ability to resist without knowing how or why it has happened. It is an art of war for delicate times.

I want to take you away from thinking of seduction as just the sort of thing that men do to women or women do to men. It's something that permeates our culture. It's in advertising. It's in marketing. It's on the internet. It's in politics.

It's slightly different in each case. Of course, a sexual seduction is not exactly the same as a politician seducing the American public or an influencer seducing her followers. But the dynamics, the casting of the spell, the enchantment, the process is similar.

I tell people it's like when you're watching a movie and you feel like the movie is casting a spell on you. It's drawing you into the story. It's having an emotional impact on you. It's taking you out of your life, out of the banal day-to-day work, and on a ride of enchantment. By the end of the movie, you're moved to tears or laughter or whatever it is. That is a form of seduction. Your psychology has been penetrated by the director, the writer, the actors, and actresses.

People are dying for more of this kind of seduction in their lives. They want some enchantment. They want some drama. They want pleasure. They want to be taken on a ride, an adventure.

It's a desire cemented in childhood. Seduction is like reaching the child in a person. When you were a child, what was the greatest pleasure? It was being picked up by your mother or father and being whirled around and taken through the air and twisting and turning. The sense that someone was taking you somewhere, that you were under their control— it made you laugh, it gave you this incredible joy. That's what's happening when you're watching that movie: it's taking you on this journey where you don't exactly where you're going or what's happening.

People don't have enough of that in their lives. It's an amazing power that you could have.

It starts with the desire to be a seducer. You might be tempted to think, "Oh, I don't want to be a seducer, I'm not interested in seduction." Yes, you do. Yes, you are. Think of the walls that people normally have up—you can't get through to your kids, you can't get through to your spouse, that employee, those coworkers. They're closed off to you. It makes you so frustrated. Now think of a time in your life where you sensed that you had power over another person, that someone was under your spell, that the things you said excited them and interested them. There's electricity in your back and forth. It's amazing. It's powerful. You want more of that. You want to be able to seduce. You want to penetrate the walls people typically keep around their hearts and minds.

That's the first thing: you want seduction in your life.

The next thing is: you have a misconception about seduction. Most people do. It's not about figuring out these very cold, calculating strategies. There's got to be a naturalness to it. If you're someone that does too much calculation in the seduction process—this is what I'm going to do, step A then B then C—it's not seductive. People can smell your coldness. We sense that the other person is trying too hard, that they've read *The Art of Seduction*, that they're applying the twenty-four strategies. It doesn't work.

You must bring out natural qualities that you have. And I maintain that every person has natural qualities that make him or her authentically seductive. It's in you. It's latent. It wants to come out. And that's what will make you an interesting and good seducer.

That, and adopting the seducer's approach to life: It is all a game, an arena for play. Knowing that the moralists, the crabbed repressed types who croak about the evils of the seducer, secretly envy their power, they do not concern themselves with other people's opinions. They do not deal in moral judgments—nothing could be less seductive.

Everything is pliant, fluid, like life itself. Seduction is a form of deception, but people want to be led astray, they yearn to be seduced.

Get rid of any moralizing tendencies, adopt the seducer's playful philosophy, and you will find the rest of the process easy and natural.

Look at the World through the Eyes of a Seducer

To have seductive power does not require a total transformation in your character or any kind of physical improvement in your looks. Seduction is a game of psychology, not beauty, and it is within the grasp of any person to become a master at the game. All that is required is that you look at the world differently, through the eyes of a seducer. A seducer sees all of life as theater, everyone an actor. Most people feel they have constricted roles in life, which makes them unhappy. Seducers, on the other hand, can be anyone and can assume many roles. Seducers take pleasure in performing and are not weighed down by their identity, or by some need to be themselves, or to be natural. This freedom of theirs, this fluidity in body and spirit, is what makes them attractive. What people lack in life is not more reality but illusion, fantasy, play. The clothes that seducers wear, the places they take you to, their words and actions, are slightly heightened—not overly theatrical but with a delightful edge of unreality, as if the two of you were living out a piece of fiction or were characters in a film.

Daily Law: Seduction is a kind of theater in real life, the meeting of illusion and reality.

The Art of Seduction, Preface

Delay Satisfaction

The ability to delay satisfaction is the ultimate art of seduction—while waiting, the victim is held in thrall. Coquettes are the grand masters of this game, orchestrating a back-and-forth movement between hope and frustration. They bait with the promise of reward—the hope of physical pleasure, happiness, fame by association, power—all of which, however, proves elusive; yet this only makes their targets pursue them the more. Coquettes seem totally self-sufficient: they do not need you, they seem to say, and their narcissism proves devilishly attractive. You want to conquer them, but they hold the cards. The strategy of the Coquette is never to offer total satisfaction. Imitate the alternating heat and coolness of the Coquette and you will keep the seduced at your heels. You must understand a critical property of love and desire: the more obviously you pursue a person, the more likely you are to chase them away. Too much attention can be interesting for a while, but it soon grows cloying and finally becomes claustrophobic and frightening. It signals weakness and neediness, an unseductive combination. How often we make this mistake, thinking our persistent presence will reassure. But Coquettes have an inherent understanding of this particular dynamic. Masters of selective withdrawal, they hint at coldness, absenting themselves at times to keep their victim off balance, surprised, intrigued. Their withdrawals make them mysterious, and we build them up in our imaginations. (Familiarity, on the other hand, undermines what we have built.) A bout of distance engages the emotions further; instead of making us angry, it makes us insecure. Perhaps they don't really like us, perhaps we have lost their interest. Once our vanity is at stake, we succumb to the Coquette just to prove we are still desirable.

Daily Law: The essence of the Coquette lies not in the tease and temptation but in the subsequent step back, the emotional withdrawal. That is the key to enslaving desire.

The Art of Seduction: The Coquette

Direct Your Gaze Outward

Seducers are never self-absorbed. Their gaze is directed outward, not inward. The reasons for this are several. First, self-absorption is a sign of insecurity; it is anti-seductive. Everyone has insecurities, but seducers manage to ignore them, finding therapy for moments of self-doubt by being absorbed in the world. This gives them a buoyant spirit—we want to be around them. Second, getting into someone's skin, imagining what it is like to be them, helps the seducer gather valuable information, learn what makes that person tick, what will make them lose their ability to think straight and fall into a trap. Armed with such information, a seducer can provide focused and individualized attention—a rare commodity in a world in which most people see us only from behind the screen of their own prejudices.

Daily Law: When you meet someone your first move is to get inside that person's skin, to see the world through their eyes.

The Art of Seduction, Preface

The Empathic Attitude

The greatest danger you face is your general assumption that you really understand people and that you can quickly judge them. Instead, you must begin with the assumption that you are ignorant and that you have natural biases that will make you judge people incorrectly. Each person you meet is like an undiscovered country, with a very particular psychological chemistry that you will carefully explore. This flexible, open spirit is similar to creative energy—a willingness to consider more possibilities and options. In fact, developing your empathy will also improve your creative powers. The best place to begin this transformation in your attitude is in your numerous daily conversations. Try reversing your normal impulse to talk and give your opinion, desiring instead to hear the other person's point of view. You have tremendous curiosity in this direction. Cut off your incessant interior monologue as best you can. Give full attention to the other. What matters here is the quality of your listening, so that in the course of the conversation you can mirror back to the other person things they said, or things that were left unsaid but that you sensed. This will have a tremendous seductive effect.

Daily Law: Let go of your tendency to make snap judgments. Open your mind to seeing people in a new light. Do not assume that you are similar or that they share your values.

The Laws of Human Nature, 2: Transform Self-Love into Empathy—The Law of Narcissism

JULY 5

Stir Up the Transgressive and Taboo

People may be straining to remove restrictions on private behavior, to make everything freer, in the world today, but that only makes seduction more difficult and less exciting. Do what you can to reintroduce a feeling of transgression and crime, even if it is only psychological or illusory. There must be obstacles to overcome, social norms to flout, laws to break, before the seduction can be consummated. It might seem that a permissive society imposes few limits; find some. There will always be limits, sacred cows, behavioral standards—endless ammunition for stirring up the transgressive and taboo. Once the desire to transgress draws your targets to you, it will be hard for them to stop.

Daily Law: Take them further than they imagined—the shared feeling of guilt and complicity will create a powerful bond.

The Art of Seduction: Stir Up the Transgressive and Taboo

The Soft Sell

Let us say your goal is to sell yourself—as a personality, a trendsetter, a candidate for office. There are two ways to go: the hard sell (the direct approach) and the soft sell (the indirect approach). In the hard sell you state your case strongly and directly. You tout your achievements, quote statistics, bring in expert opinions, even go so far as to induce a bit of fear if the audience ignores your message. Some people will be offended, resisting your message, even if what you say is true. Others will feel you are manipulating them—who can trust experts and statistics, and why are you trying so hard? The soft sell, on the other hand, has the potential to draw in millions because it is entertaining, gentle on the ears, and can be repeated without irritating people. The technique was invented by the great charlatans of seventeenth-century Europe. To peddle their elixirs and alchemic concoctions, they would first put on a show—clowns, music, vaudeville-type routines—that had nothing to do with what they were selling. A crowd would form, and as the audience laughed and relaxed, the charlatan would come onstage and briefly and dramatically discuss the miraculous effects of the elixir. In the centuries since, publicists, advertisers, political strategists, and others have taken this method to new heights, but the rudiments of the soft sell remain the same: bring pleasure by creating a positive atmosphere around your name or message.

Daily Law: Never seem to be selling something—that will look manipulative and suspicious. Instead, let entertainment value and good feelings take center stage, sneaking the sale through the side door.

The Art of Seduction: Soft Seduction—How to Sell Anything to the Masses

Appear to Be an Object of Desire

Most of the time we prefer one thing to another because that is what
our friends already prefer or because that object has marked social
significance. . . . When we say of a man or woman that he or she is
desirable, what we really mean is that others desire them.

—SERGE MOSCOVICI

Few are drawn to the person whom others avoid or neglect; people gather
around those who have already attracted interest. We want what other
people want. To draw your victims closer and make them hungry to possess you, you must create an aura of desirability—of being wanted and
courted by many. It will become a point of vanity for them to be the
preferred object of your attention, to win you away from a crowd of ad-
mirers. Manufacture the illusion of popularity by surrounding yourself
with members of the opposite sex—friends, former lovers, present suitors.
Create triangles that stimulate rivalry and raise your value.

Daily Law: Build a reputation that precedes you: if many have succumbed to your charms, there must be a reason.

The Art of Seduction: Appear to Be an Object of Desire—Create Triangles

The Anti-Seducer

Anti-Seducers come in many shapes and kinds, but almost all of them share a single attribute, the source of their repellence: insecurity. We are all insecure, and we suffer for it. Yet we are able to surmount these feelings at times; a seductive engagement can bring us out of our usual self-absorption, and to the degree that we seduce or are seduced, we feel charged and confident. Anti-Seducers, however, are insecure to such a degree that they cannot be drawn into the seductive process. Their needs, their anxieties, their self-consciousness close them off. They interpret the slightest ambiguity on your part as a slight to their ego; they see the merest hint of withdrawal as a betrayal, and are likely to complain bitterly about it. It seems easy: Anti-Seducers repel, so be repelled—avoid them. Unfortunately, however, many Anti-Seducers cannot be detected as such at first glance. They are more subtle, and unless you are careful they will ensnare you in a most unsatisfying relationship. You must look for clues to their self-involvement and insecurity: perhaps they are ungenerous, or they argue with unusual tenacity, or are excessively judgmental. Perhaps they lavish you with undeserved praise, declaring their love before knowing anything about you. Or, most important, they pay no attention to details. Since they cannot see what makes you different, they cannot surprise you with nuanced attention. They lack the subtlety to create the promise of pleasure that seduction requires.

Daily Law: Rid yourself of any anti-seductive tendencies by getting outside yourself and your insecurities and into their spirit.

The Art of Seduction: The Anti-Seducer

Make Them Want to Spoil You

People often mistakenly believe that what makes a person desirable and seductive is physical beauty, elegance, or overt sexuality. Yet Cora Pearl was not dramatically beautiful; her body was boyish, and her style was garish and tasteless. Even so, the most dashing men of Europe vied for her favors, often ruining themselves in the process. It was Cora's spirit and attitude that enthralled them. Spoiled by her father, she imagined that spoiling her was natural—that all men should do the same. The consequence was that, like a child, she never felt she had to try to please. It was Cora's powerful air of independence that made men want to possess her. The lesson is simple: It may be too late to be spoiled by a parent, but it is never too late to make other people spoil you. It is all in your attitude. People are drawn to those who expect a lot out of life, whereas they tend to disrespect those who are fearful and undemanding.

Daily Law: Wild independence has a provocative effect on us: it appeals to us, while also presenting us with a challenge—we want to be the one to tame it, to make the spirited person dependent on us.

The Art of Seduction: The Natural

Set Off Viral Effects

The moment people know you are after something—a vote, a sale—they become resistant. But disguise your sales pitch as a news event and not only will you bypass their resistance, you can also create a social trend that does the selling for you. To make this work, the event you set up must stand out from all the other events that are covered by the media, yet it cannot stand out too far or it will seem contrived. An event that is picked up by the news has the imprimatur of reality. It is important to give this manufactured event positive associations. Associations that are patriotic, say, or subtly sexual, or spiritual—anything pleasant and seductive—take on a life of their own. Who can resist? People essentially persuade themselves to join the crowd without even realizing that a sale has taken place. The feeling of active participation is vital to seduction. No one wants to feel left out of a growing movement. Announce your message as a trend and it will become one. The goal is to create a kind of viral effect in which more and more people become infected with the desire to have whatever you are offering.

Daily Law: Seem to be in the vanguard of a trend or lifestyle and the public will lap you up for fear of being left behind.

The Art of Seduction: Soft Seduction—How to Sell Anything to the Masses

Friend to Lover

I do not approach her, I merely skirt the periphery of her
existence. . . . This is the first web into which she must be spun.
—SØREN KIERKEGAARD

To move from friendship to love can win success without calling attention
to itself as a maneuver. First, your friendly conversations with your targets
will bring you valuable information about their characters, their tastes,
their weaknesses, the childhood yearnings that govern their adult behavior. Second, by spending time with your targets you can make them comfortable with you. Believing you are interested only in their thoughts, in
their company, they will lower their resistance, dissipating the usual tension between the sexes. Now they are vulnerable, for your friendship with
them has opened the golden gate to their body: their mind. At this point
any offhand comment, any slight physical contact, will spark a different
thought, which will catch them off guard: perhaps there could be something else between you. Once that feeling has stirred, they will wonder
why you haven't made a move, and will take the initiative themselves,
enjoying the illusion that they are in control. There is nothing more effective in seduction than making the seduced think that they are the ones
doing the seducing.

**Daily Law: Cultivate a relatively neutral relationship, moving gradually
from friend to lover.**

The Art of Seduction: Create a False Sense of Security—Approach Indirectly

Flout Their Expectations

Too constant a peace is productive of a deadly ennui. Uniformity
kills love, for as soon as the spirit of method mingles in an affair of
the heart, the passion disappears, languor supervenes, weariness
begins to wear, and disgust ends the chapter.

—NINON DE L'ENCLOS

Familiarity is the death of seduction. If the target knows everything
about you, the relationship gains a level of comfort but loses the elements
of fantasy and anxiety. Without anxiety and a touch of fear, the erotic
tension is dissolved. Remember: reality is not seductive. Maintain some
mystery or be taken for granted. You will have only yourself to blame for
what follows.

Daily Law: Keep some dark corners in your character, flout expectations, use absences to fragment the clinging, possessive pull that allows familiarity to creep in.

The Art of Seduction: Beware the Aftereffects

Make Use of Contrasts

Careful exploitation of people who are dull or unattractive may enhance your desirability by comparison. At a social affair, for instance, make sure that your target has to chat with the most boring person available. Come to the rescue and your target will be delighted to see you. In *The Seducer's Diary*, by Søren Kierkegaard, Johannes has designs on the innocent young Cordelia. Knowing that his friend Edward is hopelessly shy and dull, he encourages this man to court her; a few weeks of Edward's attentions will make her eyes wander in search of someone else, anyone else, and Johannes will make sure that they settle on him. Johannes chose to strategize and maneuver, but almost any social environment will contain contrasts you can make use of almost naturally.

Daily Law: Make use of contrasts—either develop and display those attractive attributes (humor, vivacity, and so on) that are the scarcest in your own social group, or choose a group in which your natural qualities are rare, and will shine.

The Art of Seduction: Appear to Be an Object of Desire—Create Triangles

Create Calculated Surprises

A child is usually a willful, stubborn creature who will deliberately do the opposite of what we ask. But there is one scenario in which children will happily give up their usual willfulness: when they are promised a surprise. Perhaps it is a present hidden in a box, a game with an unforeseeable ending, a journey with an unknown destination, a suspenseful story with a surprise finish. In those moments when children are waiting for a surprise, their willpower is suspended. They are in your thrall for as long as you dangle possibility before them. This childish habit is buried deep within us, and is the source of an elemental human pleasure: being led by a person who knows where they are going, and who takes us on a journey. In seduction, you need to create constant tension and suspense, a feeling that with you nothing is predictable. The moment people feel they know what to expect from you, your spell on them is broken. More: you have ceded them power. The only way to lead the seduced along and keep the upper hand is to create suspense, a calculated surprise. People love a mystery, and this is the key to luring them further into your web. Behave in a way that leaves them wondering, What are you up to? Doing something they do not expect from you will give them a delightful sense of spontaneity—they will not be able to foresee what comes next. You are always one step ahead and in control. Give them a thrill with a sudden change of direction.

Daily Law: There are all kinds of calculated surprises you can spring on your victims—sending a message out of the blue, showing up unexpectedly, taking them to a place they have never been. But best of all are surprises that reveal something new about your character.

The Art of Seduction: Keep Them in Suspense—What Comes Next?

Heighten the Experience

In Marcel Proust's novel *Remembrance of Things Past*, the character Swann finds himself gradually seduced by a woman who is not really his type. He is an aesthete and loves the finer things in life. She is of a lower class, less refined, even a little tasteless. What poeticizes her in his mind is a series of exuberant moments they share together, moments that from then on he associates with her. One of these is a concert in a salon that they attend, in which he is intoxicated by a little melody in a sonata. Whenever he thinks of her, he remembers this little phrase. Little gifts she has given him, objects she has touched or handled, begin to assume a life of their own. You must find a way to share such moments with your targets—a concert, a play, a spiritual encounter, whatever it takes—so that they associate something elevated with you. Shared moments of exuberance have immense seductive pull. Also, any kind of object can be imbued with poetic resonance and sentimental associations. The gifts you give and other objects can become imbued with your presence; if they are associated with pleasant memories, the sight of them keeps you in mind and accelerates the poeticization process.

Daily Law: Any kind of heightened experience, artistic or spiritual, lingers in the mind much longer than normal experience.

The Art of Seduction: Poeticize Your Presence

Enter Their Spirit

> The great, the implacable amorous passions are all linked to the
> fact that a being imagines he sees his most secret self spying upon
> him behind the curtain of another's eyes.
>
> —ROBERT MUSIL

All of us are narcissists. When we were children our narcissism was physical: we were interested in our own image, our own body, as if it were a
separate being. As we grow older, our narcissism grows more psychological: we become absorbed in our own tastes, opinions, experiences. A hard
shell forms around us. Paradoxically, the way to entice people out of this
shell is to become more like them, in fact a kind of mirror image of them.
You do not have to spend days studying their minds; simply conform to
their moods, adapt to their tastes, play along with whatever they send
your way. In doing so you will lower their natural defensiveness. Their
sense of self-esteem does not feel threatened by your strangeness or different habits. People truly love themselves, but what they love most of all is
to see their ideas and tastes reflected in another person. This validates
them. Their habitual insecurity vanishes. Hypnotized by their mirror image, they relax. Now that their inner wall has crumbled, you can slowly
draw them out, and eventually turn the dynamic around. Once they are
open to you, it becomes easy to infect them with your own moods and
heat. Entering the other person's spirit is a kind of hypnosis; it is the most
insidious and effective form of persuasion known to man.

Daily Law: Lure people out of their natural intractability and self-
obsession by entering their spirit. Soon you can shift the dynamic: once
you have entered their spirit you can make them enter yours, at a point
when it is too late to turn back.

The Art of Seduction: Enter Their Spirit

Create Temptation

The only way to get rid of temptation is to yield to it.

—OSCAR WILDE

What people want is not temptation; temptation happens every day. What people want is to give in to temptation, to yield. That is the only way to get rid of the tension in their lives. It costs much more to resist temptation than to surrender. Your task, then, is to create a temptation that is stronger than the daily variety. It has to be focused on them, aimed at them as individuals—at their weakness. Understand: everyone has a principal weakness, from which others stem. Find that childhood insecurity, that lack in their life, and you hold the key to tempting them. Their weakness may be greed, vanity, boredom, some deeply repressed desire, a hunger for forbidden fruit. They signal it in little details that elude their conscious control: their style of clothing, an offhand comment. Their past, and particularly their past romances, will be littered with clues. Give them a potent temptation, tailored to their weakness, and you can make the hope of pleasure that you stir in them figure more prominently than the doubts and anxieties that accompany it.

> Daily Law: Find that weakness of theirs, that fantasy that has yet to be realized, and hint that you can lead them toward it. It could be wealth, it could be adventure, it could be forbidden and guilty pleasures; the key is to keep it vague.

The Art of Seduction: Create Temptation

Prove Yourself

Making your deed as dashing and chivalrous as possible will elevate the seduction to a new level, stir up deep emotions, and conceal any ulterior motives you may have. The sacrifices you are making must be visible; talking about them, or explaining what they have cost you, will seem like bragging. Lose sleep, fall ill, lose valuable time, put your career on the line, spend more money than you can afford. You can exaggerate all this for effect, but don't get caught boasting about it or feeling sorry for yourself: cause yourself pain and let them see it. Since almost everyone else in the world seems to have an angle, your noble and selfless deed will be irresistible.

Daily Law: Choose a dramatic, difficult action that reveals the painful time and effort involved.

The Art of Seduction: Prove Yourself

Lure Others into Your Fantasy World

From very early on, Josephine Baker could not stand the feeling of having no control over the world. Her solution was something children often do: confronted with a hopeless environment, she closed herself off in a world of her own making, oblivious to the ugliness around her. This world was filled with dancing, clowning, dreams of great things. Let other people wail and moan; Josephine would smile, remain confident and self-reliant. Almost everyone who met her, from her earliest years to her last, commented on how seductive this quality was. Her refusal to compromise, or to be what she was expected to be, made everything she did seem authentic and natural. A child loves to play, and to create a little self-contained world. When children are absorbed in make believe, they are hopelessly charming. They infuse their imaginings with such seriousness and feeling. Adult Naturals do something similar, particularly if they are artists: they create their own fantasy world, and live in it as if it were the real one. Fantasy is so much more pleasant than reality, and since most people do not have the power or courage to create such a world, they enjoy being around those who do.

Daily Law: Learn to play with your image, never taking it too seriously. The key is to infuse your play with the conviction and feeling of a child, making it seem natural. The more absorbed you seem in your own joy-filled world, the more seductive you become.

The Art of Seduction: The Natural

Be a Source of Pleasure

No one wants to hear about your problems and troubles. Listen to your targets' complaints, but more important, distract them from their problems by giving them pleasure. (Do this often enough and they will fall under your spell.) An energetic presence is more charming than lethargy, which hints at boredom, an enormous social taboo; and elegance and style will usually win out over vulgarity, since most people like to associate themselves with whatever they think elevated and cultured.

Daily Law: Being lighthearted and fun is always more charming than being serious and critical.

The Art of Seduction: The Charmer

The Law of Covetousness

From the beginning, Coco Chanel made sure her clothes were seen every-where. Observing other women wearing such clothes stimulated compet-itive desires to have the same and not be left out. In truth, the boater hats she originally designed were nothing more than common objects anyone could buy in a department store. The clothes she first designed were made out of the cheapest materials. The perfume was a mix of ordinary flowers. It was pure psychological magic that transformed them into objects that stimulated such intense desires to possess them. Just like Chanel, you need to reverse your perspective. Instead of focusing on what you want and covet in the world, you must train yourself to focus on others, on their repressed desires and unmet fantasies. You must train yourself to see how they perceive the objects you make, as if you were looking at yourself and your work from the outside. This will give you the almost limitless power to shape people's perceptions about these objects and excite them. People do not want truth and honesty, no matter how much we hear such nonsense endlessly repeated. They want their imaginations to be stimu-lated and to be taken beyond their banal circumstances. Create an air of mystery around you and your work. Associate it with something new, unfamiliar, exotic, progressive, and taboo. Do not define your message but leave it vague.

Daily Law: Create an illusion of ubiquity—your object is seen every-where and desired by others. Then let the covetousness so latent in all humans do the rest, setting off a chain reaction of desire.

The Laws of Human Nature, 5: Become an Elusive Object of Desire—The Law of Covetousness

JULY 22

Create a Wound

In Plato's dialogue *Symposium*—the West's oldest treatise on love, and a text that has had a determining influence on our ideas of desire—the courtesan Diotima explains to Socrates the parentage of Eros, the god of love. Eros's father was Contrivance, or Cunning, and his mother was Poverty, or Need. Eros takes after his parents: he is constantly in need, which he is constantly contriving to fill. As the god of love, he knows that love cannot be induced in another person unless they too feel need. And that is what his arrows do: piercing people's flesh, they make them feel a lack, an ache, a hunger. This is the essence of your task as a seducer. Like Eros, you must create a wound in your victim, aiming at their soft spot, the chink in their self-esteem. If they are stuck in a rut, make them feel it more deeply, "innocently" bringing it up and talking about it. What you want is a wound, an insecurity you can expand a little, an anxiety that can best be relieved by involvement with another person, namely you.

Daily Law: Try to position yourself as coming from outside, as a stranger of sorts. You represent change, difference, a breakup of routines. Make your victims feel that by comparison their lives are boring and their friends less interesting than they had thought.

The Art of Seduction: Create a Need—Stir Anxiety and Discontent

Pay Attention to Detail

When we were children, our senses were much more active. The colors of a new toy, or a spectacle such as a circus, held us in thrall; a smell or a sound could fascinate us. In the games we created, many of them reproducing something in the adult world on a smaller scale, what pleasure we took in orchestrating every detail. We noticed everything. As we grow older our senses get dulled. We no longer notice as much, for we are constantly hurrying to get things done, to move on to the next task. In seduction, you are always trying to bring the target back to the golden moments of childhood. A child is less rational, more easily deceived. A child is also more attuned to the pleasures of the senses. So when your targets are with you, you must never give them the feeling they normally get in the real world, where we are all rushed, ruthless, out for ourselves. You need to deliberately slow things down, and return them to the simpler times of their youth. The details that you orchestrate—colors, gifts, little ceremonies—are aimed at their senses, at the childish delight we take in the immediate charms of the natural world. Their senses filled with delightful things, they grow less capable of reason and rationality. Pay attention to detail and you will find yourself assuming a slower pace; your targets will not focus on what you might be after because you seem so considerate, so attentive. In the childish realm of the senses in which you envelop them, they get a clear sense that you are involving them in something distinct from the real world—an essential ingredient of seduction.

Daily Law: Lofty words and grand gestures can be suspicious: Why are you trying so hard to please? The details of a seduction—the subtle gestures, the offhand things you do—are often more charming and revealing.

The Art of Seduction: Pay Attention to Detail

Make Them Fetishize You

When Marlene Dietrich entered a room, or arrived at a party, all eyes inevitably turned to her. First there were her startling clothes, chosen to make heads turn. Then there was her air of nonchalant indifference. Men, and women too, became obsessed with her, fetishizing her long after other memories of the evening had faded. She had a distance from her own self: she could study her face, her legs, her body, as if she were someone else. This gave her the ability to mold her look, transforming her appearance for effect. She was like a beautiful object, something to fetishize and admire the way we admire a work of art. If you see yourself as an object, then others will too. An ethereal, dreamlike air will heighten the effect. Consider yourself a blank screen. Float through life noncommittally and people will want to seize you and consume you. Of all the parts of your body that draw this fetishistic attention, the strongest is the face; so learn to tune your face like an instrument, making it radiate a fascinating vagueness for effect. And since you will have to stand out from other Stars in the sky, you will need to develop an attention-getting style. Dietrich was the great practitioner of this art; her style was chic enough to dazzle, weird enough to enthrall.

Daily Law: Your own image and presence are materials you can control. The sense that you are engaged in this kind of play will make people see you as superior and worthy of imitation.

The Art of Seduction: The Star

Play with Ambiguity

To capture and hold attention, you need to show attributes that go against your physical appearance, creating depth and mystery. If you have a sweet face and an innocent air, let out hints of something dark, even vaguely cruel in your character. It is not advertised in your words, but in your manner. Do not worry if this underquality is a negative one, like danger, cruelty, or amorality; people will be drawn to the enigma anyway, and pure goodness is rarely seductive.

Daily Law: No one is naturally mysterious, at least not for long; mystery is something you have to work at, a ploy on your part, and something that must be used early on in the seduction.

The Art of Seduction: Send Mixed Signals

Know When to Withdraw

Love never dies of starvation but often of indigestion.
—NINON DE L'ENCLOS

The Russian seductress Lou Andreas-Salomé had an intense presence; when a man was with her, he felt her eyes boring into him, and often became entranced with her coquettish ways and spirit. But then, almost invariably, something would come up—she would have to leave town for a while, or would be too busy to see him. It was during her absences that men fell hopelessly in love with her, and vowed to be more aggressive next time they were with her. Your absences at this latter point of the seduction should seem at least somewhat justified. You are insinuating not a blatant brush-off but a slight doubt: perhaps you could have found some reason to stay, perhaps you are losing interest, perhaps there is someone else.

Daily Law: In your absence, their appreciation of you will grow. They will forget your faults, forgive your sins. The moment you return, they will chase after you as you desire. It will be as if you had come back from the dead.

The Art of Seduction: Give Them Space to Fall—The Pursuer Is Pursued

Know When to Be Bold

The more timidity a lover shows with us the more it concerns our pride to goad him on; the more respect he has for our resistance, the more respect we demand of him. We would willingly say to you men. Ah, in pity's name do not suppose us to be so very virtuous; you are forcing us to have too much of it.

—NINON DE L'ENCLOS

No one is born timid; timidity is a protection we develop. If we never stick our necks out, if we never try, we will never have to suffer the consequences of failure or success. If we are kind and unobtrusive, no one will be offended—in fact, we will seem saintly and likable. In truth, timid people are often self-absorbed, obsessed with the way people see them, and not at all saintly. And humility may have its social uses, but it is deadly in seduction. You need to be able to play the humble saint at times; it is a mask you wear. But in seduction, take it off. Boldness is bracing, erotic, and absolutely necessary to bring the seduction to its conclusion. Done right, it tells your targets that they have made you lose your normal restraint, and gives them license to do so as well. People are yearning to have a chance to play out the repressed sides of their personality.

Daily Law: At the final stage of a seduction, boldness eliminates any awkwardness or doubts.

The Art of Seduction: Master the Art of the Bold Move

Communicate to People's Senses

Free yourself from the need to communicate in the normal direct manner and you will present yourself with greater opportunities for the soft sell. Make the words you say unobtrusive, vague, alluring. And pay much greater attention to your style, the visuals, the story they tell. Convey a sense of movement and progress by showing yourself in motion. Express confidence not through facts and figures but through colors and positive imagery, appealing to the infant in everyone. Let the media cover you unguided and you are at their mercy. So turn the dynamic around—the press needs drama and visuals? Provide them. It is fine to discuss issues or "truth" as long as you package it entertainingly. Remember: images linger in the mind long after words are forgotten. Do not preach to the public—that never works. Learn to express your message through visuals that insinuate positive emotions and happy feelings. The audience may focus superficially on the content or moral you are preaching, but they are really absorbing the visuals, which get under their skin and stay there longer than any words or preachy pronouncements.

Daily Law: Pay more attention to the form of your message than to the content. Images are more seductive than words, and visuals should actually be your real message.

The Art of Seduction: Soft Seduction—How to Sell Anything to the Masses

The Pursuer Is Pursued

I retreat and thereby teach her to be victorious as she pursues me. I continually fall back, and in this backward movement I teach her to know through me all the powers of erotic love, its turbulent thoughts, its passion, what longing is, and hope, and impatient expectancy.

—SØREN KIERKEGAARD

Each gender has its own seductive lures, which come naturally to them. When you seem interested in someone but do not respond sexually, it is disturbing and presents a challenge: they will find a way to seduce you. To produce this effect, first reveal an interest in your targets, through letters or subtle insinuation. But when you are in their presence, assume a kind of sexless neutrality. Be friendly, even warm, but no more. You are pushing them into arming themselves with the seductive charms that are natural to their sex—exactly what you want.

Daily Law: Create the illusion that the seducer is being seduced.

The Art of Seduction: Give Them Space to Fall—The Pursuer Is Pursued

The Thrill of Illusion

Theater creates a sense of a separate, magical world. The actors' makeup, the fake but alluring sets, the slightly unreal costumes—these heightened visuals, along with the story of the play, create illusion. To produce this effect in real life, you must fashion your clothes, makeup, and attitude to have a playful, artificial edge—a feeling that you have dressed for the pleasure of your audience. This is the goddesslike effect of a Marlene Dietrich. Your encounters with your targets should also have a sense of drama, achieved through the settings you choose and through your actions. The target should not know what will happen next. Create suspense through twists and turns that lead to the happy ending; you are performing.

> Daily Law: Whenever your targets meet you, give them the vague feeling of being in a play, the thrill of wearing masks, of playing a different role from the one your life has allotted you.

The Art of Seduction: Appendix A—Seductive Environment/Seductive Time

Poeticize Your Presence

He who does not know how to poetize himself into a girl so that it is
from her that everything proceeds as he wants it—he is and remains a
bungler. . . . To poetize oneself into a girl is an art.

—SØREN KIERKEGAARD

In a world that is harsh and full of disappointment, it is a great pleasure
to be able to fantasize about a person you are involved with. This makes
the seducer's task easy: people are dying to be given the chance to fantasize about you. Do not spoil this golden opportunity by overexposing
yourself or becoming so familiar and banal that the target sees you exactly as you are. You do not have to be an angel, or a paragon of virtue—
that would be quite boring. You can be dangerous, naughty, even
somewhat vulgar, depending on the tastes of your victim.

**Daily Law: Never be ordinary or limited. In poetry (as opposed to
reality), anything is possible.**

The Art of Seduction: Poeticize Your Presence

August

The Master Persuader

SOFTENING PEOPLE'S RESISTANCE

We humans cannot avoid trying to influence others. Everything we say or do is examined and interpreted by others for clues as to our intentions. As social animals we cannot avoid constantly playing the game, whether we are conscious of this or not. Most people do not want to expend the effort that goes into thinking about others and figuring out a strategic entry past their defenses. They are lazy. They want to simply be themselves, speak honestly, or do nothing, and justify this to themselves as stemming from some great moral choice. Since the game is unavoidable, better to be skillful at it than in denial or merely improvising in the moment. In the end, being good at influence is actually more socially beneficial than the moral stance. Becoming proficient at persuasion requires that we immerse ourselves in the perspective of others, exercising our empathy. The month of August will teach you the maneuvers and strategies that will instruct you on how to create a spell, break down people's resistance, give movement and force to your persuasion, and induce surrender in your target.

I'm often asked why I talk to the reader through stories.

I'm very focused on the reader. I'm always thinking when I'm writing, how are they going to absorb this information?

There's a problem that psychologists have noted. If you're a teacher, you assume that your students have the same knowledge you have. This makes them bad teachers. I know that my readers don't necessarily know what I'm talking about. If I'm talking about Carl Jung, for instance, and I just throw out jargon, the reader is not going to get it. So I have to make it understandable to the average person.

In *The Art of Seduction,* I talk about how telling a story lowers people's resistance. Stories make the mind open up.

From the time we're kids—being carried by our parents or playing peek-a-boo—the sense of not knowing what comes next is very deeply ingrained in human psychology.

So if I tell a story about Rockefeller to illustrate aggression, I know that as the reader is being pulled into this story, they don't know where I'm going, or who the aggressor is in this story, or the lesson that I'm trying to derive. So they're going to want to read. They're going to want to go further and further and further. I've tricked them into coming to page eight. Whereas if I immediately hit them with Jung and this or that study and some sociology jargon, their minds close off. They're falling asleep.

That's the mistake 98 percent of people who write books out there make. They don't think about the reader. They assume that the reader is as interested in the material as they are. You have to seduce the reader. You have to persuade them that what you have to say is worth the time. That's why I tell stories.

People make the same mistake in the social realm, in trying to persuade or influence others. If you want someone to do you're bidding, to help you, to finance your film or whatever it is—if you come at it only thinking about what you want or deserve, it has no effect. But if you think in terms of how they think, the stories they want to hear, what will please them, what will interest them—the game changes. You have the power to influence them.

Just as I have the power to influence the reader when I start thinking about what the reader wants, you have the power to influence people when you start thinking about what they want.

The Hypnotist's Art

The goal of persuasive speech is often to create a kind of hypnosis: you are distracting people, lowering their defenses, making them more vulnerable to suggestion. Learn the hypnotist's lessons of repetition and affirmation, key elements in putting a subject to sleep. Repetition involves using the same words over and over, preferably a word with emotional content: "taxes," "liberals," "bigots." The effect is mesmerizing—ideas can be permanently implanted in people's unconscious simply by being repeated often enough. Affirmation is simply the making of strong positive statements, like the hypnotist's commands. Seductive language should have a kind of boldness, which will cover up a multitude of sins. Your audience will be so caught up in your bold language that they won't have time to reflect on whether or not it is true. Never say, "I don't think the other side made a wise decision"; say, "We deserve better," or "They have made a mess of things." Affirmative language is active language, full of verbs, imperatives, and short sentences.

Daily Law: Cut out "I believe," "Perhaps," "In my opinion." Head straight for the heart.

The Art of Seduction: Use the Demonic Power of Words to Sow Confusion

Play on Their Competitive Spirit

In 1948 the director Billy Wilder was casting for his new film, *A Foreign Affair*, which was to be set in Berlin just after the war. One of the main characters was a woman named Erika von Schluetow, a German cabaret singer with suspicious ties to various Nazis during the war. Wilder knew that Marlene Dietrich would be the perfect actress to play the part, but Dietrich had publicly expressed her intense dislike of anything having to do with the Nazis and had worked hard for various Allied causes. When first approached about the role, she found it too distasteful, and that was the end of the discussion. Wilder did not protest or plead with her, which would have been futile, given Dietrich's famed stubbornness. Instead he told her he had found two perfect American actresses to play the part, but he wanted her opinion on which would be better. Would she view their tests? Feeling bad that she had turned down her old friend Wilder, Dietrich naturally agreed to this. But Wilder had cleverly tested two well-known actresses whom he knew would be quite terrible for the role, making a mockery of the part of a sexy German cabaret singer. The ploy worked like a charm. The very competitive Dietrich was aghast at their performances and immediately volunteered to do the part herself.

Daily Law: Your attempts at influence must always follow a similar logic: how can you get others to perceive what you want them to do as something they are choosing to do?

The Laws of Human Nature, 7: Soften People's Resistance by Confirming Their Self-Opinion—The Law of Defensiveness

Make Them the Star of the Show

Most men . . . seek less to be instructed, and even to be amused,
than to be praised and applauded.

—JEAN DE LA BRUYÈRE

Influence over people and the power that it brings are gained in the opposite way from what you might imagine. Normally we try to charm
people with our own ideas, showing ourselves off in the best light. We
hype our past accomplishments. We promise great things about ourselves. We ask for favors, believing that being honest is the best policy.
What we do not realize is that we are putting all of the attention on
ourselves. In a world where people are increasingly self-absorbed, this
only has the effect of making others turn more inward in return and
think more of their own interests rather than ours. The royal road to influence and power is to go the opposite direction: Put the focus on others.
Let them do the talking. Let them be the stars of the show. Their opinions
and values are worth emulating. The causes they support are the noblest.
Such attention is so rare in this world, and people are so hungry for it,
that giving them such validation will lower their defenses and open their
minds to whatever ideas you want to insinuate.

Daily Law: In conversation, try getting others to do 70 percent of the
talking without them noticing, and see the effect.

The Laws of Human Nature, 7: Soften People's Resistance by Confirming
Their Self-Opinion—The Law of Defensiveness

Channel Overpowering Emotions

Malcolm X spoke all over the United States. He never read from a text; looking out at the audience, he made eye contact, pointed his finger. His anger was obvious, not so much in his tone—he was always controlled and articulate—as in his fierce energy, the veins popping out on his neck. Many earlier Black leaders had used cautious words, and had asked their followers to deal patiently and politely with their social lot, no matter how unfair. What a relief Malcolm was. He ridiculed the racists, he ridiculed the liberals, he ridiculed the president; no white person escaped his scorn. If whites were violent, Malcolm said, the language of violence should be spoken back to them, for it was the only language they understood. "Hostility is good!" he cried out. "It's been bottled up too long." Malcolm X had a bracing effect on many who felt the same anger he did but were frightened to express it. He was a Charismatic of Moses's kind: he was a deliverer. The power of this sort of Charismatic comes from his or her expression of dark emotions that have built up over years of oppression. That's the essence of charisma—it's an overpowering emotion that communicates itself in your gestures, in your tone of voice, in subtle signs that are the more powerful for being unspoken. You feel something more deeply than others, and no emotion is more powerful and more capable of creating a charismatic reaction than hatred, particularly if it comes from deep-rooted feelings of oppression. Express what others are afraid to express and they will see great power in you. Say what they want to say but cannot.

Daily Law: Learn how to channel your emotions. Nothing is more charismatic than the sense that someone is struggling with great emotion rather than simply giving in to it.

The Art of Seduction: The Charismatic

Win through Your Actions

During his extremely long career as England's most celebrated architect, Sir Christopher Wren was often told by his patrons to make impractical changes in his designs. Never once did he argue or offend. He had other ways of proving his point. In 1688 Wren designed a magnificent town hall for the city of Westminster. The mayor, however, was not satisfied; in fact he was nervous. He told Wren he was afraid the second floor was not secure, and that it could all come crashing down on his office on the first floor. He demanded that Wren add two stone columns for extra support. Wren, the consummate engineer, knew that these columns would serve no purpose, and that the mayor's fears were baseless. But build them he did, and the mayor was grateful. It was only years later that workmen on a high scaffold saw that the columns stopped just short of the ceiling. They were dummies. But both men got what they wanted: the mayor could relax, and Wren knew posterity would understand that his original design worked and the columns were unnecessary.

Daily Law: Demonstrate, do not explicate.

The 48 Laws of Power, Law 9: Win through Your Actions, Never through Argument

Keep Them Guessing

Only months after arriving in Paris in 1926, Josephine Baker had completely charmed and seduced the French public with her wild dancing. But less than a year later she could feel their interest wane. Since childhood she had hated feeling out of control of her life. Why be at the mercy of the fickle public? She left Paris and returned a year later, her manner completely altered—now she played the part of an elegant Frenchwoman, who happened to be an ingenious dancer and performer. The French fell in love again; the power was back on her side. If you are in the public eye, you must learn from this trick of surprise. People are bored, not only with their own lives but with people who are meant to keep them from being bored. The minute they feel they can predict your next step, they will eat you alive. The artist Andy Warhol kept moving from incarnation to incarnation, and no one could predict the next one—artist, filmmaker, society man. Always keep a surprise up your sleeve.

Daily Law: To keep the public's attention, keep them guessing. Let the moralists accuse you of insincerity, of having no core or center. They are actually jealous of the freedom and playfulness you reveal in your public persona.

The Art of Seduction: Keep Them in Suspense—What Comes Next?

Consider Their Self-Interest

Most men are so thoroughly subjective that nothing really
interests them but themselves.

—ARTHUR SCHOPENHAUER

The quickest way to secure people's minds is by demonstrating, as simply as possible, how an action will benefit them. Self-interest is the strongest motive of all: a great cause may capture minds, but once the first flush of excitement is over, interest will flag—unless there is something to be gained. Self-interest is the solider foundation. The causes that work best use a noble veneer to cover a blatant appeal to self-interest; the cause seduces but the self-interest secures the deal.

Daily Law: Show people what's in it for them.

The 48 Laws of Power, Law 43: Work on the Hearts and Minds of Others

Avoid Argument

Never argue. In society nothing must be discussed; give only results.
—BENJAMIN DISRAELI

The Arguer does not understand that words are never neutral, and that by arguing with a superior he impugns the intelligence of one more powerful than he. He also has no awareness of the person he is dealing with. Since each man believes that he is right, and words will rarely convince him otherwise, the arguer's reasoning falls on deaf ears. When cornered, he only argues more, digging his own grave. Once he has made the other person feel insecure and inferior in his beliefs, the eloquence of Socrates could not save the situation. It is not simply a question of avoiding an argument with those who stand above you. We all believe we are masters in the realm of opinions and reasoning.

Daily Law: You must be careful to always try to demonstrate the correctness of your ideas indirectly.

The 48 Laws of Power, Law 9: Win through Your Actions, Never through Argument

The Moral Effect

The power of verbal argument is extremely limited, and often accomplishes the opposite of what is intended. As Gracián remarks, "The truth is generally seen, rarely heard." The Moral Effect is a perfect way to demonstrate your ideas through action. Quite simply, you teach others a lesson by giving them a taste of their own medicine. In the Moral Effect, you mirror what other people have done to you, and do so in a way that makes them realize you are doing to them exactly what they did to you. You make them feel that their behavior has been unpleasant, as opposed to hearing you complain and whine about it, which only gets their defenses up. And as they feel the result of their actions mirrored back at them, they realize in the profoundest sense how they hurt or punish others with their unsocial behavior.

Daily Law: Objectify the qualities you want them to feel ashamed of and create a mirror in which they can gaze at their follies and learn a lesson about themselves.

The 48 Laws of Power, Law 44: Disarm and Infuriate with the Mirror Effect

Anchor Their Ego

Think of people's ego and vanity as a kind of front. When they are attacking you and you don't know why, it is often because you have inadvertently threatened their ego, their sense of importance in the world. Whenever possible, you must work to make people feel secure about themselves. Use whatever works: subtle flattery, a gift, an unexpected promotion, an offer of alliance, a presentation of you and they as equals, a mirroring of their ideas and values. All these things will make them feel anchored in their frontal position relative to the world, lowering their defenses and making them like you. Secure and comfortable, they are now set up for persuasion. This is particularly devastating with a target whose ego is delicate.

Daily Law: When people feel secure about themselves, when you anchor the ego they front, they are disarmed and maneuverable.

The 33 Strategies of War, Strategy 18: Expose and Attack Your Opponent's Soft Flank—The Turning Strategy

Master the Art of Insinuation

No persuader can hope to succeed without mastering the language and art of insinuation. Slips of the tongue, apparently inadvertent "sleep on it" comments, alluring references, statements for which you quickly apologize— all of these have immense insinuating power. They get under people's skin like a poison and take on a life of their own. The key to succeeding with your insinuations is to make them when your targets are at their most relaxed or distracted, so that they are not aware of what is happening. Polite banter is often the perfect front for this; people are thinking about what they will say next, or are absorbed in their own thoughts. Your insinuations will barely register, which is how you want it. There is too little mystery in the world; too many people say exactly what they feel or want. We yearn for something enigmatic, for something to feed our fantasies. Because of the lack of suggestion and ambiguity in daily life, the person who uses them suddenly seems to have something alluring and full of promise.

Daily Law: Insinuation is the supreme means of influencing people. Hints, suggestions, and insinuations bypass people's natural resistance. Make everything suggestive.

The Art of Seduction: Master the Art of Insinuation

AUGUST 12

Use Their Emotions

In the book *Change*, the therapist authors (Paul Watzlawick, John Weakland, and Richard Fisch) discuss the case of a rebellious teenager, suspended from school by the principal because he was caught dealing drugs. He was still to do his homework at home, but was forbidden from being on campus. This would put a big dent in his drug-dealing business. The boy burned with the desire to get vengeance.

The mother consulted a therapist who told her to do the following: explain to the son that the principal believed only students who attended class in person could do well. In the principal's mind, by keeping the boy away from school he was ensuring he would fail. If he did better by working at home than at class, this would embarrass the principal. Better to not try too hard this semester, he advised her to say; instead, get on the good side of the principal by proving him right. Of course, such advice was cleverly designed to play into his rebellious nature. Now he desired nothing more than to embarrass the principal, and so threw himself into his homework with great energy, the goal of the therapist all along.

> Daily Law: In essence, the idea is not to counter people's strong emotions but move with them and find a way to channel them in a productive direction.

Robert Greene, "4 Strategies for Becoming a Master Persuader,"
Medium, November 14, 2008

Penetrate Their Minds

Machiavelli craved the power to spread his ideas and advice. Denied this power through politics, he set out to win it through books: he would convert readers to his cause, and they would spread his ideas, witting or unwitting carriers. Machiavelli knew that the powerful are often reluctant to take advice, particularly from someone apparently beneath them. He also knew that many of those not in power might be frightened by the dangerous aspects of his philosophy—that many readers would be attracted and repelled at the same time. To win over the resistant and ambivalent, Machiavelli's books would have to be strategic, indirect, and crafty. So he devised unconventional rhetorical tactics to penetrate deep behind his readers' defenses. First, he filled his books with indispensable advice—practical ideas on how to get power, stay in power, protect one's power. That draws in readers of all kinds, for all of us think first of our own self-interest. Next, Machiavelli stitched historical anecdotes throughout his writing to illustrate his ideas. People like to be shown ways to fancy themselves modern Caesars or Medicis, and they like to be entertained by a good story; and a mind captivated by a story is relatively undefended and open to suggestion. Finally, Machiavelli used stark, unadorned language to give his writing movement. Instead of finding their minds slowing and stopping, his readers are infected with the desire to go beyond thought and take action.

> Daily Law: You may have brilliant ideas, the kind that could revolutionize the world, but unless you can express them effectively, they will have no force, no power to enter people's minds in a deep and lasting way. Be strategic in your messaging.

The 33 Strategies of War, Strategy 30: Penetrate Their Minds

Leave People with a Feeling

For most of us, the conclusion of anything—a project, a campaign, an attempt at persuasion—represents a kind of wall: our work is done, and it is time to tally our gains and losses and move on. Lyndon Johnson looked at the world much differently: an ending was not like a wall but more like a door, leading to the next phase or battle. What mattered to him was not gaining a victory but where it left him, how it opened onto the next round. He kept his eye on the future, and on the kind of success that would keep him moving forward. Johnson used the same approach in his efforts to win over voters. Instead of trying to persuade people to support him with speeches and fancy words (he was not a good orator anyway), he focused on the feeling he left people with. He knew that persuasion is ultimately a process of the emotions: words can sound nice, but if a politician leaves people suspecting him of being insincere, of merely plugging for votes, they will close off to him and forget him. So Johnson worked to establish an emotional connection with voters, and he would close his conversations with them with a hearty handshake and with a look in his eye, a tremor in his voice, that sealed the bond between them. He left them feeling that they would see him again, and he stirred emotions that would erase any suspicion he might be insincere. The end of the conversation was in fact a kind of beginning, for it stayed in their minds and translated into votes.

Daily Law: Keep your eyes on the aftermath of any encounter. Think more of the feeling you leave people with—a feeling that might translate into a desire to see more of you.

The 33 Strategies of War, Strategy 22: Know How to End Things—The Exit Strategy

Create Compelling Spectacles

Using words to plead your case is risky business: Words are dangerous instruments, and often go astray. The words people use to persuade us virtually invite us to reflect on them with words of our own; we mull them over, and often end up believing the opposite of what they say. (That is part of our perverse nature.) It also happens that words offend us, stirring up associations unintended by the speaker. The visual, on the other hand, short-circuits the labyrinth of words. It strikes with an emotional power and immediacy that leave no gaps for reflection and doubt. Like music, it leaps right over rational, reasonable thoughts. The best way to use visuals is to organize images and symbols into a grand spectacle that awes people and distracts them from unpleasant realities. This is easy to do: People love what is grand, spectacular, and larger than life. Appeal to their emotions and they will flock to your spectacle in hordes. The visual is the easiest route to their hearts.

Daily Law: Stage spectacles for those around you, then, full of arresting visuals and radiant symbols that heighten your presence. Dazzled by appearances, no one will notice what you are really doing.

The 48 Laws of Power, Law 37: Create Compelling Spectacles

Use Their Rigidity

A pawnbroker's son once came to the great eighteenth-century Zen master Hakuin with the following problem: he wanted to get his father to practice Buddhism, but the man pretended to be too busy with his bookkeeping to have time for even a single chant or prayer. Hakuin knew the pawnbroker—he was an inveterate miser who was only using this as an excuse to avoid religion, which he considered a waste of time. Hakuin advised the boy to tell his father that the Zen master himself would buy from him each prayer and chant that he did on a daily basis. It was strictly a business deal. Of course the pawnbroker was very happy with the deal—he could shut his son up and make money in the process. Each day he presented Hakuin with his bill for the prayers, and Hakuin duly paid him. But on the seventh day, he failed to show up. It seemed that he had gotten so caught up in the chanting that he had forgotten to count how many prayers he had done. A few days later he admitted to Hakuin he had become completely taken up with the chants, felt so much better, and did not need to be paid anymore. He soon became a very generous donor to Hakuin's temple. When people are rigid in their opposition to something, it stems from deep fear of change and the uncertainty it could bring. They must have everything on their terms and feel in control. You play into their hands if you try with all your advice to encourage change— it gives them something to react against and justifies their rigidity. They become more stubborn. Stop fighting with such people and use the actual nature of their rigid behavior to effect a gentle change that could lead to something greater.

Daily Law: People often won't do what others ask them to do, because they simply want to assert their will. If you heartily agree with their rebellion, they will rebel again and assert their will in the opposite direction, which is what you wanted all along—the essence of reverse psychology.

The Laws of Human Nature, 7: Soften People's Resistance by Confirming Their Self-Opinion—The Law of Defensiveness

Persuade with a Light Touch

The most anti-seductive form of language is argument. How many silent enemies do we create by arguing? There is a superior way to get people to listen and be persuaded: humor and a light touch. The nineteenth-century English politician Benjamin Disraeli was a master at this game. In Parliament, to fail to reply to an accusation or slanderous comment was a deadly mistake: silence meant the accuser was right. Yet to respond angrily, to get into an argument, was to look ugly and defensive. Disraeli used a different tactic: he stayed calm. When the time came to reply to an attack, he would slowly make his way to the speaker's table, pause, then utter a humorous or sarcastic retort. Everyone would laugh. Now that he had warmed people up, he would proceed to refute his enemy, still mixing in amusing comments; or perhaps he would simply move on to another subject, as if he were above it all. His humor took out the sting of any attack on him. Laughter and applause have a domino effect: once your listeners have laughed, they are more likely to laugh again. In this lighthearted mood they are also more apt to listen.

Daily Law: A subtle touch and a bit of irony give you room to persuade them, move them to your side, mock your enemies. That is the seductive form of argument.

The Art of Seduction: Use the Demonic Power of Words to Sow Confusion

Make Them Feel Your Point

A heckler once interrupted Nikita Khrushchev in the middle of a speech in which he was denouncing the crimes of Stalin. "You were a colleague of Stalin's," the heckler yelled, "why didn't you stop him then?" Khrushchev apparently could not see the heckler and barked out, "Who said that?" No hand went up. No one moved a muscle. After a few seconds of tense silence, Khrushchev finally said in a quiet voice, "Now you know why I didn't stop him." Instead of just arguing that anyone facing Stalin was afraid, knowing that the slightest sign of rebellion would mean certain death, he had made them feel what it was like to face Stalin—had made them feel the paranoia, the fear of speaking up, the terror of confronting the leader, in this case Khrushchev. The demonstration was visceral and no more argument was necessary. The power of demonstrating is that your opponents do not get defensive, and are therefore more open to persuasion.

Daily Law: Your goal must be to make them literally and physically feel your meaning, rather than pouring words over them.

The 48 Laws of Power, Law 9: Win through Your Actions, Never through Argument

Let Them Win on the Minor Points

In 1782 the French playwright Pierre-Augustin Caron de Beaumarchais put the finishing touches on his great masterpiece *The Marriage of Figaro*. The approval of King Louis XVI was required, and when he read the manuscript, he was furious. Such a play would lead to a revolution, he said: "This man mocks everything that must be respected in a government." After much pressure, he agreed to have it privately performed in a theater at Versailles. The aristocratic audience loved it. The king allowed more performances, but he directed his censors to get their hands on the script and alter its worst passages before it was presented to the public, To bypass this, Beaumarchais commissioned a tribunal of academics, intellectuals, courtiers, and government ministers to go over the play with him. A man who attended the meeting wrote, "M. de Beaumarchais announced that he would submit unreservedly to every cut and change that the gentlemen and even the ladies present might deem appropriate. . . . Everyone wanted to add something of his own. . . . M. de Breteuil suggested a witticism, Beaumarchais accepted it and thanked him. . . . 'It will save the fourth act.' Mme de Matignon contributed the color of the little page's ribbon. The color was adopted and became fashionable." Beaumarchais was indeed very clever. By allowing others to make even the smallest changes to his masterpiece, he greatly flattered their egos and their intelligence. Of course, on the larger changes later requested by Louis's censors, Beaumarchais did not relent. By then he had so won over the members of his own tribunal that they stridently defended him, and Louis had to back down.

Daily Law: Learn to lower people's defenses by agreeing to matters that are not so important. This will give you great latitude to move them in the direction you desire and get them to concede to your desires on more important matters.

The Laws of Human Nature, 7: Soften People's Resistance by Confirming Their Self-Opinion—The Law of Defensiveness

How to Deal with the Irritating

Earlier on in his career, when the renowned psychotherapist Milton Erickson was a medical professor at a university, he had to deal with a very smart student named Anne, who always showed up late to classes, then apologized profusely and very sincerely. She happened to be a straight-A student. She always promised to be on time for the next class but never was. This made it difficult for her fellow students; she frequently held up lectures or laboratory work. And on the first day of one of Erickson's lecture classes, she was up to her old tricks, but Erickson was prepared. When she entered late, he had the entire class stand up and bow down to her in mock reverence; he did the same. Even after class, as she walked down the hall, the students continued their bowing. The message was clear—"We see through you"—and feeling embarrassed and ashamed, she stopped showing up late.

Daily Law: Teach the irritating a lesson by giving them a taste of their own medicine or showing them you see through them.

The Laws of Human Nature, 16: See the Hostility Behind the Friendly
Façade—The Law of Aggression

The Master Motivator

On the eve of his army's first battle with the fearsome Roman legions, Hannibal somehow had to bring his worn-out men alive. He decided to put on a show: he brought in a group of prisoners and told them that if they fought one another to the death in a gladiatorial contest, the victors would win freedom and a place in the Carthaginian army. The prisoners agreed, and Hannibal's soldiers were treated to hours of bloody entertainment. When the fighting was over, Hannibal addressed his men. You soldiers, said Hannibal, are in exactly the same position as the prisoners. You are many miles from home, on hostile territory, and you have nowhere to go. It is either freedom or slavery, victory or death. But fight as these men fought today and you will prevail. The contest and speech got hold of Hannibal's soldiers, and the next day they fought with deadly ferocity and defeated the Romans. Hannibal was a master motivator of a rare kind. Where others would harangue their soldiers with speeches, he knew that to depend on words was to be in a sorry state: words only hit the surface of a soldier, and a leader must grab his men's hearts, make their blood boil, get into their minds, alter their moods. Hannibal reached his soldiers' emotions indirectly, by relaxing them, calming them, taking them outside their problems, and getting them to bond. Only then did he hit them with a speech that brought home their precarious reality and swayed their emotions.

> Daily Law: Motivating people is a subtle art. You must aim indirectly at people's emotions. By setting up your emotional appeal, you will get inside instead of just scratching the surface.

The 33 Strategies of War, Strategy 7: Transform Your War into a Crusade—Morale Strategies

AUGUST 22

The Lure of the Unfamiliar

One of the perverse parts of human nature is that we always desire what we don't have. We look on the other side of the fence—the grass is always greener, the neighbor has a better car, their children are better behaved. We're always desiring what other people have. We think what we don't have is better. That's the nature of desire. When we actually attain something, it's not such a great feeling. The importance of desire is to always be pursuing something, something outside of ourselves. We want what is unfamiliar, what is exotic, what we've never had in our lives before. We want what is transgressive, what is the taboo, what other people don't have, what is new or fresh. You have to create that object of desire—in whatever you're creating in life. You have to give people the feeling that there's something a little bit taboo and transgressive about it, which was what I did with *The 48 Laws of Power.* When you pick up that book, you feel like you're doing something a little bit dirty and nasty. You want to create the feeling that what you are offering is not something familiar.

Daily Law: When a person or an object is familiar, we have a bit of disdain. But when it's distant and alluring and mysterious and something out there that we don't have—that sparks our desire. That's the key to any sort of marketing or soft sell.

Robert Greene in conversation at Live Talks Los Angeles, February 11, 2019

Find Their Thumbscrew

Find out each man's thumbscrew. 'Tis the art of setting their wills in action. It needs more skill than resolution. You must know where to get at anyone. Every volition has a special motive which varies according to taste. All men are idolaters, some of fame, others of self-interest, most of pleasure. Skill consists in knowing these idols in order to bring them into play. Knowing any man's mainspring of motive you have as it were the key to his will.

—BALTASAR GRACIÁN

We all have resistances. We live with a perpetual armor around ourselves to defend against change and the intrusive actions of friends and rivals. We would like nothing more than to be left to do things our own way. Constantly butting up against these resistances will cost you a lot of energy. One of the most important things to realize about people, though, is that they all have a weakness, some part of their psychological armor that will not resist, that will bend to your will if you find it and push on it. Some people wear their weaknesses openly, others disguise them. Those who disguise them are often the ones most effectively undone through that one chink in their armor.

Daily Law: Everyone has a thumbscrew, a gap in the castle wall. Once found, it is a thumbscrew you can turn to your advantage.

The 48 Laws of Power, Law 33: Discover Each Man's Thumbscrew

Mix Harshness and Kindness

Napoleon was the greatest man manager in history: he took millions of unruly, undisciplined, unsoldierly young men, recently liberated by the French Revolution, and molded them into one of the most successful fighting forces ever known. Of all Napoleon's techniques, none was more effective than his use of punishments and rewards, all staged for the greatest dramatic impact. His personal rebukes were rare, but when he was angry, when he punished, the effect was devastating: the target felt disowned, outcast. As if exiled from the warmth of his family, he would struggle to win back the general's favor and then never to give him a reason to be angry again. Promotions, rewards, and public praise were equally rare, and when they came, they were always for merit, never for some political calculation. Caught between the poles of wanting never to displease Napoleon and yearning for his recognition, his men were pulled into his sway, following him devotedly but never quite catching up. Learn from the master: the way to manage people is to keep them in suspense. First, create a bond between your soldiers and yourself. They respect you, admire you, even fear you a little. To make the bond stronger, hold yourself back, create a little space around yourself; you are warm yet with a touch of distance. Once the bond is forged, appear less often. Make both your punishments and your praises rare and unexpected, whether for mistakes or for successes that may seem minor at the time but have symbolic meaning. Understand: once people know what pleases you and what angers you, they turn into trained poodles, working to charm you with apparent good behavior.

Daily Law: Keep them in suspense—make them think of you constantly and want to please you but never know just how to do it. Once they are in the trap, you will have a magnetic pull over them. Motivation will become automatic.

The 33 Strategies of War, Strategy 7: Transform Your War into a Crusade—Morale Strategies

Cultivate the Third Eye

In 401 BC, ten thousand Greek mercenary soldiers suddenly found themselves on the losing side of a battle, trapped deep in the heart of Persia. They wandered through their camp bemoaning their fate. Among them was the writer Xenophon, who had gone along with the soldiers as a kind of roving reporter. Xenophon had studied philosophy as a student of Socrates. He believed in the supremacy of rational thinking, of seeing the entire picture, the general idea behind the fleeting appearances of daily life. One night he had a vision of how the Greeks could escape their trap and return home. He saw them moving swiftly and stealthily through Persia, sacrificing everything for speed. He saw them leaving right away, using the element of surprise to gain some distance. He thought ahead—of the terrain, the route to take, the many enemies they would face, how they could help and use citizens who revolted against the Persians. In the space of a few hours, he had conjured up the details of the retreat, all inspired by his overall vision of their fast zigzag route to the Mediterranean and home. Although he had no military experience, his vision was so complete, and he communicated it with such confidence, that the soldiers nominated him as their de facto leader. This story embodies the essence of all authority and the most essential element in establishing it. Most people are locked in the moment. They are prone to overreacting and panicking, to seeing only a narrow part of the reality facing the group. They cannot entertain alternative ideas or prioritize. Those who maintain their presence of mind and elevate their perspective above the moment tap into the visionary powers of the human mind and cultivate that third eye for unseen forces and trends. They stand out from the group and fulfill the true function of leadership.

Daily Law: Create the aura of authority by seeming to possess the god-like ability to read the future. This is a power that can be practiced and developed and applied to any situation.

The Laws of Human Nature, 15: Make Them Want to Follow You—The Law of Fickleness

Appeal to Their Unrealized Greatness

Most people believe themselves to be inwardly greater than they outwardly appear to the world. They are full of unrealized ideals: they could be artists, thinkers, leaders, spiritual figures, but the world has crushed them, denied them the chance to let their abilities flourish. This is the key to their seduction—and to keeping them seduced over time. Appeal only to people's physical side, as many amateur seducers do, and they will resent you for playing upon their basest instincts. But appeal to their better selves, to a higher standard of beauty, and they will hardly notice that they have been seduced.

Daily Law: Make your targets feel elevated, lofty, spiritual, and your power over them will be limitless.

The Art of Seduction: The Ideal Lover

Transform Yourself into a Deep Listener

You know your own thoughts only too well. You are rarely surprised. Your mind tends to circle obsessively around the same subjects. But each person you encounter represents an undiscovered country full of surprises. Imagine for a moment that you could step inside people's minds and what an amazing journey that could be. People who seem quiet and dull often have the strangest inner lives for you to explore. Even with boors and fools, you can educate yourself as to the origins and nature of their flaws.

Daily Law: Transforming yourself into a deep listener will not only prove more amusing as you open your mind to their mind but will also provide the most invaluable lessons about human psychology. The secret to this: finding other people endlessly fascinating.

The Laws of Human Nature, 7: Soften People's Resistance by Confirming Their Self-Opinion—The Law of Defensiveness

Instill a Feeling of Inner Security

When you try to convince people of something, one of three things will happen. First, you might inadvertently challenge a particular aspect of their self-opinion. Second, you can leave their self-opinion in a neutral position—neither challenged nor confirmed. Third, you can actively confirm their self-opinion. In this case, you are fulfilling one of people's greatest emotional needs. We can imagine that we are independent, intelligent, decent, and self-reliant, but only other people can truly confirm this for us. And in a harsh and competitive world in which we are all prone to continual self-doubt, we almost never get this validation that we crave. When you give it to people, you will have the magical effect that occurred when you yourself were drunk, or at a rally, or in love. You will make people relax. No longer consumed by insecurities, they can direct their attention outward. Their minds open, making them susceptible to suggestion and insinuation. If they decide to help you, they feel like they are doing this of their own free will.

> Daily Law: Your task is simple: instill in people a feeling of inner security. Mirror their values, show that you like and respect them, make them feel you appreciate their wisdom and experience.

The Laws of Human Nature, 7: Soften People's Resistance by Confirming
Their Self-Opinion—The Law of Defensiveness

Infect People with the Proper Mood

If you are relaxed and anticipating a pleasurable experience, this will communicate itself and have a mirror-like effect on the other person. One of the best attitudes to adapt for this purpose is one of complete indulgence. You do not judge other people; you accept them as they are. In the novel *The Ambassadors*, the writer Henry James paints the portrait of this ideal in the form of Marie de Vionnet, an older French woman of impeccable manners, who surreptitiously uses an American named Lambert Strether to help her in a love affair. From the very moment he meets her, Strether is captivated. She seems a "mix of lucidity and mystery." She listens deeply to what he says and, without responding, gives him the feeling she completely understands him. She envelops him in her empathy. She acts from the beginning as if they have become good friends, but it is in her manner, nothing she says. He calls her indulgent spirit "a beautiful conscious mildness," and it has a hypnotic power over him. Well before she even asks for his help, he is completely under her spell and will do anything for her. Such an attitude replicates the ideal mother figure—unconditional in her love. It is not expressed so much in words as in looks and body language. It works equally well on men and women and has a hypnotic effect on almost anyone.

Daily Law: As social animals, we are extremely susceptible to the moods of other people. Use this power to subtly infuse into people the appropriate mood for influencing them.

The Laws of Human Nature, 7: Soften People's Resistance by Confirming Their Self-Opinion—The Law of Defensiveness

Imagine Them in the Best Light

Keep in mind that your expectations about people are communicated to them nonverbally. It has been demonstrated, for instance, that teachers who expect greater things from their pupils can, without ever saying anything, have a positive effect on their work and grades. By feeling particularly excited when you're meeting someone, you will communicate this to him or her in a powerful way. Some have claimed to get great results by simply thinking the other person is handsome or good-looking.

Daily Law: If there is a person of whom you will eventually ask a favor, try imagining him or her in the best light—generous and caring—if that is possible.

The Laws of Human Nature, 7: Soften People's Resistance by Confirming Their Self-Opinion—The Law of Defensiveness

Come to Terms with Your Own Self-Opinion

Finally, when it comes to your own self-opinion, try to have some ironic distance from it. Make yourself aware of its existence and how it operates within you. Come to terms with the fact that you are not as free and autonomous as you like to believe. You do conform to the opinions of the groups you belong to; you do buy products because of subliminal influence; you can be manipulated. Realize as well that you are not as good as the idealized image of your self-opinion. Like everyone else, you can be quite self-absorbed and obsessed with your own agenda. With this awareness, you will not feel the need to be validated by others.

Daily Law: Work at making yourself truly independent and concerned with the welfare of others, as opposed to staying attached to the illusion of your self-opinion.

The Laws of Human Nature, 7: Soften People's Resistance by Confirming
Their Self-Opinion—The Law of Defensiveness

September

The Grand Strategist

RISING OUT OF TACTICAL HELL

≈

Strategy is an art that requires not only a different way of thinking but an entirely different approach to life itself. Too often there is a chasm between our ideas and knowledge on the one hand and our actual experience on the other. We absorb trivia and information that take up mental space but get us nowhere. We read books that divert us but have little relevance to our daily lives. We have lofty ideas that we do not put into practice. We also have many rich experiences that we do not analyze enough, that do not inspire us with ideas, whose lessons we ignore. Strategy requires a constant contact between the two realms. It is practical knowledge of the highest form. Events in life mean nothing if you do not reflect on them in a deep way, and ideas from books are pointless if they have no application to life as you live it. In strategy all of life is a game that you are playing. This game is exciting but also requires deep and serious attention. The stakes are so high. What you know must translate into action, and action must translate into knowledge. In this way strategy becomes a lifelong challenge and the source of constant pleasure in surmounting difficulties and solving problems. The month of September aims to transform you into a strategic warrior in daily life.

In my book *The 33 Strategies of War*, I make the point that most of us exist in a realm that I call tactical hell. This hell consists of all the people around us who are vying for power or some kind of control, and whose actions intersect our lives in a thousand different directions. We are constantly having to react to what this person does or says, getting emotional in the process. Once you sink into this hell, it is very difficult to raise your mind above it. You are dealing with one battle after another, and none of them end with any resolution. It is very hard for you to see the hell for what it is; you are too close to it, too mired in it to think of it any other way. Because there are so many people now vying for power in this world, and our attentions are so distracted in many different directions, this dynamic only gets worse and worse.

Strategy is the only answer. This is not some dry academic point of contention. It is actually a matter of grave importance, the difference between a life of misery and one of balance and success. Strategy is a mental process in which your mind elevates itself above the battlefield. You have a sense of a larger purpose for your life, where you want to be down the road, what you were destined to accomplish. This makes it easier to decide what is truly important, what battles to avoid. You are able to control your emotions, to view the world with a degree of detachment.

If a person tries to suck you into their battles or problems, you have the necessary distance and perspective to keep away or help them without losing your balance. You see everything as a strategic concern, including how the group you lead is structured—for mobility, for morale. Once you are on this track, everything becomes easier. A defeat or setback is a lesson to be learned, not a personal affront. Success does not go to your head, make you overreach.

There are false strategists in this world who are nothing more than master tacticians. They look like strategists because they are able to manage immediate problems with a degree of aplomb. They know how to fix problems. They get ahead, or rather, they are able to just raise their heads above the water. But they inevitably slip up. I consider President Bill Clinton to be an example of this, as compared to an Abraham Lincoln or Franklin Delano Roosevelt, who were true strategists.

There are others who also seem to have a vision, to have a large plan in life. They look like strategists as well, but their plans have no relation to reality. Their plans and goals are really reflections of their desires. And in the execution we can see this. Everything turns into friction. President Bush's "grand strategy" to remold the Middle East is an example of this. It looks large and encompassing, on paper it makes some sense, but in practice it is a massive failure, because it has no relation to the reality on the ground. Strategists are realists if nothing else—they can look at the world and themselves with a higher degree of objectivity than others.

My books have been described as evil and immoral, and me as someone who is creating more harm in this world by writing them. I don't take this personally, but the truth as I see it is that the books are not evil at all. I believe far more bad things occur in this world because people do not know how to operate effectively, or strategically. They launch wars without knowing where they are headed; they start businesses that are on shaky ground and get nowhere; they direct political campaigns that are badly thought out and fail; they waste valuable time and energy on things that do not matter. It is tempting for people to talk about good and evil from their armchairs. Nothing is easier. But to translate those ideas into reality requires strategic thinking. Even Gandhi knew that.

To the ancient Greeks, far more harm is caused in this world by stupidity and incompetence than outright evil. Those who are overtly evil can be combated, because they are easy to recognize and fight against. The incompetent and stupid are far more dangerous because we are never quite sure where they are leading us, until it is too late. The greatest military disasters in history have more often than not originated from leaders who lack strategic wisdom.

It is almost a religious matter: Will you convert to the light side, to strategy? Or will you keep yourself in tactical hell? The mental commitment to being more of a strategist in life is half of the battle. It is all that I ask of my readers.

Elevate Yourself Above the Battlefield

[Strategy] is more than a science: it is the application of knowledge to
practical life, the development of thought capable of modifying the
original guiding idea in the light of ever-changing situations; it is the
art of acting under the pressure of the most difficult conditions.

—HELMUTH VON MOLTKE

In war, strategy is the art of commanding the entire military operation.
Tactics, on the other hand, is the skill of forming up the army for battle
itself and dealing with the immediate needs of the battlefield. Most of us
in life are tacticians, not strategists. We become so enmeshed in the conflicts we face that we can think only of how to get what we want in the
battle we are currently facing. To think strategically is difficult and unnatural. You may imagine you are being strategic, but in all likelihood
you are merely being tactical. To have the power that only strategy can
bring, you must be able to elevate yourself above the battlefield, to focus
on your long-term objectives, to craft an entire campaign, to get out of
the reactive mode that so many battles in life lock you into. Keeping your
overall goals in mind, it becomes much easier to decide when to fight and
when to walk away. That makes the tactical decisions of daily life much
simpler and more rational.

Daily Law: Tactical people are heavy and stuck in the ground; strategists are light on their feet and can see far and wide. Where are you on
that spectrum?

The 33 Strategies of War, Preface

Control the Entire Chessboard

The film director Alfred Hitchcock made this strategy a life principle. His every action a setup designed to yield results down the road, he calmly thought ahead and moved step by step. His goal was to make a film that matched his original vision, uncorrupted by the influence of the actors, producers, and other staff who necessarily came along later. By controlling every detail of the film's screenplay, he made it almost impossible for the producer to interfere. Should the producer try to meddle during the actual shooting, Hitchcock would have a camera ready on set with no film in it. He could pretend to take the extra shots that the producer wanted, letting the producer feel powerful without risk to the end result. Hitchcock did the same with actors: instead of telling them directly what to do, he would infect them with the emotion he wanted—fear, anger, desire—by the way he treated them on set. Every step on the campaign trail fit perfectly into the next one.

Daily Law: Maintain control of your emotions and plot your moves in advance, seeing the entire chessboard.

The 33 Strategies of War, Strategy 12: Lose Battles but Win the War—Grand Strategy

Attack the Center of Gravity

The first principle is that the ultimate substance of enemy strength
must be traced back to the fewest possible sources, and ideally to one
alone. . . . By constantly seeking out the center of his power, by daring
all to win all, will one really defeat the enemy.

—CARL VON CLAUSEWITZ

It is the nature of power to present a forceful front, to seem menacing and intimidating, strong and decisive. But this outward display is often exaggerated or even downright deceptive, since power does not dare show its weaknesses. And beneath the display is the support on which power rests—its "center of gravity." The phrase is von Clausewitz's, who elaborated it as "the hub of all power and movement, on which everything depends." To attack this center of gravity, to neutralize or destroy it, is the ultimate strategy, for without it the whole structure will collapse. Hitting the enemy's center of gravity there is the best way to end a conflict definitively and economically. In looking for those centers, it is crucial not to be misled by the intimidating or dazzling exterior, mistaking the outward appearance for what sets it in motion. You will probably have to take several steps, one by one, to uncover this ultimate power source, peeling away layer after layer.

Daily Law: When you look at your rivals, search for the center of gravity that holds the entire structure together. That center can be their wealth, their popularity, a key position, a winning strategy. Hitting them there will inflict disproportionate pain.

The 33 Strategies of War, Strategy 16: Hit Them Where It Hurts—The
Center-of-Gravity Strategy

Avoid Tactical Hell

Often we see this dynamic in marital spats: it is no longer about repairing the relationship but about imposing one's point of view. At times, caught in these battles, you feel defensive and petty, your spirit drawn downward. This is almost a sure sign that you have descended into tactical hell. Our minds are designed for strategic thinking—calculating several moves in advance toward our goals. In tactical hell you can never raise your perspective high enough to think in that manner. You are constantly reacting to the moves of this or that person, embroiled in their dramas and emotions, going around in circles. The only solution is to back out temporarily or permanently from these battles, particularly if they are occurring on several fronts. You need some detachment and perspective. Get your ego to calm down. Remind yourself that winning an argument or proving your point really gets you nowhere in the long run. Win through your actions, not your words. Start to think again about your long-term goals.

Daily Law: Create a ladder of values and priorities in your life, reminding yourself of what really matters to you. If you determine that a particular battle is in fact important, with a greater sense of detachment you can now plot a more strategic response.

The Laws of Human Nature, 7: Soften People's Resistance by Confirming Their Self-Opinion—The Law of Defensiveness

Place Yourself in Shih

To separate yourself from the mechanical and reactive types, you need to get rid of a common misconception: the essence of strategy is not to carry out a brilliant plan that proceeds in steps; it is to put yourself in situations where you have more options than the enemy does. Instead of grasping at Option A as the single right answer, true strategy is positioning yourself to be able to do A, B, or C depending on the circumstances. That is strategic depth of thinking, as opposed to formulaic thinking. Sun Tzu expressed this idea differently: what you aim for in strategy, he said, is shih, a position of potential force—the position of a boulder perched precariously on a hilltop, say, or of a bowstring stretched taut. A tap on the boulder, the release of the bowstring, and potential force is violently unleashed. The boulder or arrow can go in any direction; it is geared to the actions of the enemy. What matters is not following preordained steps but placing yourself in shih and giving yourself options.

Daily Law: Rid yourself of the illusion that strategy is a series of steps to be followed toward a goal. Run in the opposite direction of any expert or guru proclaiming to possess a secret formula for success and power.

The 33 Strategies of War, Strategy 6: Segment Your Forces—The Controlled-Chaos Strategy

Never Attack Your Opponents Head-On

"It is by turning the enemy, by attacking his flank, that battles are won."
—NAPOLEON BONAPARTE

One of Napoleon's favorite strategies was what he called the *manoeuvre sur les derrières*. Its success was based on two truths: First, generals like to place their armies in a strong frontal position. Napoleon would often play on this tendency to face forward in battle by seeming to engage the enemy frontally; in the fog of battle, it was hard to tell that really only half of his army was deployed here, and meanwhile he would sneak the other half to the side or rear. Second, an army sensing attack from the flank is alarmed and vulnerable and must turn to face the threat. This moment of turning contains great weakness and confusion. Learn from the great master himself: Attacking from the front is rarely wise. Go for the flank, the vulnerable side. This principle is applicable to conflicts or encounters of any scale. Individuals often show their flank, signal their vulnerability, by its opposite, the front they show most visibly to the world. This front can be an aggressive personality, a way of dealing with people by pushing them around. It can be their most cherished beliefs and ideas; it can be the way they make themselves liked. The more you get people to expose this front, to show more of themselves and the directions they tend to move in, the more their unprotected flanks will come into focus—unconscious desires, gaping insecurities, precarious alliances, uncontrollable compulsions. Once you move on their flanks, your targets will turn to face you and lose their equilibrium. All enemies are vulnerable from their sides. There is no defense against a well-designed flanking maneuver.

Daily Law: When you attack people head-on, you stiffen their resistance and make your task that much harder. Instead: distract your opponents' attention to the front, then attack them from the side, where they least expect it.

The 33 Strategies of War, Strategy 18: Expose and Attack Your Opponent's Soft Flank—The Turning Strategy

Divide and Conquer

Japan's great seventeenth-century swordsman Miyamoto Musashi on several occasions faced bands of warriors determined to kill him. The sight of such a group would intimidate most people. Another tendency would be to lash out violently, trying to kill as many of the attackers as possible all at once, but at the risk of losing control of the situation. Musashi, however, was above all else a strategist, and he solved these dilemmas in the most rational way possible. He would place himself so that the men would have to come at him in a line or at an angle. Then he would focus on killing the first man and move swiftly down the line. Instead of being overwhelmed or trying too hard, he would break the band into parts. Then he just had to kill opponent number one, while leaving himself in position to deal with opponent number two and preventing his mind from being clouded and confused. The effect was that he could retain his focus while keeping his opponents off balance, for as he proceeded down the line, they would become the ones who were intimidated and flustered. Whether you are beset by many small problems or by one giant problem, make Musashi the model for your mental process. If you let the complexity of the situation confuse you and either hesitate or lash out without thought, you will lose mental control, which will only add momentum to the negative force coming at you. Always divide up the issue at hand, first placing yourself in a central position, then proceeding down the line, killing off your problems one by one. It is often wise to begin with the smallest problem while keeping the most dangerous one at bay. Solving that one will help you create momentum that will help you overwhelm all the rest.

Daily Law: Take problems one by one.

The 33 Strategies of War, Strategy 17: Defeat Them in Detail

SEPTEMBER 8

Exploit the Chaos

Chaos—where brilliant dreams are born.

—THE I CHING

Think of your mind as an army. Armies must adapt to the complexity and chaos of modern war by becoming more fluid and maneuverable. The ultimate extension of this evolution is guerrilla warfare, which exploits chaos by making disorder and unpredictability a strategy. The guerrilla army never stops to defend a particular place or town; it wins by always moving, staying one step ahead. By following no set pattern, it gives the enemy no target. The guerrilla army never repeats the same tactic. It responds to the situation, the moment, the terrain where it happens to find itself. There is no front, no concrete line of communication or supply, no slow-moving wagon. The guerrilla army is pure mobility. That is the model for your new way of thinking. Apply no tactic rigidly; do not let your mind settle into static positions, defending any particular place or idea, repeating the same lifeless maneuvers. Staying in constant motion you show your enemies no target to aim at. You exploit the chaos of the world instead of succumbing to it.

Daily Law: Attack problems from new angles, adapting to the landscape and to what you're given.

The 33 Strategies of War, Strategy 2: Do Not Fight the Last War—The Guerrilla-War-of-the-Mind Strategy

See the Larger Dangers That Loom in the Future

Experience shows that, if one foresees from far away the designs to be undertaken, one can act with speed when the moment comes to execute them.

—CARDINAL RICHELIEU

According to the cosmology of the ancient Greeks, the gods were thought to have complete vision into the future. They saw everything to come, right down to the intricate details. Men, on the other hand, were seen as victims of fate, trapped in the moment and their emotions, unable to see beyond immediate dangers. Those heroes, such as Odysseus, who were able to look beyond the present and plan several steps ahead, seemed to defy fate, to approximate the gods in their ability to determine the future. The comparison is still valid—those among us who think further ahead and patiently bring their plans to fruition seem to have a godlike power. Because most people are too imprisoned in the moment to plan with this kind of foresight, the ability to ignore immediate dangers and pleasures translates into power.

Daily Law: Overcome the natural human tendency to react to things as they happen, and instead train yourself to step back, imagine the larger things taking shape beyond your immediate vision.

The 48 Laws of Power, Law 29: Plan All the Way to the End

Never Seem Defensive

Man: Kick him—he'll forgive you. Flatter him—he may or may
not see through you. But ignore him and he'll hate you.
—IDRIES SHAH, *Caravan of Dreams*

The Renaissance writer Pietro Aretino often boasted of his aristocratic lineage, which was, of course, a fiction, since he was actually the son of a shoemaker. When an enemy of his finally revealed the embarrassing truth, word quickly spread, and soon all of Venice (where he lived at the time) was aghast at Aretino's lies. Had he tried to defend himself, he would have only dragged himself down. His response was masterful: he announced that he was indeed the son of a shoemaker, but this only proved his greatness, since he had risen from the lowest stratum of society to its very pinnacle. From then on he never mentioned his previous lie, trumpeting instead his new position on the matter of his ancestry. Remember: the powerful responses to niggling, petty annoyances and irritations are contempt and disdain. Never show that something has affected you, or that you are offended—that only shows you have acknowledged a problem. Contempt is a dish that is best served cold and without affectation.

Daily Law: By acknowledging a petty problem you give it existence and credibility. The less interest you reveal, the more superior you seem.

The 48 Laws of Power, Law 36: Disdain Things You Cannot Have—
Ignoring Them Is the Best Revenge

The Warrior's Creed

Reality can be defined by a sharp series of limitations on every living thing, the final boundary being death. We have only so much energy to expend before we tire; only so much in the way of food and resources is available to us; our skills and capacities can go only so far. An animal lives within those limits: it does not try to fly higher or run faster or expend endless energy amassing a pile of food, for that would exhaust it and leave it vulnerable to attack. It simply tries to make the most of what it has. A cat, for instance, instinctively practices an economy of motion and gesture, never wasting effort. People who live in poverty, similarly, are acutely aware of their limits: forced to make the most of what they have, they are endlessly inventive. Necessity has a powerful effect on their creativity. The problem faced by those of us who live in societies of abundance is that we lose a sense of limit. Abundance makes us rich in dreams, for in dreams there are no limits. But it makes us poor in reality. It makes us soft and decadent, bored with what we have and in need of constant shocks to remind us that we are alive. In life you must be a warrior, and war requires realism. While others may find beauty in endless dreams, warriors find it in reality, in awareness of limits, in making the most of what they have. Like the cat, they look for the perfect economy of motion and gesture—the way to give their blows the greatest force with the least expenditure of effort. Their awareness that their days are numbered—that they could die at any time—grounds them in reality. There are things they can never do, talents they will never have, lofty goals they will never reach; that hardly bothers them. Warriors focus on what they do have, the strengths that they do possess and that they must use creatively. Knowing when to slow down, to renew, to retrench, they outlast their opponents. They play for the long term.

Daily Law: Sometimes in strategy you have to ignore your greater strength and force yourself to get the maximum out of the minimum. Even if you have the technology, fight the peasant's war.

The 33 Strategies of War, Strategy 8: Pick Your Battles Carefully—The Perfect-Economy Strategy

Time Is All You Have

Space I can recover. Time, never.
—NAPOLEON BONAPARTE

Time is just as important as space in strategic thought, and knowing how to use time will make you a superior strategist, giving an added dimension to your attacks and defense. To do this you must stop thinking of time as an abstraction: in reality, beginning the minute you are born, time is all you have. It is your only true commodity. People can take away your possessions, but—short of murder—not even the most powerful aggressors can take time away from you unless you let them. Even in prison your time is your own, if you use it for your own purposes. To waste your time in battles not of your choosing is more than just a mistake, it is stupidity of the highest order.

Daily Law: Resist the urge to respond to trivial annoyances. Time lost can never be regained.

The 33 Strategies of War, Strategy 11: Trade Space for Time—The Nonengagement Strategy

Think of the Unintended Consequences

The years teach much which the days never know.

—RALPH WALDO EMERSON

In ancient Rome, a group of men loyal to the Republic feared that Julius Caesar was going to make his dictatorship permanent and establish a monarchy. In 44 BC they decided to assassinate him, thereby restoring the Republic. In the ensuing chaos and power vacuum, Caesar's great-nephew Octavius quickly rose to the top, assumed power, and permanently ended the Republic by establishing a de facto monarchy. After Caesar's death it came out that he had never intended to create a monarchical system. The conspirators brought about precisely what they had tried to stop. Invariably in these cases, people's thinking is remarkably simple and lazy: kill Caesar and the Republic returns, action A leads to result B. Understand: Any phenomenon in the world is by nature complex. The people you deal with are equally complex. Any action sets off a limitless chain of reactions. It is never so simple as A leads to B. B will lead to C, to D, and beyond. Other actors will be pulled into the drama and it is hard to predict their motivations and responses. You cannot possibly map out these chains or get a complete handle on consequences. But by making your thinking more consequential you can at least become aware of the more obvious negative consequences that could ensue, and this often spells the difference between success and disaster. You want depth of thinking, to go to several degrees in imagining the permutations, as far as your mind can go.

Daily Law: Game out all of the possible consequences of a strategy or line of action.

The Laws of Human Nature, 6: Elevate Your Perspective—The Law of Shortsightedness

Crowd Out Panic

Lord Yamanouchi, an aristocrat of eighteenth-century Japan, once asked his tea master to accompany him on a visit to Edo (later Tokyo). Now, the tea master knew everything there was to know about the tea ceremony, but little else. He dressed, however, like a samurai. One day, the tea master was accosted by a samurai who challenged him to a duel. Though not a swordsman, to turn the challenge down would disgrace both his family and Lord Yamanouchi. He accepted—knowing that meant certain death—requesting only that the duel be put off to the next day. His wish was granted. In panic, the tea master hurried to the nearest fencing school. If he were to die, he wanted to learn how to die honorably. The fencing master listened to his story and agreed to teach the poor visitor the art of dying, but first he wanted to be served some tea. As the tea master proceeded to perform the ritual, the fencing master yelled out in excitement, "No need for you to learn the art of death! The state of mind you're in now is enough for you to face any samurai. When you see your challenger, imagine you're about to serve tea to a guest." This ritual completed, the tea master was to raise his sword in the same alert spirit. Then he would be ready to die. The tea master agreed to do as his teacher said. The next day, he went to meet the samurai, who could not help but notice the completely calm and dignified expression on his opponent's face as he took off his coat. The samurai thought this fumbling tea master must actually be a skilled swordsman. He begged pardon for his behavior and hurried away. When circumstances scare us, our imagination tends to take over, filling our minds with endless anxieties. You need to gain control of your imagination. A focused mind has no room for anxiety or for the effects of an overactive imagination.

Daily Law: Give yourself such control by forcing the mind to concentrate on something relatively simple—a calming ritual, a repetitive task that you are good at. You are creating the kind of composure you naturally have when your mind is absorbed in a problem.

The 33 Strategies of War, Strategy 3: Amidst the Turmoil of Events, Do Not Lose Your Presence of Mind—The Counterbalance Strategy

Drop Your Preconceived Notions

If you put an empty gourd on the water and touch it, it will slip to one
side. No matter how you try, it won't stay in one spot. The mind of
someone who has reached the ultimate state does not stay with
anything, even for a second. It is like an empty gourd on
the water that is pushed around.

—TAKUAN SŌHŌ

The greatest generals, the most creative strategists, stand out not because
they have more knowledge but because they are able, when necessary, to
drop their preconceived notions and focus intensely on the present moment. That is how creativity is sparked and opportunities are seized.
Knowledge, experience, and theory have limitations: no amount of thinking in advance can prepare you for the chaos of life, for the infinite possibilities of the moment. The great philosopher of war Carl von Clausewitz
called this "friction": the difference between our plans and what actually
happens. Since friction is inevitable, our minds have to be capable of
keeping up with change and adapting to the unexpected. The better we
can adapt our thoughts to changing circumstances, the more realistic our
responses to them will be. The more we lose ourselves in predigested
theories and past experiences, the more inappropriate and delusional our
response. It can be valuable to analyze what went wrong in the past, but
it is far more important to develop the capacity to think in the moment.
In that way you will make far fewer mistakes to analyze.

**Daily Law: Think of the mind as a river: the faster it flows, the better
it keeps up with the present and responds to change.**

The 33 Strategies of War, Strategy 2: Do Not Fight the Last War—The
Guerrilla-War-of-the-Mind Strategy

Force Them Off the Negative

It is always easier to argue from the negative side—criticizing other people's actions, dissecting their motives, etc. And that is why most people will opt for this. If they had to describe a positive vision of what they want in the world, or how they would accomplish a particular task, this would open them up to all kinds of attacks and criticisms. It takes effort and thought to establish a positive position. It takes less effort to work on what other people have done, and poke endless holes. It also makes you look tough and insightful, because people delight in hearing someone tear an idea apart. Facing these negative-mongers in a debate or argument is infuriating. They can come at you from all angles: hit you with sarcasm and snide comments, weave all kinds of abstractions that can make you look bad. If you lower yourself to their position, you end up like a boxer throwing punches into thin air. These opponents give you nothing to hit. (In war, it is always easier to hold ground than take ground.) Your task is to force them off this position by getting them to commit to some positive position. Now, you have a target. If they resist or refuse to do this, you can attack them for this resistance.

Daily Law: Avoid the temptation to fight back on the same level as the opponent. You must always shift the terms of the battle onto the terrain of your choice. In that moment of shifting, you have the initiative and the upper hand.

Robert Greene, "Only the Dull and Stupid Fight Head-on:
Some Strategic Thoughts," powerseductionandwar.com, July 15, 2007

Balance Ends and Means

Wise generals through the ages have learned to begin by examining the means they have at hand and then to develop their strategy out of those tools. They always think first of the givens—the makeup of their own army and of the enemy's, their respective proportions of cavalry and infantry, the terrain, their troops' morale, the weather. That would give them the foundation not only for their plan of attack but also for the ends they wanted to achieve in a particular encounter. Instead of being locked in to a way of fighting, they constantly adjust their ends to their means. The next time you launch a campaign, try an experiment: do not think about either your solid goals or your wishful dreams, and do not plan out your strategy on paper. Instead think deeply about what you have—the tools and materials you will be working with. Ground yourself not in dreams and plans but in reality: think of your own skills, any political advantage you might have, the morale of your troops, how creatively you can use the means at your disposal. Then, out of that process, let your plans and goals blossom. Not only will your strategies be more realistic, they will be more inventive and forceful. Dreaming first of what you want and then trying to find the means to reach it is a recipe for exhaustion, waste, and defeat.

Daily Law: Constantly balance ends and means: you might have the best plan to achieve a certain end, but unless you have the means to accomplish it, your plan is worthless.

The 33 Strategies of War, Strategy 8: Pick Your Battles Carefully—The Perfect-Economy Strategy.

The Piecemeal Strategy

To multiply small successes is precisely to build one
treasure after another. In time one becomes rich without
realizing how it has come about.

—FREDERICK THE GREAT

The problem that many of us face is that we have great dreams and ambitions. Caught up in the emotions of our dreams and the vastness of our
desires, we find it very difficult to focus on the small, tedious steps usually necessary to attain them. We tend to think in terms of giant leaps
toward our goals. But in the social world as in nature, anything of size
and stability grows slowly. The piecemeal strategy is the perfect antidote
to our natural impatience: it focuses us on something small and immediate, a first bite, then how and where a second bite can get us closer to our
ultimate objective. It forces us to think in terms of a process, a sequence
of connected steps and actions, no matter how small, which has immea-
surable psychological benefits as well. Too often, the magnitude of our
desires overwhelms us; taking that small first step makes them seem re-
alizable. There is nothing more therapeutic than action.

Daily Law: Have a clear sense of your objective, but then identify the
small composite steps. Now, attaining your dreams is easy: step-
by-step.

The 33 Strategies of War, Strategy 29: Take Small Bites—The Fait Accompli Strategy

Make Use of the Cat's-Paw

*Important affairs often require rewards and punishments. Let only
the good come from you and the evil from others.*
—BALTASAR GRACIÁN

In the fable, the Monkey grabs the paw of his friend, the Cat, and uses it
to fish chestnuts out of the fire, thus getting the nuts he craves, without
hurting himself.

If there is something unpleasant or unpopular that needs to be done,
it is far too risky for you to do the work yourself. You need a cat's-paw—
someone who does the dirty, dangerous work for you. The cat's-paw grabs
what you need, hurts whom you need hurt, and keeps people from noticing that you are the one responsible.

Daily Law: Let someone else be the executioner, or the bearer of bad
news, while you bring only joy and glad tidings.

The 48 Laws of Power, Law 26: Keep Your Hands Clean

Hit from Unexpected Angles

People expect your behavior to conform to known patterns and conventions. Your task as a strategist is to upset their expectations. Surprise them with chaos and unpredictability—which they try desperately to keep at bay. To Sun Tzu and the ancient Chinese, doing something extraordinary had little effect without a setup of something ordinary. You had to mix the two—to fix your opponent's expectations with some banal, ordinary maneuver, a comfortable pattern that they would then expect you to follow. With the enemy sufficiently mesmerized, you would then hit it with the extraordinary, a show of stunning force from an entirely new angle. Framed by the predictable, the blow would have double the impact.

Daily Law: Operate according to your own rhythms, adapting strategies to your idiosyncrasies, not the other way around. Refusing to follow common patterns will make it hard for people to guess what you'll do next.

Robert Greene, "What Muhammad Ali Can Teach Us about Success and an Authentic Life," *The Observer*, July 22, 2015

Get Them to Reveal Their Intentions

*If you have reason to suspect that a person is telling you a lie,
look as though you believed every word he said. This will give him
courage to go on; he will become more vehement in his
assertions, and in the end betray himself.*

—ARTHUR SCHOPENHAUER

In the realm of power, your goal is a degree of control over future events. Part of the problem you face, then, is that people won't tell you all their thoughts, emotions, and plans. Controlling what they say, they often keep the most critical parts of their character hidden—their weaknesses, ulterior motives, obsessions. The result is that you cannot predict their moves, and are constantly in the dark. The trick is to find a way to probe them, to find out their secrets and hidden intentions, without letting them know what you are up to. The French politician Talleyrand was one of the greatest practitioners of this art. He had an uncanny ability to worm secrets out of people in polite conversation. A contemporary of his, Baron de Vitrolles, wrote, "Wit and grace marked his conversation. He possessed the art of concealing his thoughts or his malice beneath a transparent veil of insinuations, words that imply something more than they express. Only when necessary did he inject his own personality." The key here is Talleyrand's ability to suppress himself in the conversation, to make others talk endlessly about themselves and inadvertently reveal their intentions and plans.

Daily Law: Suppress yourself in conversation. Let others talk endlessly.

The 48 Laws of Power, Law 14: Pose as a Friend, Work as a Spy

Create Maximum Disorder

*So to win a hundred victories in a hundred battles is not the
highest excellence; the highest excellence is to subdue the
enemy's army without fighting at all.*

—SUN TZU

Your enemy depends on being able to read you, to get some sense of your intentions. The goal of your maneuvers should be to make that impossible, to send the enemy on a wild-goose chase for meaningless information, to create ambiguity as to which way you are going to jump.

Daily Law: The more you break down people's ability to reason about you, the more disorder you inject into their system.

The 33 Strategies of War, Strategy 20: Maneuver Them into Weakness—The
Ripening-for-the-Sickle Strategy

Develop Your Fingerspitzengefühl

Presence of mind depends not only on your mind's ability to come to your aid in difficult situations but also on the speed with which this happens. Waiting until the next day to think of the right action to take does you no good at all. "Speed" here means responding to circumstances with rapidity and making lightning-quick decisions. This power is often read as a kind of intuition, what the Germans call *Fingerspitzengefühl* (fingertip feel). Erwin Rommel, who led the German tank campaign in North Africa during World War II, had great fingertip feel. He could sense when the Allies would attack and from what direction. He didn't just study his men, his tanks, the terrain, and the enemy—he got inside their skin, understood the spirit that animated them, what made them tick. Having felt his way into these things, in battle he entered a state of mind in which he did not have to think consciously of the situation. The totality of what was going on was in his blood, at his fingertips. He had *Fingerspitzengefühl*. Whether or not you have the mind of a Rommel, there are things you can do to help you respond faster and bring out that intuitive feel that all animals possess. Deep knowledge of the terrain will let you process information faster than your enemy, a tremendous advantage. Getting a feel for the spirit of men and material, thinking your way into them instead of looking at them from outside, will help to put you in a different frame of mind, less conscious and forced, more unconscious and intuitive.

Daily Law: Get your mind into the habit of making lightning-quick decisions, trusting your fingertip feel. And you will develop this by knowing as deeply as possible all the details in any situation.

The 33 Strategies of War, Strategy 3: Amidst the Turmoil of Events, Do Not Lose Your Presence of Mind—The Counterbalance Strategy

Retreat to Gain Perspective

To remain disciplined and calm while waiting for disorder to appear
amongst the enemy is the art of self-possession.

—SUN TZU

The problem we all face in strategy, and in life, is that each of us is unique and has a unique personality. Our circumstances are also unique; no situation ever really repeats itself. But most often we are barely aware of what makes us different—in other words, of who we really are. Our ideas come from books, teachers, all kinds of unseen influences. We respond to events routinely and mechanically instead of trying to understand their differences. In our dealings with other people too, we are easily infected by their tempo and mood. All this creates a kind of fog. We fail to see events for what they are; we do not know ourselves. Your task as a strategist is simple: to see the differences between yourself and other people, to understand yourself, your side, and the enemy as well as you can, to get more perspective on events, to know things for what they are. In the hubbub of daily life, this is not easy—in fact, the power to do it can come only from knowing when and how to retreat. If you are always advancing, always attacking, always responding to people emotionally, you have no time to gain perspective. Your strategies will be weak and mechanical, based on things that happened in the past or to someone else. Like a monkey, you will imitate instead of create.

> Daily Law: Retreating shows not weakness but strength. It is something you must do every now and then, to find yourself and detach yourself from infecting influences.

The 33 Strategies of War, Strategy 11: Trade Space for Time—The Nonengagement Strategy

Stay Away from the Corners

In almost all board games—chess, go (wei chi), backgammon, et cetera—the corners spell defeat and death. These corners also exist on higher, more abstract planes. As you are right now, in your profession or relationships or battles that you face, you could be backing yourself into a corner. And the thing is, you are rarely aware of it as it happens, because often it is when you are excited and emotional, feeling engaged and moving in some direction, or that you have solved a problem, that you inadvertently trap yourself. There are always ways to get yourself out, in a tactical sense, but the wisest course is to become a strategist in the Sun Tzu sense of the term. What matters in the Sun Tzu universe are not positions of strength and power, but situations in which you have options, full of potential force. On a career level, for instance, I always advise people to look ahead and be open to changes in direction. That job that seems so good now can easily turn into a nightmare if you do not see the possible corners it can land you in. I know, because working in Hollywood, seduced by the pay, I backed myself into such a corner. I only got out by thinking far ahead and plotting a much different direction in my life. Instead of aiming at becoming a screenwriter, a trapped position if ever there is one, I aimed at writing books on subjects that excited me and presented endless possibilities for going in this or that direction, even returning to screenwriting, if I wanted to, but on my terms.

Daily Law: Strategists think differently than the way many are used to, in which so much revolves around moving toward a goal. That is linear thinking. What you want is to always aim to increase your options for power and mobility.

"Corners," powerseductionandwar.com

Let Go of the Past

Thus one's victories in battle cannot be repeated—they take their form
in response to inexhaustibly changing circumstances.

—SUN TZU

What limits individuals as well as nations is the inability to confront
reality, to see things for what they are. As we grow older, we become more
rooted in the past. Habit takes over. Something that has worked for us
before becomes a doctrine, a shell to protect us from reality. Repetition
replaces creativity. We rarely realize we're doing this, because it is almost
impossible for us to see it happening in our own minds. Then, suddenly,
a young Napoleon crosses our path, a person who does not respect tradition, who fights in a new way. Only then do we see that our ways of
thinking and responding have fallen behind the times. Never take it for
granted that your past successes will continue in the future. Actually,
your past successes are your biggest obstacle: every battle, every war, is
different, and you cannot assume that what worked before will work
today.

Daily Law: Think of the mind as a river: the faster it flows, the better
it keeps up with the present and responds to change. Obsessional
thoughts and past experiences (whether traumas or successes) are like
boulders or mud in this river.

The 33 Strategies of War, Strategy 2: Do Not Fight the Last War—The
Guerrilla-War-of-the-Mind Strategy

Give Yourself Space to Maneuver

Any project—artistic or professional or scientific—is like fighting a war. There is a certain strategic logic to the way you attack a problem, shape your work, deal with friction and the discrepancy between what you want and what you get. Directors or artists often start out with great ideas but in the planning create such a straitjacket for themselves, such a rigid script to follow and form to fit in, that the process loses all joy; there's nothing left to explore in the creation itself, and the end result seems lifeless and disappointing. On the other side, artists may start with a loose idea that seems promising, but they are too lazy or undisciplined to give it shape and form. They create so much space and confusion that in the end nothing coheres. The solution is to plan, to have a clear idea what you want, then put yourself in open space and give yourself options to work with. This means not burdening yourself with commitments that will limit your options. It means not taking stances that leave you nowhere to go. The need for space is psychological as well as physical: you must have an unfettered mind to create anything worthwhile.

Daily Law: You always want open space, never dead positions. Direct the situation but leave room for unexpected opportunities and random events.

The 33 Strategies of War, Strategy 20: Maneuver Them into Weakness—The Ripening-for-the-Sickle Strategy

Plan All the Way to the End

The most ordinary cause of people's mistakes is their being
too much frightened at the present danger, and not enough
so at that which is remote.

—CARDINAL DE RETZ

The dangers that are remote, that loom in the distance—if we can see them as they take shape, how many mistakes we avoid. How many plans we would instantly abort if we realized we were avoiding a small danger only to step into a larger one. So much of power is not what you do but what you do not do—the rash and foolish actions that you refrain from before they get you into trouble. Plan in detail before you act—do not let vague plans lead you into trouble. Unhappy endings are much more common than happy ones—do not be swayed by the happy ending in your mind.

Daily Law: Ask of every potential action: Will this have unintended consequences? Will I stir up new enemies? Will someone else take advantage of my labors?

The 48 Laws of Power, Law 29: Plan All the Way to the End

Assume Formlessness

The consummation of forming an army is to arrive at formlessness.
Victory in war is not repetitious, but adapts its form endlessly. . . .
A military force has no constant formation, water has no constant
shape: The ability to gain victory by changing and adapting
according to the opponent is called genius.

—SUN TZU

Everything in life depends on the circumstances you're in. That's why the last law in *The 48 Laws of Power* is "Assume Formlessness." The idea is that being formless like water is the highest form of power and strategy. In that chapter, I contradict my entire book and I essentially say: There are no laws. You have to be in the moment. You have to understand the circumstances you're in. Learning to adapt to each new circumstance means seeing events through your own eyes, and often ignoring the advice that people constantly peddle your way. It means that ultimately you must throw out the laws that others preach, and the books they write to tell you what to do, and the sage advice of the elder. "The laws that govern circumstances are abolished by new circumstances," Napoleon wrote, which means that it is up to you to gauge each new situation.

Daily Law: Accept the fact that nothing is certain and no law or strategy is fixed. The best way to protect yourself is to be as fluid and formless as water; never bet on stability or lasting order. Everything changes.

"Robert Greene: Mastery and Research," *Finding Mastery: Conversations with Michael Gervais*, January 25, 2017

Do Not Go Past the Mark You Aimed For

The greatest danger occurs at the moment of victory.
—NAPOLEON BONAPARTE

The essence of strategy is controlling what comes next, and the elation of victory can upset your ability to control what comes next in two ways. First, you owe your success to a pattern that you are apt to try to repeat. You will try to keep moving in the same direction without stopping to see whether this is still the direction that is best for you. Second, success tends to go to your head and make you emotional. Feeling invulnerable, you make aggressive moves that ultimately undo the victory you have gained. The lesson is simple: The powerful vary their rhythms and patterns, change course, adapt to circumstance, and learn to improvise. Rather than letting their dancing feet impel them forward, they step back and look where they are going. It is as if their bloodstream bore a kind of antidote to the intoxication of victory, letting them control their emotions and come to a kind of mental halt when they have attained success. They steady themselves, give themselves the space to reflect on what has happened, examine the role of circumstance and luck in their success. As they say in riding school, you have to be able to control yourself before you can control the horse.

Daily Law: The moment of victory is often the moment of greatest peril. Do not allow success to go to your head. There is no substitute for strategy and careful planning. Set a goal, and when you reach it, stop.

The 48 Laws of Power, Law 47: Do Not Go Past the Mark You Aimed for—In Victory, Learn When to Stop

October

The Emotional Self

COMING TO TERMS WITH OUR DARK SIDE

≈

For thousands of years, it has been our fate to largely grope in the shadows when it comes to understanding ourselves and our own nature. We have labored under so many illusions about the human animal—imagining we descended magically from a divine source, from angels instead of primates. We have found any signs of our primitive nature and our animal roots deeply distressing, something to deny and repress. We have covered up our darker impulses with all kinds of excuses and rationalizations, making it easier for some people to get away with the most unpleasant behavior. But finally we're at a point where we can overcome our resistance to the truth about who we are through the sheer weight of knowledge we have now accumulated about human nature. The month of October will help you come to terms with human nature, accept that there are patterns beyond your control, and understand your primitive roots so that you are not destroyed by them.

Over the course of several years after the publication of *The 48 Laws of Power*, I received thousands of emails from readers who came to me with their problems. I was also approached by hundreds of people who wanted one-on-one consulting for their problems.

After much deep thinking about these experiences and my own experiences with people I knew, I came to the following conclusion: We humans have a dirty little secret. It's a secret that has nothing to do with sex lives or fantasies or anything as exciting as that. Rather, the secret is that all of us, to some degree, are in pain. It's a pain that we don't discuss or even understand.

The source of this pain is other people.

What I mean is our often disappointing, superficial, unsatisfactory relationships with people. This comes in the form of relationships and connections that aren't very deep between us and those whom we consider our friends, leading to a lot of loneliness. It comes in the form of bad choices for associates and partners—leading to all this struggle and messy breakups. It comes from letting some toxic narcissist into our life—leading to all kinds of emotional trauma that can take years to get over, if we even ever do. And it also comes from our inability to persuade, to move people, to influence them, to get them interested in our ideas—generating feelings of frustration and anger.

We are deeply social animals and having dysfunctional social relationships leads to all kinds of problems. It leads to depression. It leads to recurring obsessive thoughts, to the inability to focus on our work, to eating disorders, to even physical diseases such as heart disease. We only see the surface phenomenon—the loneliness or the depression or physical ailment. We don't see the underlying source. And sometimes we're not even aware that we suffer from loneliness.

And so, in 2012, while I was writing *Mastery*, I decided what I really wanted to do next was to write a book that would help people deal with and overcome this very deep pain that I felt a lot of my readers were expressing to me. But I didn't want to just write the usual stupid self-help book that throws little formulas at you, pat phrases about how to get along with people. I wanted to write a book like I always try to do—one that gets inside of you, that changes how you think about the world, that gets under your skin and really alters your perspective about people and the world.

And so with that "modest" goal in mind, I asked myself a question like I always do when I write a book: What is the source of this pain, of this problem? The obvious answer is that we are generally very poor observers of people around us. We're poor listeners. We've become so self-absorbed with our smartphones and our technology. We're not paying attention. And when we do pay attention, we project onto people our own emotions, our own desires. Or we're very quick to judge and categorize them—that person's good, that person's evil; that person's likeable, that person's not likeable.

Seeing just a small portion of who people are, we naturally misunderstand and misjudge them—leading to all kinds of problems, to bad decisions, to bad strategies.

And so, if that is the source of our problem, then the solution is that we all just become better observers and listeners, which is what a lot of self-help books that deal with the subject say. But I found that very unsatisfying for an answer. That's not where I wanted to begin.

I thought very deeply and decided I wanted to ask another question: Are there moments in our lives in which we actually feel different? In which we are actually paying deep attention to people? In which we are actually observing them? And I said yes, there are.

First of all, as children. Children are master observers of people. They are very attuned to the emotions and moods of their parents—their survival depends on it. Con artists hate children because children can see through their phoniness, their fakeness. We were all great observers when we were children. Then, if we travel to a foreign country and everything's exotic and weird, our senses are heightened. We're paying attention to people. They seem so different—we want to understand them. Also, if we start a new job and we're a bit nervous—we're paying attention to all the little power dynamics going on. Obviously, when we fall in love—we're extremely attentive to that person. We're picking out every little sign and detail that they're emitting about whether they like us, who they are, what their character is like. And finally, strangely enough, if we read a really good novel or see a great movie. We're fascinated by the characters someone has created, and we want to get inside of their world.

What do all these experiences have in common? In these moments, our desire is engaged. We're excited. We're curious. We feel the need to pay attention to people. Our survival could even depend on it. And when we're excited and curious and we feel the necessity, suddenly our eyes come to life. We're watching. We're observing. We're getting inside people. And in these moments, there's less of our ego. We're getting outside of ourselves and into the world of other people.

Normally, we don't feel that way. We actually have low interest in the people around us. I hate to say that, but it's true. The people we deal with every day—they're too familiar to us. They don't seem exciting. We feel that our own thoughts and our own world is more interesting than theirs. We have our own needs and our own problems to deal with.

So I decided—what if I could write a book that would bring you back to those positions you had in those moments? What if I could make you feel like a child again? What if I could make you feel like those moments when you were in love or when you were traveling to a foreign country or when you were excited and curious and really wanted to probe inside the minds of the people around you?

That would change everything. You wouldn't have to suddenly imagine you were a better listener or observer. You would become a better listener and observer.

So how could I create that kind of magic? By taking you as a reader and leading you deep inside the inner worlds of the people around you. By making you see what their fantasies are, what their lives are like from the inside.

It's my contention that the people you deal with are a lot more interesting and complicated and weird than you imagine. You think that you have to travel to some foreign region like Bali or see some interesting movie to find people interesting. No, that salesperson at Rite Aid or whomever—they actually have a really deep, rich inner life. They are fascinating. You're just not realizing it.

So how am I going to be able to do this? How am I going to make you understand people rather than let them cause you pain?

By immersing you in the study of human nature. And as I said, I will alter how you perceive people from the inside out. And once I get you to go that far, you're never going to want to go back to where you were before.

The Primary Law of Human Nature

Let's start with the primary law of human nature. If I had to say what the primary law of human nature is, it is to deny that we have human nature, to deny that we are subject to these forces. We think, I'm not irrational, I'm not aggressive, I don't feel envy, I am not a narcissist. It's always the other side. It's the Republicans, it's the Spartans, it's the Ethiopians—they're the ones who are irrational and aggressive. Me? No. The truth is we all evolved from the same source, from the same small number of people. Our brains are basically the same. We are wired in a similar way. We experience the world, emotionally, the same way that hunter-gatherers experienced the world. Very little has changed in that sense. So if we all come from the same source, why would it be that only a small number of people are aggressive or are irrational? We are all the same.

Daily Law: Accept the nature you share with others. Stop separating yourself out as special or superior.

"The Laws of Human Nature: An Interview with Robert Greene," dailystoic.com, October 23, 2018

There's Nothing Stronger Than Human Nature

Man will only become better when you make him see what he is like.
—ANTON CHEKHOV

You might be tempted to imagine that this knowledge of human nature is a bit old-fashioned. After all, you might argue, we are now so sophisticated and technologically advanced, so progressive and enlightened; we have moved well beyond our primitive roots; we are in the process of rewriting our nature. But the truth is in fact the opposite—we have never been more in the thrall of human nature and its destructive potential than now. And by ignoring this fact, we are playing with fire. Look at how the permeability of our emotions has only been heightened through social media, where viral effects are continually sweeping through us and where the most manipulative leaders are able to exploit and control us. Look at the aggression that is now openly displayed in the virtual world, where it is so much easier to play out our shadow sides without repercussions. Notice how our propensities to compare ourselves with others, to feel envy, and to seek status through attention have only become intensified with our ability to communicate so quickly with so many people. And finally, look at our tribal tendencies and how they have now found the perfect medium to operate in—we can find a group to identify with, reinforce our tribal opinions in a virtual echo chamber, and demonize any outsiders, leading to mob intimidation. The potential for mayhem stemming from the primitive side of our nature has only increased. It is simple: Human nature is stronger than any individual, than any institution or technological invention. It ends up shaping what we create to reflect itself and its primitive roots. It moves us around like pawns. Ignore the laws at your own peril.

Daily Law: Refusing to come to terms with human nature simply means that you are dooming yourself to patterns beyond your control and to feelings of confusion and helplessness.

The Laws of Human Nature, Introduction

OCTOBER 3

The Inner Athena

What I fear is not the enemy's strategy but our own mistakes.

—PERICLES

In Pericles's conception, the human mind has to worship something, has to have its attention directed to something it values above all else. For most people, it is their ego; for some it is their family, their clan, their god, or their nation. For Pericles it would be *nous*, the ancient Greek word for "mind" or "intelligence." Nous is a force that permeates the universe, creating meaning and order. The human mind is naturally attracted to this order; this is the source of our intelligence. For Pericles, the nous that he worshipped was embodied in the figure of the goddess Athena. Athena was literally born from the head of Zeus, her name itself reflecting this—a combination of "god" (theos) and "mind" (nous). But Athena came to represent a very particular form of nous—eminently practical, feminine, and earthy. She is the voice that comes to heroes in times of need, instilling in them a calm spirit, orienting their minds toward the perfect idea for victory and success, then giving them the energy to achieve this. In essence, Athena stood for rationality, the greatest gift of the gods to mortals, for it alone could make a human act with divine wisdom. The voice of Athena exists within you right now, a potential you have perhaps felt in moments of calmness and focus, the perfect idea coming to you after much thinking. You are not connected to this higher power in the present because your mind is weighed down with emotions.

Daily Law: Cultivate your inner Athena and worship her. Rationality is then what you will value the most and that which will serve as your guide.

The Laws of Human Nature, 1: Master Your Emotional Self—The Law of Irrationality

Analyze, Scrutinize, Question

It's just as though one's second self were standing beside one; one is
sensible and rational oneself, but the other self is impelled to do
something perfectly senseless, and sometimes very funny; and
suddenly you notice that you are longing to do that amusing thing,
goodness knows why; that is, you want to, as it were, against your will;
though you fight against it with all of your might, you want to.

—FYODOR DOSTOYEVSKY, *A Raw Youth*

To cultivate his inner Athena, Pericles first had to find a way to master
his emotions. Emotions turn us inward, away from nous, away from reality. We dwell on our anger or our insecurities. If we look out at the world
and try to solve problems, we see things through the lens of these emotions; they cloud our vision. Pericles trained himself to never react in the
moment, to never make a decision while under the influence of a strong
emotion. Instead, he analyzed his feelings. Usually when he looked closely
at his insecurities or his anger, he saw that they were not really justified,
and they lost their significance under scrutiny. Sometimes he had to physically get away from the heated Assembly and retire to his house, where
he remained alone for days on end, calming himself down. Slowly, the
voice of Athena would come to him.

Daily Law: Look at those emotions that are continually infecting your
ideas and decisions. Learn to question yourself: Why this anger or resentment? Where does this incessant need for attention come from?

The Laws of Human Nature, 1: Master Your Emotional Self—The Law of Irrationality

OCTOBER 5

Do Not Let Success Intoxicate You

We humans possess a weakness that is latent in us all and will push us into the delusional process without our ever being aware of the dynamic. The weakness stems from our natural tendency to overestimate our skills. We normally have a self-opinion that is somewhat elevated in relation to reality. We have a deep need to feel ourselves superior to others in something—intelligence, beauty, charm, popularity, or saintliness. This can be a positive. A degree of confidence impels us to take on challenges, to push past our supposed limits, and to learn in the process. But once we experience success on any level—increased attention from an individual or group, a promotion, funding for a project—that confidence will tend to rise too quickly, and there will be an ever-growing discrepancy between our self-opinion and reality.

Daily Law: After any kind of success, analyze the components. See the element of luck that is inevitably there, as well as the role that other people, including mentors, played in your good fortune.

The Laws of Human Nature, 11: Know Your Limits—The Law of Grandiosity

See into Your Own Nature

We're very complicated. We don't know where ideas come from. We don't know where our emotions come from. But you can get closer to that. You can have some degree of clarity. You can start to see that kind of shadow side or that stranger within. And that's really the only hope because when you're in denial, you don't realize that you're being a narcissist, you don't realize that you're being governed by your emotions. You could think you're superior to other people just because of the opinion you hold. You can let your shadow side come out without even being aware of it. You need to come to terms with the fact that 95 percent of your ideas and opinions are not your own—they come from what other people have taught you, from what you're reading on the internet, from what other people are saying and doing. You're a conformist—that's who you are. I'm like that and everybody is like that and you realize that only by throwing some light on yourself and realizing that these qualities, these flaws that are built into us, they are inside you too. Only then can you begin to overcome them and use them for productive purposes. Question, question, question. Don't assume that the reason that you feel something, and that it's right just because you feel it. And in that kind of process, you will become rational, you'll become somebody who can use empathy, you will have the ability to judge people properly and accept them for who they are as opposed to continually moralizing, wishing people were something that they're not. You'll have a much smoother path through life, and you'll be much calmer and more peaceful without all that emotional baggage that drags you down. But it starts with looking inward and questioning yourself and not assuming that everything you feel or think is right.

---≈---

Daily Law: Ask yourself, "Where did I pick up this belief?" "Is it true?" "Would I agree with it if I heard it fresh today?"

"'Stop Assuming that Everything You Feel or Think Is Right'—An Interview with Robert Greene," *Quillette*, January 1, 2019

Rationality: A Simple Definition

Clearly the words rational and irrational can be quite loaded. People are always labeling those who disagree with them "irrational." What we need is a simple definition that can be applied as a way of judging, as accurately as possible, the difference between the two. The following shall serve as our barometer: We constantly feel emotions, and they continually infect our thinking, making us veer toward thoughts that please us and soothe our egos. It is impossible to not have our inclinations and feelings somehow involved in what we think. Rational people are aware of this and through introspection and effort are able, to some extent, to subtract emotions from their thinking and counteract their effect. Irrational people have no such awareness. They rush into action without carefully considering the ramifications and consequences. In all cases, the degree of awareness represents the difference. Rational people can readily admit their own irrational tendencies and the need to be vigilant. On the other hand, irrational people become highly emotional when challenged about the emotional roots of their decisions. They are incapable of introspection and learning. Their mistakes make them increasingly defensive.

Daily Law: How would you rate yourself on this scale?

The Laws of Human Nature, 1: Master Your Emotional Self—The Law of Irrationality

OCTOBER 8

The Madness of Groups

Madness is something rare in individuals—but in groups,
parties, peoples, and ages it is the rule.
—FRIEDRICH NIETZSCHE

If as individuals we had some plan that was clearly ridiculous, others would warn us and bring us back down to earth, but in a group the opposite happens—everyone seems to validate the scheme, no matter how delusional (such as invading Iraq and expecting to be greeted as liberators), and there are no outsiders to splash some cold water on us. Whenever you feel unusually certain and excited about a plan or idea, you must step back and gauge whether it is a viral group effect operating on you. If you can detach yourself for a moment from your excitement, you might notice how your thinking is used to rationalize your emotions, to confirm the certainty you want to feel.

Daily Law: Never relinquish your ability to doubt, reflect, and consider other options—your rationality as an individual is your only protection against the madness that can overcome a group.

The Laws of Human Nature, 14: Resist the Downward Pull of the
Group—The Law of Conformity

OCTOBER 9

The Power of Association

Humans are extremely susceptible to the moods, emotions, and even the ways of thinking of those with whom they spend their time. The incurably unhappy and unstable have a particularly strong infecting power because their characters and emotions are so intense. They often present themselves as victims, making it difficult, at first, to see their miseries as self-inflicted. Before you realize the real nature of their problems you have been infected by them. Understand this: the people you associate with are critical. The risk of associating with infectors is that you will waste valuable time and energy trying to free yourself. Through a kind of guilt by association, you will also suffer in the eyes of others.

Daily Law: Be aware of the power those with whom you associate have over you.

The 48 Laws of Power, Law 10: Infection—Avoid the Unhappy and Unlucky

OCTOBER 10

———

Think for Yourself

We human beings tend to be incredibly conventional animals. We get ideas from our parents, from our schooling, from the people around us. And that becomes how we think about everything in the world. We stop thinking for ourselves, and with social media this has become much worse. We're afraid to think for ourselves. The classic example of this cowardice in thinking comes from academics—the people who are supposed to be the most brilliant thinkers of all—many of whom have been largely indoctrinated in a particular way of looking at the world, filled with jargon and orthodoxies. They can never get outside of it—everything they write, everything they see, everything they think about is in that little bubble that they have been inculcated with in their academic training. You need to be fearless. You need to be able to get rid of everything you've ever believed in before. You need to get rid of all the strategies you've used before. All the conventional ideas.

Commandment: You need to think for yourself and not be tied to what other people have told you is reality.

Robert Greene Official, "Irrationality 2020," YouTube, August 29, 2020

Beware the Fragile Ego

Of all the human emotions, none is uglier or more elusive than envy, the sensation that others have more of what we want—possessions, attention, respect. We deserve to have as much as they do yet feel somewhat helpless to get such things. But paradoxically, envy entails the admission to ourselves that we are inferior to another person in something we value. Not only is it painful to admit this inferiority, but it is even worse for others to see that we are feeling this. And so almost as soon as we feel the initial pangs of envy, we are motivated to disguise it to ourselves—it is not envy we feel but unfairness at the distribution of goods or attention, resentment at this unfairness, even anger. The underlying sense of inferiority is too strong, leading to hostility that cannot be vented by a comment or put-down. Sitting with one's envy over a long period of time can be painful and frustrating. Feeling righteous indignation against the envied person, however, can be invigorating. Acting on envy, doing something to harm the other person, brings satisfaction, although the satisfaction is short lived because enviers always find something new to envy.

Daily Law: Envy is perhaps the ugliest human emotion. Destroy it before it destroys you. Develop your sense of self-worth from internal standards and not incessant comparisons.

The Laws of Human Nature, 10: Beware the Fragile Ego—The Law of Envy

See Things as They Are, Not as Your Emotions Color Them

You must see your emotional responses to events as a kind of disease that must be remedied. Fear will make you overestimate the enemy and act too defensively. Anger and impatience will draw you into rash actions that will cut off your options. Overconfidence, particularly as a result of success, will make you go too far. Love and affection will blind you to the treacherous maneuvers of those apparently on your side. Even the subtlest gradations of these emotions can color the way you look at events. The only remedy is to be aware that the pull of emotion is inevitable, to notice it when it is happening, and to compensate for it. When you have success, be extra wary. When you are angry, take no action. When you are fearful, know you are going to exaggerate the dangers you face.

Daily Law: Life demands the utmost in realism, seeing things as they are. The more you can limit or compensate for your emotional responses, the closer you will come to this ideal.

The 33 Strategies of War, Preface

Change Your Circumstances by Changing Your Attitude

The greatest discovery of my generation is the fact that human beings can alter their lives by altering their attitudes of mind.

—WILLIAM JAMES

Imagine the following scenario: A young American must spend a year studying in Paris. He is somewhat timid and cautious, prone to feelings of depression and low self-esteem, but he's genuinely excited by this opportunity. Once there, he finds it hard to speak the language, and the mistakes he makes and the slightly derisory attitude of the Parisians make it even harder for him to learn. He finds the people not friendly at all. The weather is damp and gloomy. The food is too rich. Even Notre Dame Cathedral seems disappointing, the area around it so crowded with tourists. He concludes that Paris is overrated and a rather unpleasant place. Now imagine the same scenario but with a young woman who is more extroverted and has an adventurous spirit. She's not bothered by making mistakes in French, nor by the occasional snide remark from a Parisian. She finds learning the language a pleasant challenge. Others find her spirit engaging. She makes friends more easily, and with more contacts, her knowledge of French improves. She finds the weather romantic and quite suitable to the place. To her, the city represents endless adventures and she finds it enchanting. In this case, two people see and judge the same city in opposite ways. The world simply exists as it is— things or events are not good or bad, right or wrong, ugly or beautiful. It is we, with our particular perspectives, who add color to or subtract it from things and people. We focus on either the beautiful Gothic architecture or the annoying tourists.

Daily Law: We, with our mindset, can make people respond to us in a friendly or unfriendly manner, depending on our anxiety or openness. We shape much of the reality that we perceive, dictated by our moods and emotions.

The Laws of Human Nature, 8: Change Your Circumstances by Changing Your Attitude—The Law of Self-sabotage

Confront Your Dark Side

Our whole being is nothing but a fight against the dark forces
within ourselves. To live is to war with trolls in heart and soul.
To write is to sit in judgment on oneself.

—HENRIK IBSEN

You have crafted a public persona that accentuates your strengths and
conceals your weaknesses. You have repressed the less socially acceptable
traits you naturally possessed as a child. You have become terribly nice
and pleasant. And you have a dark side, one that you are loath to admit
or examine. It contains your deepest insecurities, your secret desires to
hurt people, even those close to you, your fantasies of revenge, your suspicions about others, your hunger for more attention and power. This dark
side haunts your dreams. It leaks out in moments of inexplicable depression, unusual anxiety, touchy moods, sudden neediness, and suspicious
thoughts. It comes out in offhand comments you later regret. And sometimes, it even leads to destructive behavior. You will tend to blame circumstances or other people for these moods and behavior, but they keep
recurring because you are unaware of their source. Depression and anxiety
come from not being your complete self, from always playing a role. It
requires great energy to keep this dark side at bay, but at times unpleasant behavior leaks out as a way to release the inner tension.

Daily Law: Recognize and examine the dark side of your character.
Once subjected to conscious scrutiny, it loses its destructive power.

The Laws of Human Nature, 9: Confront Your Dark Side—The Law of Repression

Create Mental Space from the Group

If we looked at ourselves closely and honestly, we would have to admit that the moment we enter our workspace or any group, we undergo a change. We easily slip into more primitive modes of thinking and behaving, without realizing it. Around others, we naturally tend to feel insecure as to what they think of us. We feel pressure to fit in, and to do so, we begin to shape our thoughts and beliefs to the group orthodoxies. We unconsciously imitate others in the group—in appearances, verbal expressions, and ideas. We tend to worry a lot about our status and where we rank in the hierarchy: "Am I getting as much respect as my colleagues?" This is the primate part of our nature, as we share this obsession with status with our chimpanzee relatives. Depending on patterns from early childhood, in the group setting we become more passive or more aggressive than usual, revealing the less developed sides of our character. To resist this downward pull that groups inevitably exert on us, we must conduct a kind of experiment in human nature with a simple goal in mind—to develop the ability to detach ourselves from the group and create some mental space for true independent thinking. We begin this experiment by accepting the reality of the powerful effect that the group has on us.

Daily Law: Be brutally honest with yourself, aware of how your need to fit in can shape and warp your thinking. Does that anxiety or sense of outrage that we feel come completely from within, or is it inspired by the group?

The Laws of Human Nature, 14: Resist the Downward Pull of the Group—The Law of Conformity

Test for Envy

The root of the Latin word for envy, *invidia*, means "to look through, to probe with the eyes like a dagger." The early meaning of the word was associated with the "evil eye" and the belief that a look could actually convey a curse and physically harm someone. The eyes are indeed a telling indicator, but the envious microexpression affects the entire face. The German philosopher Arthur Schopenhauer devised a quick way to test for envy. Tell suspected enviers some good news about yourself—a promotion, a new and exciting love interest, a book contract. You will notice a very quick expression of disappointment. Their tone of voice as they congratulate you will betray some tension and strain. Equally, tell them some misfortune of yours and notice their uncontrollable microexpression of joy in your pain, what is commonly known as *schadenfreude*. Their eyes light up for a fleeting second. People who are envious cannot help feeling some glee when they hear of the bad luck of those they envy.

> Daily Law: If you see such looks in the first few encounters with someone, and they happen more than once, be on the lookout for a dangerous envier entering your life.

The Laws of Human Nature, 10: Beware the Fragile Ego—The Law of Envy

See into the Spirit of the Times

A man's shortcomings are taken from his epoch;
his virtues and greatness belong to himself.
—JOHANN WOLFGANG VON GOETHE

You must alter your attitude toward your own generation. We like to imagine that we are autonomous and that our values and ideas come from within, not without, but this is in fact not the case. Your goal is to understand as deeply as possible how profoundly the spirit of your generation, and the times that you live in, have influenced how you perceive the world. Consider yourself a kind of archaeologist digging into your own past and that of your generation, looking for artifacts, for observations that you can piece together to form a picture of the underlying spirit. When you examine your memories, try to do so with some distance, even when you recall the emotions you felt at the time. Catch yourself in the inevitable process of making judgments of good and bad about your generation or the next one, and let go of them. You can develop such a skill through practice. Forging such an attitude will play a key role in your development.

Daily Law: With some distance and awareness, you can become much more than a follower of or a rebel against your generation; you can mold your own relationship to the zeitgeist and become a formidable trendsetter.

The Laws of Human Nature, 17: Seize the Historical
Moment—The Law of Generational Myopia

Think Like a Writer

Anton Chekhov's family was large and poor, and his father, an alcoholic, mercilessly beat all of the children, including young Chekhov. Chekhov became a doctor and took up writing as a side career. He applied his training as a doctor to the human animal, his goal to understand what makes us so irrational, so unhappy, and so dangerous. In his stories and plays, he found it immensely therapeutic to get inside his characters and make sense of even the worst types. In this way, he could forgive anybody, even his father. His approach in these cases was to imagine that each person, no matter how twisted, has a reason for what they've become, a logic that makes sense to them. In their own way, they are striving for fulfillment, but irrationally. By stepping back and imagining their story from the inside, Chekhov demythologized the brutes and aggressors; he cut them down to human size. They no longer elicited hatred but rather pity.

Daily Law: Think more like a writer in approaching the people you deal with, even the worst sorts.

The Laws of Human Nature, 1: Master Your Emotional Self—The Law of Irrationality

Accept People as Facts

If you come across any special trait of meanness or stupidity . . .
you must be careful not to let it annoy or distress you, but to look
upon it merely as an addition to your knowledge—a new fact to
be considered in studying the character of humanity. Your attitude
towards it will be that of the mineralogist who stumbles upon a
very characteristic specimen of a mineral.

—ARTHUR SCHOPENHAUER

Interactions with people are the major source of emotional turmoil, but it doesn't have to be that way. The problem is that we are continually judging people, wishing they were something that they are not. We want to change them. We want them to think and act a certain way, most often the way we think and act. And because this is not possible, because everyone is different, we are continually frustrated and upset. Instead, see other people as phenomena, as neutral as comets or plants. They simply exist. They come in all varieties, making life rich and interesting. Work with what they give you, instead of resisting and trying to change them. Make understanding people a fun game, the solving of puzzles. It is all part of the human comedy. Yes, people are irrational, but so are you. Make your acceptance of human nature as radical as possible. This will calm you down and help you observe people more dispassionately, understanding them on a deeper level. You will stop projecting your own emotions on to them. All of this will give you more balance and calmness, more mental space for thinking.

Daily Law: Examine the faults you see in others and how they are in you as well.

The Laws of Human Nature, 1: Master Your Emotional Self—The Law of Irrationality

See Beyond the Moment

We humans tend to live in the moment. It is the animal part of our nature. We respond first and foremost to what we see and hear, to what is most dramatic in an event. But we are not merely animals tied to the present. Human reality encompasses the past—every event is connected to something that happened before in an endless chain of historical causation. Any present problem has deep roots in the past. It also encompasses the future. Whatever we do has consequences that stretch far into the years to come. When we limit our thinking to what our senses provide, to what is immediate, we descend to the pure animal level in which our reasoning powers are neutralized. We are no longer aware of why or how things come about. We imagine that some successful scheme that has lasted a few months can only get better. We no longer give thought to the possible consequences of anything we set in motion. We react to what is given in the moment, based on only a small piece of the puzzle. Salesmen and demagogues play on this weakness in human nature to con us with the prospect of easy gains and instant gratification. Our only antidote is to train ourselves to continually detach from the immediate rush of events and elevate our perspective.

Daily Law: Instead of merely reacting, step back and look at the wider context. Consider the ramifications of any action you take. Realize that is often better to do nothing, to not react, to let time go by and see what it reveals.

The Laws of Human Nature, 6: Elevate Your Perspective—The Law of Shortsightedness

Recognize Your Aggressive Impulses

Men are not gentle, friendly creatures wishing for love, who simply
defend themselves if attacked. . . . A powerful desire for aggression
has to be reckoned as part of their . . . endowment.

—SIGMUND FREUD

What this means is the following: All of us understand that humans have
been capable of much violence and aggression in the past and in the present. We know that out there in the world there are sinister criminals,
greedy and unscrupulous businesspeople, belligerent negotiators, and
sexual aggressors. But we create a sharp dividing line between those examples and us. We have a powerful block against imagining any kind of
continuum or spectrum when it comes to our own aggressive moments
and those of the more extreme variety in others. We in fact define the
word to describe the stronger manifestations of aggression, excluding ourselves. It is always the other who is belligerent, who starts things, who is
aggressive. This is a profound misconception of human nature. Aggression is a tendency that is latent in every single human individual. It is a
tendency wired into our species. We became the preeminent animal on
this planet precisely because of our aggressive energy, supplemented by
our intelligence and cunning. We cannot separate this aggressiveness
from the way we attack problems, alter the environment to make our lives
easier, fight injustice, or create anything on a large scale.

Daily Law: Look for signs of your own aggressive impulses in past
actions—how they led to friction or success.

The Laws of Human Nature, 16: See the Hostility Behind the Friendly
Façade—The Law of Aggression

Lost in Trivia

You feel overwhelmed by the complexity of your work. You feel the need to be on top of all the details and global trends so you can control things better, but you are drowning in information. It is hard to see the proverbial forest for the trees. This is a sure sign that you have lost a sense of your priorities—which facts are more important, what problems or details require more attention. What you need is a mental filtering system based on a scale of priorities and your long-term goals. Knowing what you want to accomplish in the end will help you weed out the essential from the nonessential. You do not have to know all the details. Sometimes you need to delegate—let your subordinates handle the information gathering.

> Daily Law: Remember that greater control over events will come from realistic assessments of the situation, precisely what is made most difficult by a brain submerged in trivia.

The Laws of Human Nature, 6: Elevate Your Perspective—The Law of Shortsightedness

The Lost Self

Your task is to let go of the rigidity that takes hold of you as you over-identify with the expected gender role. Power lies in exploring that middle range between the masculine and the feminine, in playing against people's expectations. Return to the harder or softer sides of your character that you have lost or repressed. In relating to people, expand your repertoire by developing greater empathy, or by learning to be less deferential. When confronting a problem or resistance from others, train yourself to respond in different ways—attacking when you normally defend, or vice versa. In your thinking, learn to blend the analytical with the intuitive in order to become more creative.

Do not be afraid to bring out the more sensitive or ambitious sides to your character. These repressed parts of you are yearning to be let out. In the theater of life, expand the roles that you play. Don't worry about people's reactions to any changes in you they sense. You are not so easy to categorize, which will fascinate them and give you the power to play with their perceptions of you, altering them at will.

Daily Law: Return to the harder or softer sides of your character that you have lost or repressed.

The Laws of Human Nature, 12: Reconnect to the Masculine or Feminine within You—The Law of Gender Rigidity

Know How Little You Know

When I left him, I reasoned thus with myself: I am wiser than this
man, for neither of us appears to know anything great and good; but
he fancies he knows something, although he knows nothing; whereas
I, as I do not know anything, so I do not fancy I do. In this trifling
particular, then, I appear to be wiser than he, because I do not
fancy I know what I do not know.

—SOCRATES

We like to scoff at the superstitious and irrational ideas that most people
held in the seventeenth century. Imagine how those of the twenty-fifth
century will scoff at ours. Our knowledge of the world is limited, despite
the advances of science. Our ideas are conditioned by the prejudices in-
stilled in us by our parents, by our culture, and by the historical period
we live in. They are further limited by the increasing rigidity of the
mind. A bit more humility about what we know would make us all more
curious and interested in a wider range of ideas.

Daily Law: When it comes to the ideas and opinions you hold, see
them as toys or building blocks that you are playing with. Some you
will keep, others you will knock down, but your spirit remains flexible
and playful.

The Laws of Human Nature, 7: Soften People's Resistance by Confirming
Their Self-Opinion—The Law of Defensiveness

Examine Your Emotions to Their Roots

You are angry. Let the feeling settle from within, and think about it. Was it triggered by something seemingly trivial or petty? That is a sure sign that something or someone else is behind it. Perhaps a more uncomfortable emotion is at the source—such as envy or paranoia. You need to look at this square in the eye. Dig below any trigger points to see where they started. For these purposes, it might be wise to use a journal in which you record your self-assessments with ruthless objectivity. Your greatest danger here is your ego and how it makes you unconsciously maintain illusions about yourself. These may be comforting in the moment, but in the long run they make you defensive and unable to learn or progress. Find a neutral position from which you can observe your actions, with a bit of detachment and even humor. Soon all of this will become second nature, and when the Emotional Self suddenly rears its head in some situation, you will see it as it happens and be able to step back and find that neutral position.

Daily Law: Develop the habit of examining in depth your own emotional responses. You will end up slowly eliminating unnecessary reactions.

The Laws of Human Nature, 1: Master Your Emotional Self—The Law of Irrationality

Resist Simple Explanations

It is not an enemy who taunts me—then I could bear it; it is not an
adversary who deals insolently with me—then I could hide from him.
But it is you, my equal, my companion, my familiar friend. . . . My
companion stretched out his hand against his friends, he violated his
covenant. His speech was smoother than butter, yet war was in his
heart; his words were softer than oil, yet they were drawn swords.

—PSALMS, 55:12–15, 20–21

We humans have a particular limitation to our reasoning powers that
causes us endless problems: when we are thinking about someone or
about something that has happened to us, we generally opt for the sim-
plest, most easily digestible interpretation. An acquaintance is good or
bad, nice or mean, his or her intentions noble or nefarious; an event is
positive or negative, beneficial or harmful; we are happy or sad. The truth
is that nothing in life is ever so simple. People are invariably a mix of
good and bad qualities, strengths and weaknesses. Their intentions in
doing something can be helpful and harmful to us at the same time, a
result of their ambivalent feelings toward us. Even the most positive event
has a downside. And we often feel happy and sad at the same time. Re-
ducing things to simpler terms makes them easier for us to handle, but
because it is not related to reality, it also means we are constantly misun-
derstanding and misreading.

**Daily Law: It would be of infinite benefit for us to allow more nuances
and ambiguity into our judgments of people and events.**

The 33 Strategies of War, Strategy 32: Dominate while Seeming to
Submit—The Passive-Aggression Strategy

See Your Shadow

My devil had long been caged, he came out roaring.

—DR. JEKYLL

The writer Robert Louis Stevenson expressed the law of repression in the novel *The Strange Case of Dr. Jekyll and Mr. Hyde*, published in 1886. The main character, Dr. Jekyll, is a well-respected and wealthy doctor/scientist with impeccable manners, so much like the paragons of goodness in our culture. He invents a concoction that transforms him into Mr. Hyde, the embodiment of his Shadow, who proceeds to murder and rape and indulge in the wildest of sensual pleasures. Stevenson's idea is that the more civilized and moral we outwardly become, the more potentially dangerous is the Shadow, which we so fiercely deny. The solution is not more repression and correctness. We can never alter human nature through enforced niceness. The pitchfork doesn't work. Nor is the solution to seek release for our Shadow in the group, which is volatile and dangerous. Instead the answer is to see our Shadow in action and become more self-aware. It is hard to project onto others our own secret impulses or to overidealize some cause, once we are made aware of the mechanism operating within us.

Daily Law: Through self-knowledge we can find a way to integrate the dark side into our consciousness productively and creatively. In doing so, we become more authentic and complete, exploiting to the maximum the energies we naturally possess.

The Laws of Human Nature, 9: Confront Your Dark Side—The Law of Repression

Move Closer to What You Envy

For not many men . . . can love a friend who fortune prospers without envying; and about the envious brain cold poison clings and doubles all the pain life brings him. His own woundings he must nurse, and feel another's gladness like a curse.

—AESCHYLUS

People tend to hide their problems and to put their best face forward. We only see and hear of their triumphs, their new relationships, their brilliant ideas that will land them a gold mine. If we moved closer—if we saw the quarrels that go on behind closed doors or the horrible boss that goes with that new job—we would have less reason to feel envy. Nothing is ever so perfect as it seems, and often we would see that we are mistaken if we only looked closely enough. Spend time with that family you envy and wish you had as your own, and you will begin to reassess your opinion. If you envy people with greater fame and attention, remind yourself that with such attention comes a lot of hostility and scrutiny that is quite painful. Wealthy people are often miserable. Read any account of the last ten years of the life of Aristotle Onassis (1906–1975), one of the wealthiest men in history, married to the glamorous Jacqueline Kennedy, and you will see that his wealth brought him endless nightmares, including the most spoiled and unloving of children. The process of moving closer is twofold: on the one hand, try to actually look behind the glittering facades people present, and on the other hand, simply imagine the inevitable disadvantages that go along with their position.

Daily Law: Remember that few people are as happy as the image they present. See past their facades and you will appreciate what you have.

The Laws of Human Nature, 10: Beware the Fragile Ego—The Law of Envy

Manage Your Grandiose Tendencies

Let us say that you have a project to realize. You can think of the project as a block of marble you must sculpt into something precise and beautiful. The block is much larger than you and the material is quite resistant, but the task is not impossible. With enough effort, focus, and resiliency you can slowly carve it into what you need. You must begin, however, with a proper sense of proportion—goals are hard to reach, people are resistant, and you have limits to what you can do. With such a realistic attitude, you can summon up the requisite patience and get to work. Imagine, however, that your brain has succumbed to a psychological disease that affects your perception of size and proportion. Instead of seeing the task you are facing as rather large and the material resistant, under the influence of this disease you perceive the block of marble as relatively small and malleable. Losing your sense of proportion, you believe it won't take long to fashion the block into the image you have in your mind of the finished product. You imagine that the people you are trying to reach are not naturally resistant but quite predictable. You know how they'll respond to your great idea—they'll love it. In fact, they need you and your work more than you need them. They should seek you out. The emphasis is not on what you need to do to succeed but on what you feel you deserve. You can foresee a lot of attention coming your way with this project, but if you fail, other people must be to blame, because you have gifts, your cause is the right one, and only those who are malicious or envious could stand in your way. We can call this psychological disease grandiosity.

Daily Law: Accept your limitations and work with what you have, rather than fantasize about godlike powers you can never attain. Maintain a realistic attitude.

The Laws of Human Nature, 11: Know Your Limits—The Law of Grandiosity

The Myth of Progress

A final word on the irrational in human nature: do not imagine that the more extreme types of irrationality have somehow been overcome through progress and enlightenment. Throughout history we witness continual cycles of rising and falling levels of the irrational. The great golden age of Pericles, with its philosophers and its first stirrings of the scientific spirit, was followed by an age of superstition, cults, and intolerance. This same phenomenon happened after the Italian Renaissance. That this cycle is bound to recur again and again is part of human nature. The irrational simply changes its look and its fashions. We may no longer have literal witch hunts, but in the twentieth century, not so very long ago, we witnessed the show trials of Stalin, the McCarthy hearings in the U.S. Senate, and the mass persecutions during the Chinese Cultural Revolution. Various cults are continually being generated, including cults of personality and the fetishizing of celebrities. Technology now inspires religious fervor. People have a desperate need to believe in something and they will find it anywhere. Polls have revealed that increasing numbers of people believe in ghosts, spirits, and angels, in the twenty-first century. As long as there are humans, the irrational will find its voices and means of spreading.

Daily Law: Rationality is something to be acquired by individuals, not by mass movements or technological progress. Feeling superior and beyond it is a sure sign that the irrational is at work.

The Laws of Human Nature, 1: Master Your Emotional Self—The Law of Irrationality

You Are the Obstacle

In this world, where the game is played with loaded dice, a man
must have a temper of iron, with armor proof to the blows of fate, and
weapons to make his way against men. Life is one long battle; we have to
fight at every step; and Voltaire very rightly says that if we succeed, it is
at the point of the sword, and that we die with the weapon in our hand.

—ARTHUR SCHOPENHAUER

Life is battle and struggle, and you will constantly find yourself facing
bad situations, destructive relationships, dangerous engagements. How
you confront these difficulties will determine your fate. If you feel lost
and confused, if you lose your sense of direction, if you cannot tell the
difference between friend and foe, you have only yourself to blame. Everything depends on your frame of mind and on how you look at the world.
A shift of perspective can transform you from a passive and confused
mercenary into a motivated and creative fighter.

Daily Law: As Xenophon said, your obstacles are not rivers or mountains or other people; your obstacle is yourself.

The 33 Strategies of War, Strategy 1: Declare War on Your Enemies—The Polarity Strategy

November

The Rational Human

REALIZING YOUR HIGHER SELF

≈

The lower self tends to be stronger. Its impulses pull us down into emotional reactions and defensive postures, making us feel self-righteous and superior to others. It makes us grab for immediate pleasures and distractions, always taking the path of least resistance. It induces us to adopt what other people are thinking, losing ourselves in the group. We feel the impulses of the higher self when we are drawn out of ourselves, wanting to connect more deeply with others, to absorb our minds in our work, to think instead of react, to follow our own path in life, and to discover what makes us unique. The lower is the more animal and reactive side of our nature, and one that we easily slip into. The higher is the more truly human side of our nature, the side that makes us thoughtful and self-aware. Because the higher impulse is weaker, connecting to it requires effort and insight. Bringing out this ideal self within us is what we all really want, because it is only in developing this side of ourselves that we humans feel truly fulfilled. The month of November will help you accomplish this by making you aware of the potentially positive and active elements contained within your nature.

There's a common misconception that people have about human rationality. This misconception is that rationality involves the suppression or the repression of emotions. In other words, if you're feeling fear or anger or love or hatred, you have to tamp down those emotions. You have to get rid of them in order to be rational.

In this view, rationality isn't something very fun or very exciting. It's kind of like health food. It's good for you, but it doesn't taste very good. I want to tell you that this is actually quite wrong. It's actually the opposite. Rationality involves some very important emotions that if you're not experiencing you can't begin to think rationally

Neuroscience has demonstrated this with studies of people who've had damage to the emotional centers in their brain. After, they are not capable of making rational decisions or rational thinking.

I can illustrate my idea of rationality with some examples you may have experienced.

Let's say you have a plan—something you want to accomplish in life. There's a book you want to write, or you want to lose weight or start a business. You've been feeling very frustrated and impatient with the course of your life. So you decide, I'm going to stop this, I'm going to actually get this project done, I'm going to create this business, or whatever it is. And you think about it and take gradual steps to get there.

Or let's say you're dealing with a nasty divorce situation, and you're fighting over custody of your child, whom you love very much. It's getting so ugly that you realize if it keeps going this way the child will actually be damaged by this process. And so at some point you take a step back and you think, "What's really important is the long-term health of my child, so I'm not going to get involved in this process. I'm actually going to back off, and I'm going to think of what's best for the child."

Or let us say finally, there's a very toxic person involved in your life. Some kind of raging narcissist, for instance, who's getting you enmeshed in all of this drama that's making you miserable. And at some point, you tell yourself, "Damn it, I've had enough of this person. I'm going to figure out a way to get rid of this narcissist." It's not easy because this person is entangled in your life in all these ways. So you step back, and you get control of yourself, and you think, "How can I get rid of this person?" And then you do it. Finally, the narcissist is gone, and you feel a tremendous sense of relief.

Let's look at these three examples.

In the first one—you're fed up with the fact that you're overweight or that you haven't been able to accomplish any of your dreams or desires in life. That frustration—that emotion—impels you to take action, which is to go through the steps of thinking rationally of how to get out of this state of frustration. And then, when it's over, when you finally have realized the project or goal, you feel a tremendous sense of relief and pride.

In the case of the child—you're impelled by the sense of empathy and love for the child. You're worried about them and that love makes you step back and go through this rational process. And when it's over, you feel so much better about yourself.

Or with that toxic person in your life—you're full of anger, but you step back, you take rational steps, and you get rid of them. You feel joy and relief.

So if you didn't feel these emotions at first, you would never be able to take the actions that will lead you to some kind of rational decision. And if you did not feel the rewards of pride, of empathy, and love of accomplishing something, you would never be motivated to go through the rational process again and again and again. So rationality involves emotions and thinking. Rationality is not about tamping down your emotions. It's about creating a beautiful harmony between the thinking process and the emotional animal parts of our nature. It is important to not see the path to rationality as something painful and ascetic. In fact, it brings powers that are immensely satisfying and pleasurable, much deeper than the more manic pleasures the world tends to offer us.

NOVEMBER 1

Hope for Us All

Despite our pronounced irrational tendencies, two factors should give us all hope. First and foremost is the existence throughout history and in all cultures of people of high rationality, the types who have made progress possible. They serve as ideals for all of us to aim for. These include Pericles, the ruler Aśoka of ancient India, Marcus Aurelius of ancient Rome, Marguerite de Valois in medieval France, Leonardo da Vinci, Charles Darwin, Abraham Lincoln, the writer Anton Chekhov, the anthropologist Margaret Mead, and the businessman Warren Buffett, to name but a few. All of these types share certain qualities—a realistic appraisal of themselves and their weaknesses; a devotion to truth and reality; a tolerant attitude toward people; and the ability to reach goals that they have set. The second factor is that almost all of us at some point in our lives have experienced moments of greater rationality. This often comes with what we shall call the maker's mindset. We have a project to get done, perhaps with a deadline. The only emotion we can afford is excitement and energy. Other emotions simply make it impossible to concentrate. Because we have to get results, we become exceptionally practical. We focus on the work—our mind calm, our ego not intruding. If people try to interrupt or infect us with emotions, we resent it.

Daily Law: These moments—as fleeting as a few weeks or hours—reveal the rational self that is waiting to come out. It just requires some awareness and some practice.

The Laws of Human Nature, 1: Master Your Emotional Self—The Law of Irrationality

Keep Free of the Emotional Whirlpool

To succeed, you have to master your emotions. But even if you succeed in gaining such balance and self-control, you can never control the temperamental dispositions of those around you. And this presents a great danger. Most people operate in a whirlpool of emotions, constantly reacting, churning up squabbles and conflicts. Your self-control and autonomy will only bother and infuriate them. They will try to draw you into the whirlpool, begging you to take sides in their endless battles, or to make peace for them. If you succumb to their emotional entreaties, little by little you will find your mind and time occupied by their problems. Do not allow whatever compassion and pity you possess to suck you in. You can never win in this game; the conflicts can only multiply. You may be afraid that people will condemn you as heartless, but in the end, maintaining your independence and self-reliance will gain you more respect and place you in a position of power from which you can choose to help others on your own initiative.

Daily Law: Remember that you have only so much energy and so much time. Every moment wasted on the dramas of others subtracts from your strength.

The 48 Laws of Power, Law 20: Do Not Commit to Anyone

Increase Your Reaction Time

"Trust your feelings!"—But feelings are nothing final or original;
behind feelings there stand judgments and evaluations which we
inherit in the form of . . . inclinations, aversions. The inspiration born
of a feeling is the grandchild of a judgment—and often of a false
judgment!—and in any event not a child of your own! To trust one's
feelings—means to give more obedience to one's grandfather and
grandmother and their grandparents than to the gods which
are in *us*: our reason and our experience.

—FRIEDRICH NIETZSCHE

This power comes through practice and repetition. When some event or interaction requires a response, you must train yourself to step back. This could mean physically removing yourself to a place where you can be alone and not feel any pressure to respond. Or it could mean writing that angry email but not sending it. You sleep on it for a day or two. You do not make phone calls or communicate while feeling some sudden emotion, particularly resentment. If you find yourself rushing to commit to people, to hire or be hired by them, step back and give it a day. Cool the emotions down. The longer you can take the better, because perspective comes with time.

Daily Law: Consider this like resistance training—the longer you can resist reacting, the more mental space you have for actual reflection, and the stronger your mind will become.

The Laws of Human Nature, 1: Master Your Emotional Self—The Law of Irrationality

NOVEMBER 4

Make Envy a Spur to Achievement

Instead of wanting to hurt or steal from the person who has achieved more, we should desire to raise ourselves up to his or her level. In this way, envy becomes a spur to excellence. We may even try to be around people who will stimulate such competitive desires, people who are slightly above us in skill level. To make this work requires a few psychological shifts. First, we must come to believe that we have the capacity to raise ourselves up. Confidence in our overall abilities to learn and improve will serve as a tremendous antidote to envy. Instead of wishing to have what another has and resorting to sabotage out of helplessness, we feel the urge to get the same for ourselves and believe we have the ability to do so. Second, we must develop a solid work ethic to back this up. If we are rigorous and persistent, we will be able to overcome almost any obstacle and elevate our position. People who are lazy and undisciplined are much more prone to feeling envy.

Daily Law: We cannot stop the comparing mechanism in our brains, so it is best to redirect it into something productive and creative.

The Laws of Human Nature, 10: Beware the Fragile Ego—The Law of Envy

Know Yourself Thoroughly

He who knows others is wise; he who knows himself is enlightened.

—LAO TZU

The Emotional Self thrives on ignorance. The moment you are aware of how it operates and dominates you is the moment it loses its hold on you and can be tamed. Therefore, your first step toward the rational is always inward. You want to catch that Emotional Self in action. For this purpose, you must reflect on how you operate under stress. What particular weaknesses come out in such moments—the desire to please, to bully or control, deep levels of mistrust? Look at your decisions, especially those that have been ineffective—can you see a pattern, an underlying insecurity that impels them? Examine your strengths, what makes you different from other people. This will help you decide upon goals that mesh with your long-term interests and that are aligned with your skills. By knowing and valuing what marks you as different, you will also be able to resist the pull of group bias and effect.

Daily Law: Can you look at yourself with some distance and see through the fog of self-deception?

The Laws of Human Nature, 1: Master Your Emotional Self—The Law of Irrationality

Who Is to Blame?

Whenever anything goes wrong, it is human nature to blame this person or that. Let other people engage in such stupidity, led around by their noses, seeing only what is immediately visible to the eye. You see things differently. When an action goes wrong—in business, in politics, in life—trace it back to the policy that inspired it in the first place. The goal was misguided. This means that you yourself are largely the agent of anything bad that happens to you. With more prudence, wiser policies, and greater vision, you could have avoided the danger. So when something goes wrong, look deep into yourself—not in an emotional way, to blame yourself or indulge your feelings of guilt, but to make sure that you start your next campaign with a firmer step and greater vision.

Daily Law: See the role you played in any failure; it can always be found.

The 33 Strategies of War, Strategy 12: Lose Battles but Win the War—Grand Strategy

Practice Mitfreude

The serpent that stings us means to hurt us and rejoices as it
does so; the lowest animal can imagine the pain of others. But to
imagine the joy of others and to rejoice at it is the highest
privilege of the highest animals.

—FRIEDRICH NIETZSCHE

Schadenfreude, the experience of pleasure in the pain of other people, is distinctly related to envy, as several studies have demonstrated. When we envy someone, we are prone to feel excitement, even joy, if they experience a setback or suffer in some way. But it would be wise to practice instead the opposite, what the philosopher Friedrich Nietzsche called *Mitfreude*—"joying with." This means that instead of merely congratulating people on their good fortune, something easy to do and easily forgotten, you must instead actively try to feel their joy, as a form of empathy. This can be somewhat unnatural, as our first tendency is to feel a pang of envy, but we can train ourselves to imagine how it must feel to others to experience their happiness or satisfaction. This not only cleans our brain of ugly envy but also creates an unusual form of rapport. If we are the targets of Mitfreude, we feel the other person's genuine excitement at our good fortune, instead of just hearing words, and it induces us to feel the same for them. Because it is such a rare occurrence, it contains great power to bond people.

Daily Law: Internalize other people's joy. In doing so, we increase our own capacity to feel this emotion in relation to our own experiences.

The Laws of Human Nature, 10: Beware the Fragile Ego—The Law of Envy

Supreme Patience

Time is an artificial concept that we ourselves have created to make the limitlessness of eternity and the universe more bearable, more human. Since we have constructed the concept of time, we are also able to mold it to some degree, to play tricks with it. The time of a child is long and slow, with vast expanses; the time of an adult whizzes by frighteningly fast. Time, then, depends on perception, which, we know, can be willfully altered. This is the first thing to understand in mastering the art of timing. If the inner turmoil caused by our emotions tends to make time move faster, it follows that once we control our emotional responses to events, time will move much more slowly. This altered way of dealing with things tends to lengthen our perception of future time, opens up possibilities that fear and anger close off, and allows us the patience that is the principal requirement in the art of timing.

Never seem to be in a hurry—hurrying betrays a lack of control over yourself, and over time. Always seem patient, as if you know that everything will come to you eventually. Become a detective of the right moment; sniff out the spirit of the times, the trends that will carry you to power. Learn to stand back when the time is not yet ripe, and to strike fiercely when it has reached fruition.

Daily Law: Practice patience. Wait a day before taking action on that pressing problem.

The 48 Laws of Power, Law 35: Master the Art of Timing

Channel Your Grandiose Impulses

Grandiosity is a form of primal energy we all possess. It impels us to want something more than we have, to be recognized and esteemed by others, and to feel connected to something larger. The problem is not with the energy itself, which can be used to fuel our ambitions, but with the direction it takes. Normally grandiosity makes us imagine we are greater and more superior than is actually the case. We can call this fantastical grandiosity because it is based on our fantasies and the skewed impression we get from any attention we receive. Fantastical grandiosity will make you flit from one fantastic idea to another, imagining all the accolades and attention you'll receive but never realizing any of them. You must do the opposite. You want to get into the habit of focusing deeply and completely on a single project or problem. You want the goal to be relatively simple to reach, and within a time frame of months and not years. You will want to break this down into mini steps and goals along the way. Your objective here is to enter a state of flow, in which your mind becomes increasingly absorbed in the work, to the point at which ideas come to you at odd hours. This feeling of flow should be pleasurable and addicting. If you do not enter this state of flow, you are inevitably multitasking and stopping the focus. Work on overcoming this. This could be a project you work on outside your job. It is not the number of hours you put in but the intensity and consistent effort you bring to it. Related to this, you want this project to involve skills you already have or are in the process of developing. Your goal is to see continual improvement in your skill level, which will certainly come from the depth of your focus. Your confidence will rise. That should be enough to keep you advancing.

Daily Law: Don't allow yourself to engage in fantasies about other projects on the horizon. You want to channel this grandiose energy by absorbing yourself in your work as deeply as possible.

The Laws of Human Nature, 11: Know Your Limits—The Law of Grandiosity

Transcending Tribalism

Tribalism has its roots in the deepest and most primitive parts of our nature, but it is now coupled with much greater technological prowess, which makes it all the more dangerous. What allowed us thousands of years ago to bind our group tightly and survive could now easily lead to our extinction as a species. The tribe feels its very existence at stake by the presence of the enemy. There is little middle ground. Battles can be more intense and violent between tribes. The future of the human race will likely depend on our ability to transcend this tribalism and to see our fate as interconnected with everyone else's. We are one species, all descendants of the same original humans, all brothers and sisters. Our differences are mostly an illusion. Imagining differences is part of the madness of groups. We must see ourselves as one large reality group and experience a deep sense of belonging to it. To solve the man-made problems threatening us will require cooperation on a much higher level and a practical spirit missing from the tribe. This does not mean the end of diverse cultures and the richness that comes with them. In fact, the reality group encourages inner diversity.

Daily Law: We must come to the conclusion that the primary group we belong to is that of the human race. That is our inevitable future. Anything else is regressive and far too dangerous.

The Laws of Human Nature, 14: Resist the Downward Pull of
the Group—The Law of Conformity

Ascend the Mountain

For us humans, locked in the present moment, it is as if we are living at the base of the mountain. What is most apparent to our eyes—the other people around us, the surrounding forest—gives us a limited, skewed vision of the reality. The passage of time is like a slow ascent up the mountain. The emotions we felt in the present are no longer so strong; we can detach ourselves and see things more clearly. The further we ascend with the passage of time, the more information we add to the picture. What we saw three months after the fact is not quite as accurate as what we come to know a year later. It is in the animal part of your nature to be most impressed by what you can see and hear in the present—the latest news reports and trends, the opinions and actions of the people around you, whatever seems the most dramatic. This is what makes you fall for alluring schemes that promise quick results and easy money. This is also what makes you overreact to present circumstances—becoming overly exhilarated or panicky as events turn one direction or the other. Your eyes must be on the larger trends that govern events, on that which is not immediately visible. Never lose sight of your long-term goals. With an elevated perspective, you will have the patience and clarity to reach almost any objective.

Daily Law: Manufacture the effect of time by giving yourself an expanded view in the present moment.

The Laws of Human Nature, 6: Elevate Your Perspective—The Law of Shortsightedness

NOVEMBER 12

Break the Codes of Convention

For centuries, and still to this day, gender roles represent the most powerful convention of all. What men and women can do or say has been highly controlled, to the point where it seems almost to represent biological differences instead of social conventions. Women in particular are socialized to be extra nice and agreeable. They feel continual pressure to adhere to this and mistake it for something natural and biological. Some of the most influential women in history were those who deliberately broke with these codes—performers like Marlene Dietrich and Josephine Baker, political figures such as Eleanor Roosevelt, businesswomen such as Coco Chanel. They brought out their Shadow and showed it by acting in ways that were traditionally thought of as masculine, blending and confusing gender roles. Even Jacqueline Kennedy Onassis gained great power by playing against the type of the traditional political wife. She had a pronounced malicious streak. When people displeased her, she showed it rather openly. She seemed to care little what others thought of her. And she became a sensation because of the naturalness she exuded. In general, consider this a form of exorcism. Once you show these desires and impulses, they no longer lie hidden in corners of your personality, twisting and operating in secret ways.

Daily Law: Show the Shadow. Release your demons and enhance your presence as an authentic human.

The Laws of Human Nature, 9: Confront Your Dark Side—The Law of Repression

Suffer Fools Gladly

You cannot be everywhere or fight everyone. Your time and energy are limited, and you must learn how to preserve them. Exhaustion and frustration can ruin your presence of mind. The world is full of fools—people who cannot wait to get results, who change with the wind, who can't see past their noses. You encounter them everywhere: the indecisive boss, the rash colleague, the hysterical subordinate. When working alongside fools, do not fight them. Instead think of them the way you think of children, or pets, not important enough to affect your mental balance. The ability to stay cheerful in the face of fools is an important skill.

Daily Law: Detach yourself emotionally from fools. And while you're inwardly laughing at their foolishness, indulge them in one of their more harmless ideas.

The 33 Strategies of War, Strategy 3: Amidst the Turmoil of Events, Do Not Lose Your Presence of Mind—The Counterbalance Strategy

Project Saintliness

No matter what historical period we are living through, there are certain traits that are always seen as positive and that you must know how to display. For instance, the appearance of saintliness never goes out of fashion. Appearing saintly today is certainly different in content from the sixteenth century, but the essence is the same—you embody what is considered good and above reproach. In the modern world, this means showing yourself as progressive, supremely tolerant, and open minded. You will want to be seen giving generously to certain causes and supporting them on social media. Projecting sincerity and honesty always plays well. A few public confessions of your weaknesses and vulnerabilities will do the trick. For some reason people see signs of humility as authentic, even though people might very well be simulating them. Learn how to occasionally lower your head and appear humble. If dirty work must be done, get others to do it. Your hands are clean. Never overtly play the Machiavellian leader—that only works well on television.

Daily Law: If people largely judge others by appearances, learn to take control of the dynamic by adopting the appropriate persona. An air of humility, even saintliness, always works well. Avoid any indication of hypocrisy or superiority in this.

The Laws of Human Nature, 3: See Through People's Masks—The Law of Role-Playing

Adopt a Generous Spirit

We all carry with us traumas and hurts from early childhood. In our social life, as we get older, we accumulate disappointments and slights. We are often haunted by a sense of worthlessness, of not really deserving the good things in life. We all have moments of great doubt about ourselves. These emotions can lead to obsessive thoughts that dominate our minds. They make us curtail what we experience as a way to manage our anxiety and disappointments. They make us turn to alcohol or any kind of habit to numb the pain. Without realizing it, we assume a negative and fearful attitude toward life. This becomes our self-imposed prison. But this is not how it has to be. We can free ourselves. It comes from a choice, a different way of looking at the world, a change in attitude. This freedom essentially comes from adopting a generous spirit—toward others and toward ourselves. By accepting people, by understanding and if possible even loving them for their human nature, we can liberate our minds from obsessive and petty emotions. We can stop reacting to everything people do and say. We can have some distance and stop ourselves from taking everything personally. Mental space is freed up for higher pursuits. Once we feel the exhilarating power from this new attitude, we will want to take it as far as possible.

Daily Law: When we feel generous toward ourselves and others, they feel drawn to us and want to match our spirit.

The Laws of Human Nature, 8: Change Your Circumstances by Changing Your Attitude—The Law of Self-Sabotage

Integrate the Shadow Side

From an early age, Abraham Lincoln liked to analyze himself, and a re-current theme in his self-examinations was that he had a split personality—on the one hand an ambitious almost cruel streak to his nature, and on the other a sensitivity and softness that made him frequently depressed. Both sides of his nature made him feel uncomfortable and odd. On the rough side, for instance, he loved boxing and thoroughly thrashing his opponent in the ring. In law and politics he had a rather scathing sense of humor. On his soft side, he loved poetry, felt tremendous affection for animals, and hated witnessing any kind of physical cruelty. At his worst, he was prone to fits of deep melancholy and brooding over death. All in all, he felt himself to be far too sensitive for the rough-and-tumble world of politics. Instead of denying this side of himself, he channeled it into incredible empathy for the public, for the average man and woman. Car-ing deeply about the loss of lives in the war, he put all his efforts into ending it early. He did not project evil onto the South but rather empa-thized with its plight and planned on a peace that was not retributive. He also incorporated it into a healthy sense of humor about himself, making frequent jokes about his ugliness, high-pitched voice, and brooding na-ture. By embracing and integrating such opposing qualities into his pub-lic persona, he gave the impression of tremendous authenticity. People could identify with him in a way never seen before with a political leader.

Daily Law: Your goal must be not only complete acceptance of your Shadow side but also the desire to integrate it into your present per-sonality. By doing so, you will be a more complete human and will radiate an authenticity that will draw people to you.

The Laws of Human Nature, 9: Confront Your Dark Side—The Law of Repression

Balance Imagination and Reality

Your project begins with an idea, and as you try to hone this idea, you let your imagination take flight, being open to various possibilities. At some point you move from the planning phase to execution. Now you must actively search for feedback and criticism from people you respect or from your natural audience. You want to hear about the flaws and inadequacies in your plan, for that is the only way to improve your skills. If the project fails to have the results you imagined, or the problem is not solved, embrace this as the best way to learn. Analyze what you did wrong in depth, being as brutal as possible. Once you have feedback and have analyzed the results, you then return to this project or start a new one, letting your imagination loose again but incorporating what you have learned from the experience. You keep cycling endlessly through this process, noticing with excitement how you are improving by doing so. If you stay too long in the imagination phase, what you create will tend to be grandiose and detached from reality. If you only listen to feedback and try to make the work a complete reflection of what others tell you or want, the work will be conventional and flat. By maintaining a continual dialogue between reality (feedback) and your imagination, you will create something practical and powerful.

Daily Law: By continually cycling between your imagination and people's feedback, what you produce will be both unique and connected to your audience—the perfect blend.

The Laws of Human Nature, 11: Know Your Limits—The Law of Grandiosity

Focus Outwardly

We humans are self-absorbed by nature and spend most of our time focusing inwardly on our emotions, on our wounds, on our fantasies. You want to develop the habit of reversing this as much as possible. You do this in three ways. First, you hone your listening skills, absorbing yourself in the words and nonverbal cues of others. You train yourself to read between the lines of what people are saying. You attune yourself to their moods and their needs, and sense what they are missing. You do not take people's smiles and approving looks for reality but rather sense the underlying tension or fascination. Second, you dedicate yourself to earning people's respect. You do not feel entitled to it; your focus is not on your feelings and what people owe you because of your position and greatness (an inward turn). You earn their respect by respecting their individual needs and by proving that you are working for the greater good. Third, you consider being a leader a tremendous responsibility, the welfare of the group hanging on your every decision. What drives you is not getting attention but bringing about the best results possible for the most people. You absorb yourself in the work, not your ego. You feel a deep and visceral connection to the group, seeing your fate and theirs as deeply intertwined.

Daily Law: If you exude this attitude, people will feel it, and they will be drawn to you by the simple fact that it is rare to encounter a person so sensitive to people's moods and focused so supremely on results.

The Laws of Human Nature, 15: Make Them Want to Follow You—The Law of Fickleness

Destiny

The true self of each person is the mind. Know therefore that you are a god. For a god is someone who moves, who feels, who remembers, who looks to the future, who rules over and guides and directs the body he is master of, just as that Supreme God directs the universe. And just as this eternal God controls the universe, which is partly mortal, so too your eternal spirit directs your fragile body.

—CICERO

In ancient times, many great leaders, such as Alexander the Great and Julius Caesar, felt that they were descended from gods and part divine. Such self-belief would translate into high levels of confidence that others would feed off and recognize. It became a self-fulfilling prophecy. You do not need to indulge in such grandiose thoughts, but feeling that you are destined for something great or important will give you a degree of resilience when people oppose or resist you. You will not internalize the doubts that come from such moments. You will have an enterprising spirit. You will continually try new things, even taking risks, confident in your ability to bounce back from failures and feeling destined to succeed.

Daily Law: You're destined to accomplish great things, and by thinking that, you will create a self-fulfilling dynamic.

The Laws of Human Nature, 8: Change Your Circumstances by Changing Your Attitude—The Law of Self-Sabotage

Focus and Prioritize

Nothing really belongs to us but time, which even he has who has nothing else. It is equally unfortunate to waste your precious life in mechanical tasks or in a profusion of important work.

—BALTASAR GRACIÁN

Certain activities are a waste of time. Certain people of a low nature will drag you down, and you must avoid them. Keep your eye on your long- and short-term goals, and remain concentrated and alert. Allow yourself the luxury of exploring and wandering creatively, but always with an underlying purpose.

Daily Law: In a world full of endless distractions, you must focus and prioritize.

The Laws of Human Nature, 15: Make Them Want to Follow You—The Law of Fickleness

Connect to What Is Nearest to You

Life is short and we have only so much energy. Led by our covetous desires, we can waste so much time in futile searches and changes. In general, do not constantly wait and hope for something better, but rather make the most of what you have. Reality beckons you. To absorb your mind in what is nearest, instead of most distant, brings a much different feeling. With the people in your circle, you can always connect on a deeper level. There is much you will never know about the people you deal with, and this can be a source of endless fascination. You can connect more deeply to your environment. The place where you live has a deep history that you can immerse yourself in. Knowing your environment better will present many opportunities for power. As for yourself, you have mysterious corners you can never fully understand. In trying to know yourself better, you can take charge of your own nature instead of being a slave to it. And your work has endless possibilities for improvement and innovation, endless challenges for the imagination. These are the things that are closest to you and compose your real, not virtual world.

Daily Law: In the end what you really must covet is a deeper relationship to reality, which will bring you calmness, focus, and practical powers to alter what it is possible to alter.

The Laws of Human Nature, 5: Become an Elusive Object of Desire—
The Law of Covetousness

Embrace Whatever Happens to You

> On hearing of the interesting events which have happened in the
> course of a man's experience, many people will wish that similar
> things had happened in their lives too, completely forgetting that they
> should be envious rather of the mental aptitude which lent those
> events the significance they possess when he describes them.
>
> —ARTHUR SCHOPENHAUER

By 1928 the actress Joan Crawford had a reasonably successful career in Hollywood, but she was feeling increasingly frustrated by the limited roles she was receiving. She saw other less talented actresses vault ahead of her. Perhaps the problem was that she was not assertive enough. She decided she needed to voice her opinion to one of the most powerful production chiefs on the MGM lot, Irving Thalberg. Little did she realize that Thalberg viewed this as impudence and that he was vindictive by nature. He therefore cast her in a Western, knowing that was the last thing she wanted and that such a fate was a dead end for many an actress. Joan had learned her lesson and decided to embrace her fate. She made herself love the genre. She became an expert rider. She read up on the Old West and became fascinated by its folklore. If that's what it took to get ahead, she decided to become the leading actress of Westerns. At the very least this would expand her acting skills. This became her lifelong attitude toward work and the supreme challenges an actress faced in Hollywood, where careers were generally very short. Every setback was a chance to grow and develop.

Daily Law: Embrace all obstacles as learning experiences, as means to getting stronger.

The Laws of Human Nature, 8: Change Your Circumstances by Changing Your Attitude—The Law of Self-Sabotage

Admire Human Greatness

Admiration is the polar opposite of envy—we are acknowledging people's achievements, celebrating them, without having to feel insecure. We are admitting their superiority in the arts or sciences or in business without feeling pain from this. But this goes further. In recognizing the greatness of someone, we are celebrating the highest potential of our species. We are experiencing *Mitfreude* with the best in human nature. We share the pride that comes from any great human achievement. Such admiration elevates us above the pettiness of our day-to-day life and will have a calming effect.

Daily Law: Although it is easier to admire without any taint of envy those who are dead, try to include at least one living person in our pantheon. If we are young enough, such objects of admiration can also serve as models to emulate.

The Laws of Human Nature, 10: Beware the Fragile Ego—The Law of Envy

Seek the Upward Pull of the Group

The reality for a group is as follows: It exists in order to get things done, to make things, to solve problems. It has certain resources it can draw upon—the labor and strengths of its members, its finances. It operates in a particular environment that is almost always highly competitive and constantly changing. The healthy group puts primary emphasis on the work itself, on getting the most out of its resources and adapting to all of the inevitable changes. Not wasting time on endless political games, such a group can accomplish ten times more than the dysfunctional variety. It brings out the best in human nature—people's empathy, their ability to work with others on a high level.

We like to focus on the psychological health of individuals, and how perhaps a therapist could fix any problems they might have. What we don't consider, however, is that being in a dysfunctional group can actually make individuals unstable and neurotic. The opposite is true as well: by participating in a high-functioning reality group, we can make ourselves healthy and whole. Such experiences are memorable and life-changing. We gain confidence in our own abilities, which such a group rewards. We feel connected to reality. We are brought into the upward pull of the group, realizing our social nature on the high level it was intended for. We feel a charge of energy that comes from feeling connected to others who are working with the same urgent spirit.

Daily Law: You must have a thorough understanding of the effect groups have on your thinking and emotions. With such awareness, you can attach yourself to groups that exert an upward pull.

The Laws of Human Nature, 14: Resist the Downward Pull of the
Group—The Law of Conformity

Transform Self-Love into Empathy

We imagine that we understand quite well the people we deal with. Life can be harsh and we have too many other tasks to attend to. We are lazy and prefer to rely upon predigested judgments. But in fact it is a matter of life and death and our success does depend on the development of these skills. We simply are not aware of this because we do not see the connection between problems in our lives and our constant misreading of people's moods and intentions and the endless missed opportunities that accrue from this. The first step, then, is the most important: to realize you have a remarkable social tool that you are not cultivating—empathy. The best way to see this is to try it out. Stop your incessant interior monologue and pay deeper attention to people. Attune yourself to the shifting moods of individuals and the group. Get a read on each person's particular psychology and what motivates them. Try to take their perspective, enter their world and value system. You will suddenly become aware of an entire world of nonverbal behavior you never knew existed, as if your eyes could now suddenly see ultraviolet light. Once you sense this power, you will feel its importance and awaken to new social possibilities.

Daily Law: We are all narcissists, some deeper on the spectrum than others. Our mission in life is to come to terms with this self-love and learn how to turn our sensitivity outward, toward others, instead of inward.

The Laws of Human Nature, 2: Transform Self-Love into Empathy—The Law of Narcissism

The Confirmation Bias

The test of a first-rate intelligence is the ability to hold two opposing ideas in mind at the same time and still retain the ability to function.

F. SCOTT FITZGERALD

To hold an idea and convince ourselves we arrived at it rationally, we go in search of evidence to support our view. What could be more objective or scientific? But because of the pleasure principle and its unconscious influence, we manage to find the evidence that confirms what we want to believe. This is known as confirmation bias. When investigating confirmation bias in the world, take a look at theories that seem a little too good to be true. Statistics and studies are trotted out to prove them; these are not very difficult to find, once you are convinced of the rightness of your argument. On the internet, it is easy to find studies that support both sides of an argument. In general, you should never accept the validity of people's ideas because they have supplied "evidence." Instead, examine the evidence yourself in the cold light of day, with as much skepticism as you can muster.

Daily Law: Your first impulse should always be to find the evidence that disconfirms your most cherished beliefs and those of others. That is true science.

The Laws of Human Nature, 1: Master Your Emotional Self—The Law of Irrationality

Assume You're Misjudging the People Around You

The greatest danger you face is your general assumption that you really understand people and that you can quickly judge and categorize them. Instead, you must begin with the assumption that you are ignorant and that you have natural biases that will make you judge people incorrectly. The people around you present a mask that suits their purposes. You mistake the mask for reality. Let go of your tendency to make snap judgments. Open your mind to seeing people in a new light. Do not assume that you are similar or that they share your values. Each person you meet is like an undiscovered country, with a very particular psychological chemistry that you will carefully explore. You are more than ready to be surprised by what you uncover.

Daily Law: This flexible, open spirit is similar to creative energy—a willingness to consider more possibilities and options. In fact, developing your empathy will also improve your creative powers.

The Laws of Human Nature, 2: Transform Self-Love into Empathy—The Law of Narcissism

Make the Past Come to Life

We are not aware of all this, but we in the present are motley products of all the accumulated changes in human thinking and psychology. By making the past into something dead, we are merely denying who we are. We become rootless and barbaric, disconnected from our nature. You must radically alter your own relationship to history, bringing it back to life within you. Begin by taking some era in the past, one that particularly excites you for whatever reason. Try to re-create the spirit of those times, to get inside the subjective experience of the actors you are reading about, using your active imagination. See the world through their eyes. Make use of the excellent books written in the last hundred years to help you gain a feel for daily life in particular periods (for example, *Everyday Life in Ancient Rome* by Lionel Casson or *The Waning of the Middle Ages* by Johan Huizinga). In the literature of the time you can detect the prevailing spirit. The novels of F. Scott Fitzgerald will give you a much livelier connection to the Jazz Age than any scholarly book on the subject. Drop any tendencies to judge or moralize.

Daily Law: People were experiencing their present moment within a context that made sense to them. You want to understand that from the inside out.

The Laws of Human Nature, 17: Seize the Historical Moment—
The Law of Generational Myopia

The Rider and the Horse

The ancient Greeks had an appropriate metaphor: the rider and the horse. The horse is our emotional nature continually impelling us to move. This horse has tremendous energy and power, but without a rider it cannot be guided; it is wild, subject to predators, and continually heading into trouble. The rider is our thinking self. Through training and practice, it holds the reins and guides the horse, transforming this powerful animal energy into something productive. The one without the other is useless. Without the rider, no directed movement or purpose. Without the horse, no energy, no power. In most people the horse dominates, and the rider is weak. In some people the rider is too strong, holds the reins too tightly, and is afraid to occasionally let the animal go into a gallop. The horse and rider must work together. This means we consider our actions beforehand; we bring as much thinking as possible to a situation before we make a decision. But once we decide what to do, we loosen the reins and enter action with boldness and a spirit of adventure. Instead of being slaves to this energy, we channel it. That is the essence of rationality. As an example of this ideal in action, try to maintain a perfect balance between skepticism (rider) and curiosity (horse). In this mode you are skeptical about your own enthusiasms and those of others. You do not accept at face value people's explanations and their application of "evidence." You look at the results of their actions, not what they say about their motivations. But if you take this too far, your mind will close itself off from wild ideas, from exciting speculations, from curiosity itself. You want to retain the elasticity of spirit you had as a child, interested in everything, while retaining the hard-nosed need to verify and scrutinize for yourself all ideas and beliefs. The two can coexist. It is a balance that all geniuses possess.

Daily Law: We cannot divorce emotions from thinking. The two are completely intertwined. But there is inevitably a dominant factor, some people more clearly governed by emotions than others. Learn to channel your emotions instead of following them where they lead you.

The Laws of Human Nature, 1: Master Your Emotional Self—The Law of Irrationality

Advance with a Sense of Purpose

In military history, we can identify two types of armies—those that fight for a cause or an idea, and those that fight largely for money, as part of a job. Those that go to war for a cause fight with greater intensity. They tie their individual fate to that of the cause and the nation. They are more willing to die in battle for the cause. Those in the army who are less enthusiastic get swept up in the group spirit. The general can ask more of his soldiers. The battalions are more unified, and the various battalion leaders are more creative. Fighting for a cause is known as a force multiplier—the greater the connection to the cause, the higher the morale, which translates into greater force. Such an army can often defeat one that is much larger but less motivated. We can say something similar about your life: operating with a high sense of purpose is a force multiplier. All of your decisions and actions have greater power behind them because they are guided by a central idea and purpose. The many sides to your character are channeled into this purpose, giving you more sustained energy. Your focus and your ability to bounce back from adversity give you ineluctable momentum. You can ask more of yourself.

Daily Law: In a world where so many people are meandering, those with a sense of purpose spring past the rest with ease and attract attention for this. Find yours and elevate it by making the connection as deep as possible.

The Laws of Human Nature, 13: Advance with a Sense of Purpose—The Law of Aimlessness

December

The Cosmic Sublime

EXPANDING THE MIND TO ITS FURTHEST REACHES

≈

You determine the quality of your mind by the nature of your daily thoughts. If they circle around the same obsessions and dramas, you create an arid and monotonous mental landscape, and this secretly makes you miserable. Instead, you must seek to radiate your mind outward, to unleash your imagination and intensify your experience of life. And the furthest you can expand the mind is by connecting it to the Cosmic Sublime. Consider the limitlessness of space and time, the unspeakably awesome chain of events triggered by the Big Bang. Return to the very origins of our planet by visiting certain primeval landscapes. Think of the infinite nature of the human brain as a mirror of the infinite cosmos. Meditate on our common mortality. You are in fact surrounded every day by endless marvels, and to the degree you let them into your daily consciousness, you expand your mind and reinvigorate its immense powers. The month of December will help you expand your mind to its furthest reaches: the Cosmic Sublime

Death—it's our greatest fear. But this fear has effects we are not even aware of. It infects our mental life in general. It secretly instills a fear of life. Much of the latent, chronic anxiety that plagues most of us is rooted in the inability to confront our mortality.

We live in a culture that takes death denial to the extreme, banishing the presence of death as much as is possible.

If you go back hundreds of years, you could not have failed to see people die in front of you. You might see it on the streets or in your home. Most people had to kill their own food. You saw animals being slaughtered in front of your eyes.

Death had a presence. It was constantly there. And so people were thinking about it all the time. And they had religion to help soothe the idea of their mortality.

We now live in a world where it's the complete opposite. We have to repress the very thought of it. We can't see it anywhere. It's put into hospitals where it's sanitized, where it happens behind closed doors. Nobody ever talks about it. Nobody tells you this is probably the most important life skill that you could have—to know how to deal with that fear of mortality. Nobody teaches that. Your parents don't talk about it. Your girlfriend or boyfriend—they don't talk about it. Nobody. It's a dirty little secret. But it's the only reality we have. We're all going to die.

So if you're in denial of it, if you're repressing it—which most people are—it comes out in secret ways. It makes you anxious in your daily life because you're not dealing with the one most important thing. You don't realize it, but it's infecting you in your day-to-day decisions, how you interact with people. It is very simple: you need to confront this fear and find ways to transform it into vitality and power.

Think of it this way—you could die tomorrow. You have no control over this. You could be young, you could be twenty-four years old—people die young all the time. Understand what that means—it means your time is limited. You don't have these vast decades of life in front of you. You have dreams and aspirations and things you want to accomplish—knowing the shortness and precariousness of life gives you a sense of urgency. It makes you also appreciate everything around you that you see. It makes life more vivid and intense by understanding that any day now, it could be ripped away from you.

I personally had this brought home to me like a slap in the face. Two months after I finished *The Laws of Human Nature*, I suffered a stroke. It was a rather severe stroke in which I was very fortunate to survive and not have permanent brain damage. It was just a matter of minutes and then it was over. I was in a coma, and upon waking from that the whole left side of my body was basically paralyzed. Movement slowly came back. But I had to confront this reality just after I wrote the chapter on meditating on our common mortality. And what I wrote about in the book is true.

Now, I look around me at all I see, I look at all that I have—and the experience makes everything more intense. The colors are more intense. The sounds are more intense. The feeling of being connected to other people is more intense because now I'm aware not just of my own mortality but that of the people I'm with. My girlfriend, she could be gone tomorrow. My mother and sister, they could be gone tomorrow. My friends, they could be gone tomorrow. I have to appreciate them on a higher level. I have to understand that everybody has this in them. And knowing that other people are also facing it is a way for me to connect to them, a way to deepen my empathy on a very primal human level.

The essential power that confronting your mortality will give you—I call it the Sublime. Because it also opens up this idea of how amazing the world is that we live in, and how much we take for granted because we think that we're going to live forever. It's an incredibly important concept to me and it's also very personal in the sense that I came this close to dying myself.

I compare it to standing at the shore of some vast ocean. The fear of that dark ocean makes you turn away and retreat. I want you to get into your little boat and I want you to go into that ocean and explore it.

The Infinite and the Awesome

Whereas all the other animals have their heads low, eyes fixed upon
the ground, the gods desired to give to man a sublime face, a face
that could raise its eyes to the heavens above, contemplating
the very stars in the sky.

—OVID

We can define the Cosmic Sublime in the following way: it is an encounter with any physical object that embodies or implies a sense of the infinite, in space or time. In the ancient world, our ancestors understood this deep human need. In cultures all around the world, they created rituals, often rites of initiation, that triggered an awareness of the magnificent forces that transcend the human. Shamans or wise elders often served as guides. In our culture we do not easily find such guides or accepted means for encountering the Cosmic Sublime. In fact, we find the opposite: the media that dominates our minds gluts us on trivia and the exaggerated dramas of the moment. If we seek the expansion that will pull us out of our mental ruts, we are largely on our own. Fortunately, however, this is not as difficult as we might imagine: we are surrounded by embodiments of the infinite and the awesome. The infinite comes in many forms—silence, seemingly endless horizons, blank spaces, et cetera. What matters is our level of attunement to these places—our desire to expand and transcend our usual limits, and our willingness to let go of any distractions and open ourselves to the elements. We are after an experience—not more talk.

Daily Law: Pull your mind away from the dramas of the moment and seek the expansion.

Law of the Sublime, 1: Expand the Mind to Its Furthest Reaches—The Cosmic Sublime

A Most Improbable Occurrence

The model for feeling the Sublime comes in our meditation on mortality, but we can train our minds to experience it through other thoughts and actions. For instance, when we look up at the night sky, we can let our minds try to fathom the infinity of space and the overwhelming smallness of our planet, lost in all the darkness. We can encounter the Sublime by thinking about the origin of life on earth, how many billions of years ago this occurred, perhaps at some particular moment, and how unlikely it was, considering the thousands of factors that had to converge for the experiment of life to begin on this planet. Such vast amounts of time and the actual origin of life exceed our capacity to conceptualize them, and we are left with a sensation of the Sublime. We can take this further: Several million years ago, the human experiment began as we branched off from our primate ancestors. But because of our weak physical nature and small numbers, we faced the continual threat of extinction. If that more-than-likely event had happened—as it had occurred for so many species, including other varieties of humans—the world would have taken a much different turn. In fact, the meeting of our own parents and our birth hung on a series of chance encounters that were equally unlikely.

Daily Law: This causes us to view our present existence as an individual, something we take for granted, as a most improbable occurrence, considering all of the fortuitous elements that had to fall into place.

The Laws of Human Nature, 18: Meditate on Our Common
Mortality—The Law of Death Denial

Turn and Face Your Mortality

For it's always that way with the sacred value of life. We forget it as
long as it belongs to us, and give it as little attention during the
unconcerned hours of our life as we do the stars in the light of
day. Darkness must fall before we are aware of the majesty of
the stars above our heads.

—STEFAN ZWEIG

Most of us spend our lives avoiding the thought of death. Instead, the inevitability of death should be continually on our minds. Understanding the shortness of life fills us with a sense of purpose and urgency to realize our goals. Training ourselves to confront and accept this reality makes it easier to manage the inevitable setbacks, separations, and crises in life. It gives us a sense of proportion, of what really matters in this brief existence of ours. Most people continually look for ways to separate themselves from others and feel superior. Instead, we must see the mortality in everyone, how it equalizes and connects us all.

Daily Law: By becoming deeply aware of our mortality, we intensify our experience of every aspect of life.

The Laws of Human Nature, 18: Meditate on Our Common
Mortality—The Law of Death Denial

The Universe Is within You

I am glad to the brink of fear. . . . Standing on the bare Ground,—my
head bathed by the blithe air, and uplifted into infinite spaces—all
mean egotism vanishes. I become a transparent eyeball;
I am nothing; I see all the currents of the Universal Being
circulate through me; I am part or parcel of God.

—RALPH WALDO EMERSON

The one form of infinity that is perhaps the most sublimely marvelous to contemplate is the one that is closest to you—your own brain. Consider the following: There are approximately 1 million billion synapses (the links between nerve cells) in the cortical sheet of the human brain. As the biologist Gerald Edelman speculated, if you were to count these synapses one per second, it would take you about 32 million years to complete. Then, if you tried to calculate all the possible paths these synapses could take to connect, the number would be hyperastronomical—in the vicinity of twenty followed by millions of zeros, a sum greater than all the positively charged particles in the universe, and more than all the matter that it contains. The neuroscientist Christof Koch once declared that the human brain is "the most complex object in the known Universe." Equally remarkable are the hyperspeeds with which the human brain operates. The inner space of the human brain matches the outer space of the Universe; it is nearly infinite in scope. (And all this speed and power come from an organ composed of the basic elements found in rocks.)

Daily Law: The grandeur of the Universe is truly within us.

Law of the Sublime, 1: Expand the Mind to Its Furthest Reaches—The Cosmic Sublime

Immerse the Mind in the Moment

Every morning, before I eat or do anything, I meditate for forty minutes. It's a very intense forty minutes because I'm emptying the mind. I've been doing it religiously every morning for close to a decade now, and I wish it'd been longer. You think, "only forty minutes," but it is intense and it is extremely difficult. You try stilling the mind for that amount of time, and you'll find out how incredibly difficult it is. But it's immensely powerful—the ability to focus and still the mind. The thinking, talking mind is what messes people up. You can see it in a golfer who's lining up a twenty-foot putt on the eighteenth hole or a baseball batter in the bottom of the ninth with two outs or a field-goal kicker with the game on the line—they're thinking, and that thinking interrupts the physical process. Even if you have the muscle memory mastered, the thinking will mess you up every single time. This is why samurai warriors were obsessed with Zen Buddhism and zazen meditation. You think that golfer or that batter or that kicker is in a pressure situation, but in a sword fight, it's life or death. If the samurai can't still the thinking mind, they die. Zen Buddhism was a way to alter the mental aspect. It gave them mental control. It made them one with moment.

Daily Law: This is the most powerful point you can reach in sports or any other endeavor—when you are no longer thinking, you are in the moment. Make it a daily practice: to focus intensely on the present moment.

"Robert Greene: Mastery and Research," *Finding Mastery: Conversations with Michael Gervais*, January 25, 2017

DECEMBER 6

Alive Time or Dead Time?

Vivre sans temps mort. (Live without wasted time.)

—PARISIAN POLITICAL SLOGAN

The time that you are alive is the only real possession that you have. Everything else that you have can be taken away from you—your family, your house, your cars, your job. The time that you're alive is the only thing you truly possess, and you can give it away. You can give it away by working for other people—they own your time and you can be miserable. You can give it away by reaching for external pleasures and distractions—spending the time that you have as a slave to different passions and different obsessions. Or you can make the time that you're alive your own. You can actually come and possess it and take ownership of this time and make each moment count. And when you do that, that means that time is yours. It's alive within you. It's green. It's growing. You own it and you're making it happen. Another way of looking at it—the way I've always thought of it—is making things your own. Everything that you do in life is a process of making your own—your time, your ideas, your mental life, and on and on and on.

Daily Law: Never waste a minute. Make today your own—whether you're stuck in traffic, sick in bed, or working long hours.

Daily Stoic, "Robert Greene on the Idea of Alive Time vs.
Dead Time," YouTube, May 10, 2020

The Bullet in the Side

The reality of death has come upon us and a consciousness of the power of God has broken our complacency, like a bullet in the side. A sense of the dramatic, of the tragic, of the infinite, has descended upon us, filling us with grief, but even above grief, wonder.

—FLANNERY O'CONNOR

After the onset of lupus at the age of twenty-five, Flannery O'Connor stared down the barrel of the gun pointed at her, refusing to look away, for over thirteen years. She used her proximity to death as a call to stir herself to action, to feel a sense of urgency, to deepen her religious faith and spark her sense of wonder at all mysteries and uncertainties of life. She used the closeness of death to teach her what really matters and to help her steer clear of the petty squabbles and concerns that plagued others. She used it to anchor herself in the present, to make her appreciate every moment and every encounter. We tend to read stories like Flannery O'Connor's with some distance. We can't help but feel some relief that we find ourselves in a much more comfortable position. But we make a grave mistake in doing so. By having her mortality so present and palpable, she had an advantage over us—she was compelled to confront death and make use of her aware-ness of it. We, on the other hand, are able to dance around the thought, to envision endless vistas of time ahead of us and dabble our way through life. And then, when reality hits us, when we perhaps receive our own bullet in the side in the form of an unexpected crisis in our career, or a painful breakup in a relationship, or the death of someone close, or even our own life-threatening illness—we are not usually prepared to handle it.

Daily Law: Flannery O'Connor's fate is our fate—we are all in the process of dying, all facing the same uncertainties.

The Laws of Human Nature, 18: Meditate on Our Common Mortality—The Law of Death Denial

Connect to Something Larger Than Yourself

In 1905, the twenty-three-year-old writer Virginia Woolf returned for the first time since her childhood to the seaside cottage in Cornwall, England, where her family had spent many idyllic summers. Her mother had died when she was young, and recently her father and closest stepsister had also died, and she had fallen into a deep depression. The moment she approached the cottage, she saw the ghosts of her childhood—all those who had died or moved far away—inhabiting the place. The abandoned house with its derelict furnishings spoke to her of the relentless passage of time. Outside, the rhythmic sound of the waves, a sound that had been the same for millions of years in the past and would continue for the same span of time into the future, long after she was gone, evoked an overwhelming sense of the infinite. Connected to something much larger than herself, she reexperienced the sensations and intensity of her childhood. Encountering the Cosmic Sublime put her own problems and feelings of depression into proper perspective. Over the next thirty years, she kept returning to the place to help heal her. She later immortalized these experiences in her semi-autobiographical novel *To the Lighthouse*.

Daily Law: You can try something similar as you age, by returning to places of your youth or childhood, feeling the passage of time all around you, and connecting this to the eternal cycles of nature of which you are a part.

Law of the Sublime, 1: Expand the Mind to Its Furthest Reaches—The Cosmic Sublime

Encounters with the Inhuman
and the Infinite

If the doors of perception were cleansed, everything
would appear to man as it is—infinite.

—WILLIAM BLAKE

Most of us rarely leave the human bubble we live in—we are immersed in words, symbols, physical structures, and a domesticated nature that bear our imprint on almost everything we see. To leave that bubble and travel into the wilderness is not enough. You will tend to carry with you your technology and the obsessive thoughts that trail you everywhere you go. Your brain has become too accustomed to its own patterns. To really access the Cosmic Sublime wherever you travel, you must go through the following process. First, you must visit places where the human influence is nil or barely detectable. Fortunately, you do not have to travel far for this adventure—such places are all around you and easily reachable. You need to penetrate as deeply as you can into these landscapes. Second, you must leave behind as much technology as possible. In this more naked state, you must welcome any physical challenges and even manageable dangers. Third, bereft of your usual distractions, try to let go of all previous patterns of thinking and seeing—travel back in time and feel the ancientness of these places, signs of Earth long before we humans dominated the scene. Let the elements of these landscapes fill your mind as far as possible and feel yourself merging with them. When you return back to your familiar environment, notice how different things appear to you, and any changes from within.

Daily Law: Leave the human bubble today.

Law of the Sublime, 1: Expand the Mind to Its Furthest Reaches—The Cosmic Sublime

See the Whole

We humans tend to see things in isolation. We see ourselves and others as individuals, not realizing how our very existence, our consciousness, our brains, and our physiology, depend on all those in the past before us, stretching far back in time. When we look at other animals, we imagine an unbridgeable gulf between us and them. The threads that connect all life-forms are simply not visible to us and so not a part of our daily consciousness. You must train yourself to think and feel differently, always seeking to pick out the hidden threads. Imagine that there is a Whole that every event and phenomenon is a part of—the Whole that is your psychology and all your unconscious motivations stretching back to early childhood; the Whole that is you and all the various influences in your life, including parents, friends, society, and the cultural zeitgeist; the Whole that is you and all the past generations of humans that have shaped the world you now live in; and finally the Whole that is you and all the life-forms that have led to the evolution of humans and that live within you.

Daily Law: When you look at the world, stop fixating on all the separate forms you see and view it as all one—one throbbing, pulsating web stretching from 4 billion years ago to the present, with you as a tiny but necessary speck on a single thread.

Law of the Sublime, 2: Awaken to the Strangeness of Being Alive—The Biological Sublime

The Child's Sense of Scale

If we were honest with ourselves, many of us would have to admit to feeling a certain flatness in our experience: so much seems the same, and there is little to surprise us. Something is missing in our lives, but it is hard to pinpoint what it is. Feeling restless, we travel, have a love affair, change jobs, anything to shake us up. But when the novelty wears off, the flatness returns. Instead of looking for any possible specific causes of the problem, let us try to attack it from another, more global angle. Perhaps the source lies in the overall sense of scale we develop as adults, and to understand the role this plays in our emotional states, we have to look back at our own childhood, when our perspective was much different. The fundamental reality of childhood was our smallness and weakness in comparison to almost everything around us. We were surrounded by objects and forces that dwarfed us in size and power—trees, buildings, hills and mountains, the ocean, storms, the social life of adults. This feeling of smallness sparked intense curiosity about this world. By trying to understand the world around us, in some way we could bring it down to size and make it less frightening. And because we were so small in a world so immense, everything we saw seemed novel, marvelous, and full of mystery.

Daily Law: Try to encounter the world today with the sense of scale you had as a child.

Law of the Sublime, 1: Expand the Mind to Its Furthest Reaches—The Cosmic Sublime

Life and Death

We are afraid of the old age which we may never attain.

—JEAN DE LA BRUYÈRE

We can describe the contrast between life and death in the following manner: Death is absolute stillness, without movement or change except decay. In death we are separated from others and completely alone. Life, on the other hand, is movement, connection to other living things, and diversity of life forms. By denying and repressing the thought of death, we feed our anxieties and become more deathlike from within—separated from other people, our thinking habitual and repetitive, with little overall movement and change. On the other hand, the familiarity and closeness with death, the ability to confront the thought of it has the paradoxical effect of making us feel more alive.

Daily Law: By connecting to the reality of death, we connect more profoundly to the reality and fullness of life. By separating death from life and repressing our awareness of it, we do the opposite.

The Laws of Human Nature, 18: Meditate on Our Common
Mortality—The Law of Death Denial

How to View the World

See yourself as an explorer. With the gift of consciousness, you stand before a vast and unknown universe that we humans have just begun to investigate. Most people prefer to cling to certain ideas and principles, many of them adopted early on in life. They are secretly afraid of what is unfamiliar and uncertain. They replace curiosity with conviction. By the time they are thirty, they act as if they know everything they need to know. As an explorer you leave all that certainty behind you. You are in continual search of new ideas and new ways of thinking. You see no limits to where your mind can roam, and you are not concerned with suddenly appearing inconsistent or developing ideas that directly contradict what you believed a few months before. Ideas are things to play with. If you hold on to them for too long, they become something dead. You are returning to your childlike spirit and curiosity, from before you had an ego and being right was more important than connecting to the world. You explore all forms of knowledge, from all cultures and time periods. You want to be challenged. As part of this, be open to exploring the insights that come from your own unconscious, as revealed in your dreams, in moments of tiredness, and in the repressed desires that leak out in certain moments. You have nothing to be afraid of or to repress there. The unconscious is merely one more realm for you to freely explore.

Daily Law: By opening the mind in this way, you will unleash unrealized creative powers, and you will give yourself great mental pleasure.

The Laws of Human Nature, 8: Change Your Circumstances by Changing
Your Attitude—The Law of Self-sabotage

Release Yourself from Habits and Banality

*Whereas the beautiful is limited, the sublime is limitless, so that the
mind in the presence of the sublime, attempting to imagine
what it cannot, has pain in the failure but pleasure in
contemplating the immensity of the attempt*

—IMMANUEL KANT

We can experience the Sublime by contemplating other forms of life. We
have our own belief about what is real based on our nervous and perceptual systems, but the reality of bats, which perceive through echolocation,
is of a different order. They sense things beyond our perceptual system.
What are the other elements we cannot perceive, the other realities invisible to us? (The latest discoveries in most branches of science will have
this eye-opening effect, and reading articles in any popular scientific
journal will generally yield a few sublime thoughts.) We can also expose
ourselves to places on the planet where all our normal compass points are
scrambled—a vastly different culture or certain landscapes where the human element seems particularly puny, such as the open sea, a vast expanse
of snow, a particularly enormous mountain. Physically confronted with
what dwarfs us, we are forced to reverse our normal perception, in which
we are the center and measure of everything.

Daily Law: In the face of the Sublime, we feel a shiver, a foretaste of
death itself, something too large for our minds to encompass. And for
a moment, it shakes us out of our smugness and releases us from the
deathlike grip of habit and banality.

The Laws of Human Nature, 18: Meditate on Our Common
Mortality—The Law of Death Denial

Create Physical Death Awareness

Always do what you are afraid to do.

—RALPH WALDO EMERSON

For Japanese samurai warriors, the center of our most sensitive nerves and our connection to life was in the gut, the viscera; it was also the center of our connection to death, and they meditated on this sensation as deeply as possible, to create physical death awareness. But beyond the gut, we can also feel something similar in our bones when we are weary. We can often sense its physicality in those moments before we fall asleep—for a few seconds we feel ourselves passing from one form of consciousness to another, and that slip has a deathlike sensation. There is nothing to be afraid of in this; in fact, in moving in this direction, we make major advancements in diminishing our chronic anxiety.

Daily Law: We can use our imagination in this as well, by envisioning the day our death arrives, where we might be, how it might come. We must make this as vivid as possible. It could be tomorrow.

The Laws of Human Nature, 18: Meditate on Our Common
Mortality—The Law of Death Denial

DECEMBER 16

The Near-Death Experience

You could leave life right now. Let that determine what
you do and say and think.

—MARCUS AURELIUS

There are books written by people who've had near-death experiences and
they're fascinating. The effect is usually as follows: Normally we go
through life in a very distracted, dreamlike state, with our gaze turned
inward. Much of our mental activity revolves around fantasies and resent-
ments that are completely internal and have little relationship to reality.
The proximity of death suddenly snaps us to attention as our whole body
responds to the threat. We feel the rush of adrenaline, the blood pumping
extra hard to the brain and through the nervous system. This focuses the
mind to a much higher level and we notice new details, see people's faces
in a new light, and sense the impermanence in everything around us,
deepening our emotional responses. This effect can linger for years, even
decades.

Daily Law: We cannot reproduce that experience without risking our
lives, but we can gain some of the effect through smaller doses. We
must begin by meditating on our death and seeking to convert it into
something more real and physical.

The Laws of Human Nature, 18: Meditate on Our Common
Mortality—The Law of Death Denial

Let the Impermanence of It All Sink In

If man were never to fade away like the dews of Adashino, never to vanish like the smoke over Toribeyama, but lingered on forever in the world, how things would lose their power to move us! The most precious thing in life is its uncertainty.

—YOSHIDA KENKŌ

Try to look at the world as if we were seeing things for the last time—the people around us, the everyday sights and sounds, the hum of the traffic, the sound of the birds, the view outside our window. Let us imagine these things still going on without us, then suddenly feel ourselves brought back to life—those same details will now appear in a new light, not taken for granted or half perceived. Let the impermanence of all life-forms sink in. The stability and solidity of the things we see are mere illusions. We must not be afraid of the pangs of sadness that ensue from this perception. The tightness of our emotions, usually so wound up around our own needs and concerns, is now opening up to the world and to the poignancy of life itself, and we should welcome this.

Daily Law: Today, pretend you are seeing things for the last time.

The Laws of Human Nature, 18: Meditate on Our Common
Mortality—The Law of Death Denial

Have a Sense of Urgency and Desperation

Life is a gift, life is happiness, every minute could have been an
eternity of happiness! If youth only knew! Now my life will change;
now I will be reborn. Dear brother, I swear that I shall not lose
hope. I will keep my soul pure and my heart open.
I will be reborn for the better.

—FYODOR DOSTOYEVSKY

When we unconsciously disconnect ourselves from the awareness of death, we forge a particular relationship to time—one that is rather loose and distended. We come to imagine that we always have more time than is the reality. Our minds drift to the future, where all our hopes and wishes will be fulfilled. If we have a plan or a goal, we find it hard to commit to it with a lot of energy. We'll get to it tomorrow, we tell ourselves. Perhaps we are tempted in the present to work on another goal or plan—they all seem so inviting and different, so how can we commit fully to one or another? We experience a generalized anxiety, as we sense the need to get things done, but we are always postponing and scattering our forces. Then, if a deadline is forced upon us on a particular project, that dream-like relationship to time is shattered and for some mysterious reason we find the focus to get done in days what would have taken weeks or months. The change imposed upon us by the deadline has a physical component: our adrenaline is pumping, filling us with energy and con-centrating the mind, making it more creative. It is invigorating to feel the total commitment of mind and body to a single purpose, something we rarely experience in the world today, in our distracted state.

Daily Law: We must think of our mortality as a kind of continual deadline, giving a similar effect as described above to all our actions in life.

The Laws of Human Nature, 18: Meditate on Our Common
Mortality—The Law of Death Denial

Feel Reborn

Life is a constant process of dying.

—ARTHUR SCHOPENHAUER

In December of 1849, the twenty-seven-year-old writer Fyodor Dosto-yevsky, imprisoned for participating in an alleged conspiracy against the Russian czar, found himself and his fellow prisoners suddenly transported to a square in St. Petersburg, and told that they were about to be executed for their crimes. This death sentence was totally unexpected. Dostoyevsky had only a few minutes to prepare himself before he faced the firing squad. In those few minutes, emotions he had never felt before came rushing in. He noticed the rays of light hitting the dome of a cathedral and saw that all life was as fleeting as those rays. Everything seemed more vibrant to him. He noticed the expressions on his fellow prisoners' faces, and how he could see the terror behind their brave facades. It was as if their thoughts and feelings had become transparent. At the last moment, a representative from the czar rode into the square, announcing that their sentences had been commuted to several years' hard labor in Siberia. Utterly overwhelmed by his psychological brush with death, Dostoyevsky felt reborn. And the experience remained embedded in him for the rest of his life, inspiring new depths of empathy and intensifying his observational powers. This has been the experience of others who have been exposed to death in a deep and personal way.

Daily Law: Imagine that you have been spared from a death sentence, now every day is one you didn't think you'd get. Live accordingly.

The Laws of Human Nature, 18: Meditate on Our Common
Mortality—The Law of Death Denial

Know What Matters

You act like mortals in all that you fear, and like immortals
in all that you desire.

—SENECA

We have goals to reach, projects to get done, relationships to improve.
This could be our last such project, our last battle on earth, given the
uncertainties of life, and we must commit completely to what we do.
With this continual awareness we can see what really matters, how petty
squabbles and side pursuits are irritating distractions. We want that sense
of fulfillment that comes from getting things done. We want to lose the
ego in that feeling of flow, in which our minds are at one with what we
are working on. When we then turn away from our work, the pleasures
and distractions we pursue have all the more meaning and intensity,
knowing their evanescence.

**Daily Law: Let the awareness of the shortness of life clarify our daily
actions.**

The Laws of Human Nature, 18: Meditate on Our Common
Mortality—The Law of Death Denial

Let Death Awareness Disperse Our Differences

> Another Plague Year would reconcile all these Differences, a close conversing with Death, or with Diseases that threaten Death, would scum off the Gall from our Tempers, remove the Animosities among us, and bring us to see with differing Eyes.
>
> —DANIEL DEFOE

In 1665 a terrible plague roared through London, killing close to 100,000 inhabitants. The writer Daniel Defoe was only five years old at the time, but he witnessed the plague firsthand and it left a lasting impression on him. Some sixty years later, he decided to re-create the events in London that year through the eyes of an older narrator, using his own memories, much research, and the journal of his uncle, creating the book *A Journal of the Plague Year*. As the plague raged, the narrator of the book notices a peculiar phenomenon: people tend to feel much greater levels of empathy toward their fellow Londoners; the normal differences between them, particularly over religious issues, vanish.

With our philosophy of life through death, we want to manufacture the cleansing effect that the plague has on our tribal tendencies and usual self-absorption. We want to begin this on a smaller scale, by looking first at those around us, seeing and imagining their deaths and noting how this can suddenly alter our perception of them.

Daily Law: Experience other people's vulnerability to pain and death, not just your own.

The Laws of Human Nature, 18: Meditate on Our Common Mortality—The Law of Death Denial

The Ultimate in Stupidity

There are only three events in a man's life; birth, life and death; he is
not conscious of being born, he dies in pain and he forgets to live.

—JEAN DE LA BRUYÈRE

I'm often asked what I think of Silicon Valley's obsession now with either
indefinitely prolonging death or ending death. I think it's the ultimate
stupidity and I've been ranting against it for years. It's like you're running
away from the only reality that exists. We can argue about what reality is.
We have our own reality. Our reality is not what a bat or a fly sees. We
don't have echolocation. Every creature has its own reality. But the one
thing that we can say is that we're born and we die. And the idea that you
want to escape death and prolong your life—how selfish and narcissistic
is this? What if everybody tries to extend their life for 50, 100 years?
What will happen to the planet? We already have 8 billion people on this
planet. People need to die or we won't have resources, we won't have air to
breathe, water to drink. So in trying to prolong life, you're prioritizing
yourself. You're going to go on consuming more Me, more energy, taking
up more space in the world? So now instead of 8 billion, we have 15 billion people? What kind of insanity is that? It's the ultimate form of stupidity and insanity.

Daily Law: To deny mortality and fight against it is the ultimate form
of human stupidity and the ultimate insult to human nature, as if you
can transcend nature. You can't transcend nature, it defines you.

"The Laws of Human Nature: An Interview with Robert Greene,"
dailystoic.com, October 23, 2018

Avoid the False Sublime

The problem we face today is that many of us are too sophisticated and skeptical to consider such a quaint and old-fashioned concept as the Sublime, which reeks of religious experiences we have seemingly outgrown. But whenever we humans attempt to repress or deny something so natural and embedded in our psychological makeup, all that happens is that the repressed desire returns in corrupted forms, in what we shall call the False Sublime. The False Sublime can be sought through drugs, alcohol, and any kind of stimulant that temporarily frees us from our rigid selves and gives us a feeling of expansion and power, or at least numbs the depression we experience in the modern world. It can also be sought through video games or pornography, in which the violence and level of stimulation has to be continually upped to have the same effect. Then there are all the microcauses and cults sprouting up to channel people's latent rage and restlessness. Through these groups, people can experience a temporary lift out of the banality of their lives, until the aura of the cause fades and a new one must be found. And in this age, technology itself can become the new religion. Through technology and algorithms, we tell ourselves, we can solve anything. These are all false forms for the following reason: the True Sublime can be triggered by some external source—the view of a mountain, the night sky, an encounter with an animal, the dipping of a cake in tea, an intense group experience, a deep love for a person or for nature. But in these instances, a transformation occurs *within us*. Our perceptions are altered, our minds expanded beyond the circle. From then on, we see the world differently.

Daily Law: The False Sublime comes from external sources and leaves no lasting internal changes except for increased dependency on the substance itself. All of the addictions plaguing twenty-first-century humanity are false and degraded forms of the Sublime.

Law of the Sublime, Introduction

Place Yourself on Death Ground

Leaders of armies have thought about this subject since armies existed: how can soldiers be motivated, be made more aggressive, more desperate? Some generals have relied on fiery oratory, and those particularly good at it have had some success. But over two thousand years ago, the Chinese strategist Sun Tzu came to believe that listening to speeches, no matter how rousing, was too passive an experience to have an enduring effect. Instead, Sun Tzu talked of a "death ground"—a place where an army is backed up against some geographical feature like a mountain, a river, or a forest and has no escape route. Without a way to retreat, Sun Tzu argued, an army fights with double or triple the spirit it would have on open terrain, because death is viscerally present. Sun Tzu advocated deliberately stationing soldiers on death ground to give them the desperate edge that makes men fight like the devil. The world is ruled by necessity: People change their behavior only if they have to. They will feel urgency only if their lives depend on it.

> Daily Law: Put yourself in situations where you have too much at stake to waste time or resources—if you cannot afford to lose, you won't. Place yourself on "death ground," where your back is against the wall and you have to fight like hell to get out alive.

The 33 Strategies of War, Strategy 4: Create a Sense of Urgency and Desperation—The Death-Ground Strategy

This Too Will Not Last

The human mind naturally freezes the relentless passage of time by presenting us with static images of people, our culture, and our own self-identity. But if we were truly sensitive to evolution, we would realize these are only passing shadows in a world of ceaseless flux. Every minute of every day we are aging; every encounter with others alters and shapes our ideas; we are a continuous work in progress, never quite the same. As Heraclitus once said, "You cannot step into the same river twice; it is not the same river, and you are not the same person." Evolution requires this continuous flux and periodic cycles of mass destruction to create space for new forms and experiments. We humans, however, aware of our mortality, recoil from this; we want to hold onto the past and mentally stop the flow. We want to hold onto our grievances and even our pain, as well as our pleasures—all to create an illusion of inner permanence and stability. Instead, we must learn to let go, to accept completely all the separations life forces upon us. It is the very impermanence of our experiences and all living things around us that give them poignancy and significance. Be consoled that nothing will last—not the depression nor disappointments we feel in the present. The sublimity of the world around us is heightened by knowing how short our time is to witness it.

Daily Law: Let go of the past and feel yourself carried along by the stream of life and all the power and energy that it will bring us in its wake.

Law of the Sublime, 2: Awaken to the Strangeness of Being Alive—The Biological Sublime

Journey Inside the Global Brain

You become what you think, your daily thoughts your reality. You create the rich or arid landscape of your brain. If you constrict your thoughts to the same obsessions, to the tiny realm of your smartphone, that is the world that you create for yourself. What a waste of this magnificent instrument that you have inherited! But if you attempt to move in the opposite direction, you will notice the opposite dynamic—continual expansion, mental doors opening up in every direction, creative connections and new ideas flooding your brain. You will not want to stop exploring, because your exploration becomes a continuous source of pleasure for the restless energy of the human mind. This is a choice you make. It is interesting to note that we humans have unconsciously created an analog to this infinite inner space in the form of the internet, a kind of global brain. It contains almost all of recorded history, the ideas and experiences of billions of people in all fields and endeavors; much of its content is nonsense, but some of it contains new possibilities in the form of connections between different ideas and fields.

> Daily Law: Instead of using this remarkable instrument as a means to get attention or to vent your rage and display your superiority, see the internet in this different light—an invitation to a fascinating journey inside a global brain and the surprises it can bring you by roaming freely in this vast space and making surprising connections.
>
> *Law of the Sublime*, 1: Expand the Mind to Its Furthest Reaches—The Cosmic Sublime

Amor Fati

My formula for greatness in a human being is amor fati: that one wants
nothing to be other than it is, not in the future, not in the past, not in
all eternity. Not merely to endure that which happens of
necessity . . . but to love it.

—FRIEDRICH NIETZSCHE

What *amor fati* (love of fate) means is the following: There is much in life
we cannot control, with death as the ultimate example of this. We will
experience illness and physical pain. We will go through separations with
people. We will face failures from our own mistakes and the nasty malev-
olence of our fellow humans. And our task is to accept these moments,
and even embrace them, not for the pain but for the opportunities to
learn and strengthen ourselves. In doing so, we affirm life itself, accepting
all of its possibilities. And at the core of this is our complete acceptance of
death.

Daily Law: We put this into practice by continually seeing events as
fateful—everything happens for a reason, and it is up to us to glean the
lesson.

The Laws of Human Nature, 18: Meditate on Our Common
Mortality—The Law of Death Denial

DECEMBER 28

The Sky and the Stars

The stars. . . . Every night come out these envoys of beauty, and light
the universe with their admonishing smile.

—RALPH WALDO EMERSON

On a cloudless day, alone with your own thoughts and no distractions,
look up and let your mind expand along with the infinite blue of the sky.
Try to feel the limitless space. Then glance at the sun. Normally you take
its existence for granted, but this time see it as a star like any other star,
one that was born and is in the process of dying. Try to grasp for a moment this utterly insane reality—its perfect distance from Earth to allow
for life; and life adding such variety of colors illuminated by that very
sun. Apollo astronauts who walked on the Moon remarked on the de-
pressing ashen grays and browns that dominated its lifeless landscapes.
Knowing how unlikely its existence is, see the phenomenon of color itself
as surprising and wondrous. At night, realize that when you look at the
Moon or stars, you are seeing the same sights that so dazzled and mesmerized our ancestors—the Babylonians, the ancient Egyptians and Greeks,
and the Maya, to name a few. They constructed entire myths and belief
systems out of the night sky, making the cosmos come to life. Try, as you
take it in, to drop your sophisticated modern perspective and to see the
sky as something animated—see it through pagan eyes. When you look
at the Moon, think of its origins as dust from the collision of the Earth
and Theia (a former planet in our solar system). Reflect on the fact that
when you look upon stars, you are seeing light that has taken millions,
sometimes billions, of years to reach us.

Daily Law: Look at the sky and stars as if seeing them for the first
time.

Law of the Sublime, 1: Expand the Mind to Its Furthest Reaches—The Cosmic Sublime

Meditate on the Mysteries

Begin with yourself. Your mind and body are in fact mysteries. You have no access to the source of your emotions; you cannot see inside your brain and the processes that call up certain thoughts, or the degree to which your ideas are the products of so many external influences. You also cannot see into your bodily processes, the high-level complexity of everything within you that makes you alive. Your senses only reveal to you a partial version of reality. You cannot perceive what a bat or a dolphin can see, nor hear what a cat or a dog can hear. So much remains invisible to your senses. Contemplate the total mystery that is yourself, and then expand this outward. You really have no clue as to the thoughts and inner lives of the people around you. They are far more complex than you imagine. You have no real grasp of the trends rolling through the present moment in culture, and the future that they herald. You don't understand the inner workings and experiences of other life forms, nor the origins of the very Earth you walk upon. Keep expanding. Planets in our galaxy and beyond contain endless mysteries, and even the possibilities of very strange alien life forms. The universe is mostly dark matter and energy. You are enveloped in what is truly invisible. Ponder the fact that the further science advances, the more mysteries it uncovers. On and on you voyage, finally reaching the frontiers of the known Universe—what could lie on the other side is beyond what we can envision, perhaps the ultimate mystery.

> Daily Law: Contemplate any feelings of uncertainty and even discomfort and hold fast to them. Amid such uncertainty your dormant sense of wonder will begin to stir, and things will start to appear novel and surprising as they did when you were very young.

Law of the Sublime, 1: Expand the Mind to Its Furthest Reaches—The Cosmic Sublime

Accept Your Insignificance

Begin by imagining yourself gradually shrinking in size, back to where you were as a child. For a moment, re-experience the sensation of your smallness in relation to your parents, to the school you went to, and to the physical world around you. Return to those sensations of fear and excitement in the face of what seemed immense. Then, keep shrinking to your infancy and reimagine feelings of terror that you once had in any form of darkness or shadow. Imagine continuing this further, returning to the womb, to your smallest origins as a living thing, all the way down to the cellular level, to mere molecules, then atoms, to a particle, to the point of literally dissolving into the atmosphere—a kind of reverse death process. Feel for a moment the sensation of smallness to such a degree that nothing separates you from everything in the universe.

Once you have felt from within this dissolution into nothingness, think of the following: this is your reality as an individual in relation to infinite space and time.

Daily Law: The fact that you are aware of this insignificance and smallness is paradoxically what renders you powerful and significant. It is an understanding of reality that no other animal is capable of. Such awareness can begin to restore to you that sense of awe and connection that comes from a proper sense of scale.

Law of the Sublime, 1: Expand the Mind to Its Furthest Reaches—The Cosmic Sublime

The Ultimate Freedom

Premeditation of death is premeditation of freedom. . . . He who has learned how to die has unlearned how to be a slave. Knowing how to die frees us from all subjection and constraint.

—MICHEL DE MONTAIGNE

In the end, think of this philosophy of life through death in the following terms: Since the beginning of human consciousness, our awareness of death has terrified us. This terror has shaped our beliefs, our religions, our institutions, and so much of our behavior in ways we cannot see or understand. We humans have become the slaves to our fears and our evasions. When we turn this around, becoming more aware of our mortality, we experience a taste of true freedom. We no longer feel the need to restrict what we think and do, in order to make life predictable. We can be more daring without feeling afraid of the consequences. We can cut loose from all the illusions and addictions that we employ to numb our anxiety. We can commit fully to our work, to our relationships, to all our actions.

Daily Law: Once we taste some of this freedom, we will want to explore further and expand our possibilities as far as time will allow us.

The Laws of Human Nature, 18: Meditate on Our Common Mortality—The Law of Death Denial

To continue this journey with a free daily meditation

from Robert Greene, sign up at

TheDailyLaws.com